THE CRADLE OF THE REPUBLIC

Jamestown and James River

Seal of Virginia, 1606-1652 (Obverse and Reverse.)

BY

LYON GARDINER TYLER, LL. D.

PRESIDENT OF THE COLLEGE OF WILLIAM AND MARY,
WILLIAMSBURG, VIRGINIA

RICHMOND, VA.
THE HERMITAGE PRESS, INC.
1906

JAMESTOWN.

... ... in the background of a picture of the Massacre of 1622. Printed in the Scheeps Togt van Anthony Chester. (See page 44.)

PREFACE TO THE FIRST EDITION.

In giving this book to the public I wish to express my acknowledgments to Philip Alexander Bruce and Alexander Brown for the assistance which they have rendered me through their monumental works, *The Economic History of Virginia in the Seventeenth Century* and *The First Republic in America.* My sincere thanks are also due to H. B. Smith, of the city of Williamsburg, who aided me very materially in preparing the charts of Jamestown Island and James River, and to Robert Lee Traylor, of Richmond, who placed his library at my service, and aided in correcting the proof-sheets.

LYON G. TYLER.

WILLIAMSBURG, VA., *May* 14, 1900.

PREFACE TO THE SECOND EDITION.

The first edition of this work was the first serious attempt to deal with the topographical history of Jamestown and James River. As the pioneer work, it did not escape some serious errors, which I am now able to correct by access to two new sources of information — the collection of manuscripts lately purchased by the Library of Congress from a member of the Ambler family, and the excellent monograph *The Site of Old Jamestowne,* compiled by Samuel H. Yonge, who, as engineer under the direction of the United States Engineer Department, had charge of the erection of the water guard now protecting the western end of Jamestown Island.

The Ambler collection in the Library of Congress comprises several charts and many original patents, deeds, and leases, covering a long period of time from 1640 to 1809, and showing the location of many lots and the gradual consolidation of the Island property into a few hands.

In his monograph, *The Site of Old Jamestowne,* Mr. Yonge has accurately fixed many details of the ancient habitations, and it would not now be a difficult matter to reconstruct Jamestown in wood and brick just as it stood in 1676. It is gratifying that much of the author's identification of localities has received the endorsement of Mr. Yonge. Passmore's Creek, Black Point, Pitch and Tar Swamp, Block House hill, "Friggett Landing," the glass house, etc., were all unknown quantities, until they were placed upon the map in "THE CRADLE OF THE REPUBLIC." My chief mistake consisted in following too literally Mr. Richard Randolph, who, citing the authority of the records of James City County court, put the body of the town west of the old church tower. Under this impression as to the situation of the town, while I properly located the first state house on the southern shore, I placed it west instead of east of the church tower. I was more correct in regard to the third and fourth state houses, which I placed on what Mr. Yonge calls the "third ridge," referred to in the first edition of this book as the " first ridge," i. e. the first ridge to the north of the plateau fronting the river, named "fourth ridge" by Mr. Yonge. See CRADLE OF THE REPUBLIC, 1st. ed., 19, 40, 59, 116, and index 174.

To avoid confusion, I have followed the old style, which was ten days behind the new; except that I have made the years run from January 1 instead of March 25, as was customary with our English ancestors, who dated events between January 1 and March 25, as of the previous year.

LYON G. TYLER.

WILLIAMSBURG, VA., *May* 14, 1906.

CONTENTS.

THE CRADLE OF THE REPUBLIC.

I.

NEW FOUNDLAND AND ROANOKE.

The settlements at Roanoke and Jamestown were the fruits of England's rivalry with Spain. During the latter part of the fifteenth century, Spain began that development which made her for a hundred years the greatest power of the world. In 1469, Ferdinand V. united the kingdoms of Arragon and Castile by his marriage with Queen Isabella, and in 1492 he conquered and annexed the kingdom of Granada. Then under his auspices occurred the discovery of America by Christopher Columbus, and not long afterwards began the importation into Spain of the treasures of Mexico and Peru. Ferdinand died in 1516, and the prestige of Spain was immensely increased by the election of his grandson, King Charles I., as emperor Charles V. of Germany. The son of Charles, Philip II., who succeeded to the Spanish throne in 1555, was the mightiest monarch of Europe, being master not only of the Spanish peninsula and the New World of the West, but of Naples and Milan, the richest and most fertile districts in Italy, and of the Netherlands and Flanders, at that time the great centre of the world's trade. Moreover, he was the head of the dominant religious influence and military power of Europe.

The history of England during this time is the story of the rise and development of a small kingdom into a successful rival with this gigantic power. Although John and Sebastian Cabot had acquired for England in 1497 the glory of being the first kingdom to make discovery of the continent of North America their enterprise did not reflect the spirit of the English people. At the beginning of the sixteenth century English commerce was of small dimensions. The discovery was not followed up, and Sebastian Cabot left England, and enlisted in the service of the king of Spain.

For half a century, only one substantial connection existed between England and America. The fisheries on the Banks of New Foundland encouraged a few to take long voyages, and there gradually grew up in England a band of hardy and experienced seamen.

Meanwhile, the Protestant reformation swept over Europe, and in 1534 Henry VIII. disavowed allegiance to the Pope, and asserted his supremacy of the Anglican Church. Thus England gradually became the champion of the Protestant cause as opposed to Spain, who represented the Catholic Church. About the same time as Henry's quarrel with the Pope, industrial activity began in England on a wide scale. The treasures of Mexico and Peru, introduced into Spain, diverted the people from serious labor into speculative enterprises, and England was called upon to supply Spain and her American possessions with most of their clothing and other manufactured goods.

In 1549, this widely spread activity of the English people struck out boldly from the shores. The new era began with the return of the grand old seaman, Sebastian Cabot, from Spain, where he had been for many years. He was made grand pilot of England, and under his auspices a company for discovery was formed to create new lines of commerce with foreign countries. Fear of Spain caused the energies of this company to be employed during the reigns of Edward VI. and Queen Mary in creating trade relations with Eastern countries rather than with the Western Continent. Russia was discovered, and lines of commerce were speedily established with Barbary, Persia and Turkey. But when in 1558 Elizabeth ascended the throne, a spirit more daring than ever before prevailed in England, which found expression in the career of the bold Sir John Hawkins, the first to throw down the barriers withholding English ships from this continent. He carried negro slaves from Guinea, and contrary to the laws of Spain, who wanted the slave trade all to herself, entered into a profitable communication with the West India planters.

His example was followed by the great seaman, Sir Francis Drake, who, in 1577–1580, visited the west coast of the South American continent, plundered the Spanish settlements, and in his ship, loaded with treasure, circumnavigated the globe. The spirit of adventure became general, and Drake's exploits were repeated by Sir Thomas Cavendish, while Sir Martin Frobisher and Captain John Davis performed their glorious voyages to the northwest and left their names upon the icy waters of Labrador and British America.

QUEEN ELIZABETH, 1558–1603

Scarcely less adventurous, but of far higher purpose, was Sir Humphrey Gilbert, of Devonshire, who conceived the noble design of planting an English colony in America, as the best means of weakening Spain and promoting the grandeur of England. In 1578, he obtained from Queen Elizabeth a patent of colonization — which gave him full power to inhabit and fortify all lands, not yet possessed by any Christian prince or people. Under this charter he attempted two expeditions to New Foundland, both of which proved futile and in the second of which he lost his life. His last words as his ship went down will ever be kept in precious remembrance: "We are as near to Heaven by sea as by land."

Sir Walter Raleigh renewed the undertaking for which his heroic half-brother Gilbert had sacrificed his life. After sending out an exploring party in 1584, he dispatched in 1585 an expedition to Roanoke Island in North Carolina under a brave soldier named Captain Ralph Lane with 108 settlers. These were of that daring, pushing material of which the pioneers of the world have ever been made, but the example of the Spaniards disposed them to despise stock raising and to rest their hopes of a plantation upon the discovery of a gold mine or the South Sea. Consequently, when neither was found, they became discouraged and returned to England. Then Raleigh sent out in 1587 a new expedition under Captain John White, consisting of 150 settlers, of whom seventeen were women and nine were children.

They intended to go to Chesapeake Bay, but the pilot would

not take them there; and so they settled again on Roanoke Island. Four weeks after their landing, Governor White's daughter Eleanor, wife of Ananias Dare, one of his councillors, was delivered of a daughter, and she was christened Virginia, because she was the first Christian child born in Virginia — a name given by Queen Elizabeth to all North America. By unanimous consent,

SIR HUMPHREY GILBERT.

White was sent back to England to hasten on the supplies, but a weary time passed before he succeeded in returning to his charge.

When he reached home in November, 1587, he found all England in a ferment over the expected attack of the Spaniards, who had collected a large army and an enormous fleet for the subjugation of England. In 1588, a great naval battle was fought in the English Channel with the Spanish Armada, and the English under Lord Charles Howard, assisted by Raleigh, Drake, Hawkins, Cavendish, Frobisher, and Lane won a great victory, the most fortunate in the annals of the world; as it saved not only England, but North America, to the English.

It was not until 1591, more than three years after his return home, that White was able to carry assistance to his friends in Virginia. But when he reached Roanoke, he found no sign of the colonists except the word *Croatoan* engraved upon a tree at the fort. The ships weighed anchor for this place, which was a sandy island on the outer coast of North Carolina; but a storm arose, and the crew, becoming afraid to linger longer during that dangerous season of the year, not only refused to go to *Croatoan*, but returned to England.

This was a sad ending of the voyage, but Raleigh sent out ships and kept up the search for eleven years longer; yet somehow it was the same old story of misfortune, and no word came from the lost colony. Years afterwards, when Jamestown was settled, some Indians who professed to know the Roanoke colonists related that, after living at *Croatoan* till about the time of the arrival of the colony on James River, they were cruelly massacred at the instigation of Powhatan, only seven of them — four men, two boys, and a young maid—being preserved from slaughter by a friendly chief.[1]

SIR WALTER RALEIGH.

Despite their reverses, Sir Humphrey Gilbert and Sir Walter Raleigh will always be esteemed the true parents of North American colonization. They are glorious twin spirits who stand on the threshold of American history. If the one started the idea and sacrificed his fortune and his life for it, the other popularized it beyond any other man. It was through Raleigh's enterprise that two of the products of that country — the potato and tobacco were popularized in England, and to him is due the ultimate selection of the Chesapeake Bay region as the proper place of settlement. Raleigh never lost hope in America, and in 1603, just before his confinement in the Tower, he wrote to Sir Robert Cecil regarding the rights which he had in that country, and used these memorable words: "I shall yet live to see it an English nation."

[1] Strachey, *Travaile into Virginia*, 26, 85.

HISTORICAL SUMMARY.

1492–1602.

From the discovery of America (1492) *to Samuel Mace's voyage* (1602)

Oct.   12, 1492.— Discovery of America by Christopher Columbus.

June   24, 1497.— John Cabot and Sebastian, his son, discover North America.

       1549.— Sebastian Cabot made grand pilot of England, and organizes a company of discovery.

       1562.— Sir John Hawkins opens the way to America by engaging in the Slave trade with the Spanish Planters in the West Indies.

   1572–1580.— Sir Francis Drake ravages the Spanish settlements in South America, and sails around the world.

   1576–1578.— Sir Martin Frobisher's explorations of the Northeast coast of North America.

Nov.   19, 1578.— Sir Humphrey Gilbert leaves Plymouth, England, upon his first voyage to plant a colony in America.

June   11, 1583.— He leaves Plymouth on his second voyage to America.

Sept.   10, 1583.— He is drowned at sea.

April   27, 1584.— Sir Walter Raleigh sends Arthur Barlow and Philip Amidas from England to explore America for the seat of a colony.

April   9, 1585.— Raleigh's first colony to Roanoke Island, under Captain Ralph Lane, leaves Plymouth, England.

   1585–1587.— Captain John Davis explores the waters of Labrador, and discovers Davis's Strait.

July   21, 1586.— Thomas Cavendish sails to plunder the Spanish settlements on the west coast of South America, and circumnavigates the world.

May   8, 1587.— Raleigh's second colony under Captain John White leaves Plymouth, England.

July 29 } 1588.— Defeat of the Spanish Armada in the English Channel
Aug. 7 }   by the English fleet under Lord Charles Howard.

March,   1591.— Captain John White goes in search of "The Lost Colony" of Roanoke Island.

       1596.— Victory of the English fleet under Lord Howard in the harbor of Cadiz.

       1602.— Voyage of Samuel Mace, sent by Sir Walter Raleigh, in search of "The Lost Colony."

COLONIES OF THE LONDON AND PLYMOUTH COMPANIES.

Sir Walter Raleigh was executed in 1618 upon an absurd charge of conspiring against King James, but he lived long enough to be comforted by the realization of his confident hope of an English nation in Virginia. From 1602 to 1605 Bartholomew Gosnold, Martin Pring and George Weymouth conducted exploring expeditions to the coast of New England and brought back good accounts of the country; and in the latter year Spain, humbled and shorn of power, made peace with England. Relieved of their fear of Spain the English people once more directed their energies to the settlement of America; but now, in the place of private enterprises like Gilbert's and Raleigh's, organized capital undertook the solution of the problem. Raleigh could not take an active part, but his friends and relations

KING JAMES I., 1603-1624.

were foremost in the new colonization schemes. Two large associations were formed, one composed of knights and merchants of London, and the other of persons resident in the cities of Bristol, Exeter and Plymouth; and they obtained from King James in 1606 a joint charter, which defined Virginia as the portion of North America lying between the 34th and 45th parallels of north latitude — practically the present United States. In this vast extent of country, the company first named, called the London Company, was permitted to establish a settlement anywhere between 34 and 41 degrees; and the second, called the Plymouth Company, anywhere between 38 and 45 degrees. The actual jurisdiction of each company was represented by a rectangle extending north and south of the place of settlement 100 miles, and east and west 100 miles inland and 100 miles to sea.[1]

Neither the company nor the colonists were to have any share in the government, but the management of both sections of Virginia, including the very limited grants to the companies, was conferred upon one royal council, which was to name a local council for each of the colonies in America; and both superior and subordinate councils were to govern "according to laws, ordinances, and instructions" to be given by the king.

These "laws, &c." when issued provided that the property of the two companies should be held in a "joint stock," and the local councils were authorized to elect or remove their presidents, to remove any of their members, to supply their own vacancies, and to decide all cases occurring in the colony civil as well as criminal not affecting life or limb.[2]

The Plymouth Company, in August, 1606, sent out exploring ships, and in May, 1607, they dispatched a colony to the mouth of the Kennebec in Maine, but after a Winter of great severity these emigrants abandoned their settlement and returned to England. The single product of their stay in Maine was the pinnace *Virginia, the first ship built by Englishmen in America,* and which was destined three years later in the South Virginia colony to perform a memorable part.[3]

SIR THOMAS SMITH,
First treasurer, or president, of the
London Company

The expedition of the London Company was more successful. It consisted of three vessels — the *Sarah Constant* of 100 tons, the *Godspeed* of 40 tons and

1 Hening, *Statutes at Large,* I., 57–66.
2 Ibid., I., 67–76.
3 Strachey, *Travaile into Virginia,* 162–180.

the *Discovery* of 20 tons, commanded respectively by Christopher Newport, Bartholomew Gosnold and John Ratcliffe — old sailors renowned for discovery and daring. The ships carried 104 men and the crews, and among the leading men, besides the three named, were Edward Maria Wingfield, who had served gallantly in the Low Countries; George Percy, brother to the Earl of Northumberland, who had been trained also in that school of war; John Smith, already distinguished for a career of romance and adventure; George Kendall, a cousin of Sir Edwin Sandys; Gabriel Archer, a lawyer and member of Gosnold's expedition to New England in 1602; John Martin, who was commander of one of the vessels in Drake's voyage in 1585-1586; and Rev. Robert Hunt, a pious and exemplary minister, recommended by Richard Hakluyt, the naval historian of England and friend of Sir Walter Raleigh.

The expedition left London December 20, 1606, but, as the colonists went by way of the West Indies, they were four months on the voyage. In the West Indies, Smith and Wingfield had a quarrel, and the latter charged Smith with plotting mutiny, so that he was arrested and confined till some weeks after Virginia was reached.

April 26, 1607, they saw the capes of Virginia, and some of them landing at Cape Henry were fiercely assaulted by Indians, who wounded Gabriel Archer and Mathew Morton. That night the sealed box which contained the names of the councillors was opened, and they were found to be Wingfield, Gosnold, Newport, Smith, Ratcliffe, Martin and Kendall.

April 29, they set up a cross at Cape Henry, and next day visited the Indian town of Kecoughtan, on the east side of Hampton River, after which Captain Newport and some of the settlers coasted in a shallop up the main river in advance of the ships, seeking a place of settlement. They went as far as Appomattox River, and, May 12, returned to the ships. The same day they discovered a point of land, which they called Archer's Hope in honor of Captain Gabriel Archer; and "if it had not been disliked because the ships could not ride neare, we had settled there to all the colonies contentment." On the next day the ships came to the west end of a peninsula in the

Paspahegh country five miles above Archer's Hope, which they chose for a place of settlement and called it Jamestown, in honor of James I., king of England.

HISTORICAL SUMMARY.

1602–1607.

From the voyage of Bartholomew Gosnold (1602) to the settlement at Jamestown Island (1607).

March 26, 1602.— Bartholomew Gosnold and Bartholomew Gilbert sail from Falmouth, England, to the New England coast.

April 10, 1603.— Captain Pring sails to visit the New England coast.

March 31, 1605.— Voyage of Captain George Weymouth to the Kennebec River.

April 10, 1606.— Charter granted to the Plymouth and London Companies by King James I.

Aug. 12, 1606.— Henry Challons sent out by the Plymouth Company on a trial voyage.

Oct., 1606.— Trial voyage of Thomas Hanham and Martin Pring.

Dec. 20, 1606.— The colony sent out by the London Company leaves London.

Jan. 5, 1607.— They anchor at the Downs.

About Feb. 8, 1607.— They leave the coast of England.

April 26, 1607.— They reach the Virginia coast.

May 13, 1607.— They reach Jamestown Island.

COAT-OF-ARMS OF THE LONDON COMPANY.

III.

At the time of the arrival of the English in Virginia, the Indians inhabiting the Tide-water section were united in a confederacy, of which Powhatan was the head war-chief or werowance. They belonged to the Algonquin race, and were far less barbarous than the wild inhabitants of the Mississippi region. Each tribe had a territory defined by natural bounds, and they lived on rivers and creeks in fixed villages, consisting of huts called wigwams, oval in shape, and made of bark set upon a frame-work of saplings. Sometimes their houses were of great length accommodating many families at once, and at Uttamussick in the peninsula formed by the Pamunkey and Mattapony were three such structures sixty feet in length, where the Indians kept the bodies of their dead werowances under the care of seven priests or medicine men. Near every wigwam there was a cleared spot, in which corn, tobacco, gourds, pumpkins, beans and cymlings were planted. The tribes received their werowances from Powhatan, and these petty werowances numbered in all about thirty-four.

On the south side of Chesapeake Bay the Chesapeake Indians had their cornfields and villages. It would appear from Strachey that they were new-comers in that region, and successors of others who had fallen victims to the jealousy and cruelty of Powhatan. "It is not long since," says[1] Strachey, "that his priests told Powhatan that from the Chesapeake Bay a nation should arise which should dissolve and give end to his empire, for which not many years since (perplext with this divelish oracle and divers understanding thereof), according to the ancyent and gentile customs, he destroyed and put to sword all such who might lye under any doubtful construccion of the said prophesie, as all the inhabitants, the werowance, and his subjects of that province." Perhaps it was the memory of this event and this prophecy that made the Indians in the

---

[1] For accounts of the Indians in Virginia see Smith, *Works* (Arber's ed.), 47–82, 360–378; Spelman, in Smith, *Works* (Arber's ed.), cv–cxiv; Strachey, *Travaile into Virginia*, 44–114; Beverley, *History of Virginia* (Campbell's reprint, 1855), 126–185.

Chesapeake region so quick to resent the landing of the whites at Cape Henry, April 26, 1607.

Above the Chesapeakes, on the same side, were the Nansemonds, governed by four werowances — Weyhohomo, Amapetough, Weyingopo and Tirchtough. Their villages were, for the most part, on the Nansemond River, which meant a neck " where there was a fishing place "—(Naus-amung).

Next came the Warrascoyacks residing in the county of Isle of Wight. Their chief town was probably near " Old Town," on Pagan River, " where a Bay wherein falleth 3 or 4 prettie brookes and creekes halfe intrench the inhabitants of Warrascoyac,"[1] — a word meaning " point of land." At Pagan Point there was a small village called Mokete and on Burwell's Bay another small village called Mathomank. The Werowance was Sasenticum and his son was Kaintu.

The neighbors of the Warrascoyacks were the Quiyoughcohanocks, whose territory extended through Surry and Prince George counties. The werowance was Pepiscumah, called for short Pipisco, who kept on good terms with the whites. However, in 1610, he had been deposed by Powhatan, and one of Powhatan's wives, Oholasc, was queen in the minority of her son Tatacope, who lived at Chawopo with Chopoke, one of Pipisco's brothers.[2] Quiyoughcohanock was on Upper Chippokes Creek, near the present Claremont.

The name " Tapahanah " was for a time wrongfully applied to Quiyoughcohanock by the whites. When in the Spring of 1607 the Indians in Virginia heard of the arrival of the ships in James River, some of them from a distance came to the banks of the James and temporarily established habitations there, in order to assist in resisting the landing of the explorers. Among these Indians were the chief Tapahanah or Tapahanock, and a body of his men from the Rappahannock or Tappahannock River. The extensive marsh at Brandon, famous for its wild ducks, still preserves the evidence of this mistake — being known as " Tapahana (Tappahannock) marsh." [3]

---

[1] Smith, *Works* (Arber's ed.), 346.
[2] Strachey, *Travaile into Virginia*, 57. In Surry County there was a plantation near " Four Mile Tree," called Pipisco, probably an adaptation of *Pipisco*.
[3] Tooker, *Some Powhatan Names*, in *American Anthropologist* (N. S.), VI., No. v.

AN INDIAN VILLAGE

Quiyoughcohanock was one of the ceremonial places of the Indians, where the boys intended to be priests or Quiyough-quisocks were initiated into the mysteries of their cult.

Next in order were the Weyanokes, who had towns on both sides of the river. Their chief town, situated on the south side, was known as " Weanock," or "Wyanoke," or "Wynauk," meaning " the going around place " or " place about which the river winds itself." A land grant[1] issued in 1650 located " Weyanoke Old Town " at the head of Powell's creek on Flowerdew Hundred plantation. Numerous Indian relics have been found there, and earth-works evidently thrown up for fortification are still extant. The place in 1705 was known as Powhatan town, and there was a ferry connecting it with Swineyards on the north side of the James.[2] The chief of the Weyanokes in 1612 was Kaquothocun.

Above the Weyanokes were the people of the Appomattox country between the river of that name and the James. The bestowal of the name on the stream was done by the colonists and not by the natives, and the same is true of all the naming of rivers noted on Smith's map. In explaining the etymology, some have derived it from Apameteku, "a sinuous tidal estuary," indicative of the curls in the river at that locality. But the eminent anthropologist, William Wallace Tooker, explains it as meaning " the resting tree " or " bower," from the mulberry tree under which Queen Opussoquionuske, sitting on a mat, received the voyagers in 1607. Above the Falls of the River resided the hereditary enemies of the Pow-hatans — the Manakins or Monacans — on the site of whose chief town in Nicholson's administration the French Hugenots were established.

Along the north side of the James River there were several tribes, and the first met with was the Powhatans, whose chief village stood on a hill opposite to an island about three miles from the Falls, and was separated from the river by a meadow of 300 acres planted with Indian corn, tobacco, pumpkins, gourds and other vegetables. The word Powhatan is derived from Powwow-atan meaning the " Powwow hill," or the hill

---

[1] *William and Mary Coll. Quart.*, X., 25.
[2] Campbell, *History of Virginia, 129, note.*

where the great chief held his powwows. Here Powhatan was born, but at the coming of the English the werowance at the Falls was Parahunt, one of Powhatan's sons, called Tanx Powhatan, "Little Powhatan."

Below the Powhatans were the Arrohatecks, whose chief town was just above the Dutch Gap Canal, in Henrico County, opposite Proctor's Creek, in Chesterfield County. A farm in that quarter, owned by the Cox family for many years, still retains the Indian name. The word Arrohateck is cognate with Natick *ahanehtan* "he laughs at him," and the idea is expressed in "Arrohatecks Joy" applied by Gabriel Archer to the village of the Indian werowance Ashuaquid.[1]

Adjoining them was the territory of the Weyanokes, whose chief town was, however, on the south side of the river as already observed.

Next to the Arrohateck Country was the territory of the Paspahegh Indians, from about Sturgeon Point, in Charles City County, to Skiffes Creek, in James City County. As Jamestown was in this district, these Indians and their chief Wowinchopunk were brought into more important relations with the whites than any other of the tribes. Their chief town was formerly about a mile from the Island called "Old Paspaheghs," but at the time of the coming of the English, Wowinchopunk resided at Sandy Point, nearly opposite to Quiyoughcohanock. The etymology of the term Paspahegh had reference to the mouth of the Chickahominy, which opened into the James in the Paspahegh territory. The same term was applied to the mouth of the Connecticut River, and in the Indian deed for Gardiner's Island we find "Pashpeshauks als Saybrook Forte;" while on Long Island it occurs as "Puspatick, a locality at the mouth of a creek." "Paspeiouk" meant land "at the flowing out," or at a stream's mouth.

Finally, near the mouth of the James was the district of the Kecoughtans — a word which meant "great town," identical with the Natick "Keihtotan." Some years before the English arrived, the Kecoughtan tribe was very powerful, and their country was sometimes the seat of as many as a thousand

---

[1] Tooker, in *William and Mary Coll. Quart.*, XIV., 62.

Indians and three hundred houses. There was a large open district in the neighborhood of nearly two or three thousand acres, and the fishing was excellent. Powhatan regarded the power of the tribe with suspicion, and while things were in confusion, on account of the death of the old Kecoughtan werowance, he suddenly invaded the territory, killed the new chief and most of the tribe, and transported the survivors over the York, where he quartered them with his own people. After much suit, these survivors obtained from him the country of Pianketank, in Mathews County, which country he likewise dispeopled in 1608. When Captain Smith and his company, in January, 1609, visited Werowocomoco, they saw the scalps of the unfortunate Pianketanks hanging on a line between two trees. In the room of the former inhabitants at Kecoughtan, Powhatan placed his son Pochins and some of his own men on whom he could rely; and at the arrival of the English their chief village was on the left side of Hampton River, near the Soldier's Home.[1]

The fighting strength of these Indian tribes was estimated by Strachey, as follows: Chesapeakes, 100 warriors; Nansemonds, 200; Warrascoyacks, 60; Tapahanas, or Quiyoughcohanocks, 60; Weyanokes, 100; Appomattocos, 120; Powhatans, 50; Arrohatecks, 60; Paspaheghs, 40; and Kecoughtans, 30 — in all, 820 warriors.

Close by, on the York River, were numerous other tribes, the nearest of whom were the Chiskiacks, two miles above Yorktown under their werowance, Ottahotin. The name of the tribe meant "wide land," "broad place," and is quite descriptive of the locality where the Indians resided, which is still known as "Indian Fields." Upon the Pamunkey River, a branch of the York, were the villages of Powhatan's three brothers, Opitchapan, Opechancanough and Kecatough.

Along the Chickahominy, where there were fine bottom lands, lived a tribe of three hundred fighting men, who, while they paid tribute to Powhatan, did not receive any werowances from him, but were governed by their priests, assisted by their old men, whom they called Cawcawwassoughes. Ac-

---

1 Strachey, *Travaile into Virginia Britannia*, 60, 61; Smith, *Works* (Arber's ed.), 378.

cording to Mr. Tooker, Chickahominy was not a place name, but the designation of a people who contributed corn to the colonists, thus saving them from starvation. He gives its etymology as *Chick-aham-min-anaugh* "coarse pounded corn people" or in brief "hominy people."

The extent of Powhatan's dominions was greater than any of his predecessors in authority ever had. He had inherited only the countries of Powhatan, Arrohateck, Appomattox, Pamunkey, Youghtamund and Mattapanient; but he had by craft and arms extended his dominions till they included all the country from the Roanoke River on the south to a palisaded town called Tockwogh, standing at the head of Chesapeake Bay, in forty degrees north latitude, or thereabouts. He was known among the Indians in 1607 as Powhatan from the place of his birth at the Falls, but his proper name was Wahunsenacawh. He had other titles, and the Indians sometimes referred to him as Ottaniack and sometimes as Mannatowick, which last signified "Great King." He had several "seates or houses," but his chief abode,[1] when the whites came into the country, was upon the north side of York River at Portan Bay (i. e. Poetan or Powhatan Bay), fifteen or sixteen miles from West Point. On the earliest chart of York River (Tindall's chart), the place is called Poetan, but it was generally known as Werowocomoco, meaning the house of the werowance, or "Kings-house," as Strachey says. In 1609, becoming uneasy at the neighborhood of the whites, he removed to a place "at the top of the river Chickahomania between Youghtamund (Pamunkey) River and Powhatan (James) River.[2]" This new seat was called Orapaks, being a combination of Oro "solitary" and paks (peakes) "a little water place," aptly descriptive of "White Oak Swamp" near Richmond.

This terrible old chief was over seventy years old, when the English first intruded upon his dominions. He bore his years well; and in stature he was tall and powerfully framed. His thin grey hair floated over his broad shoulders, and his countenance was furrowed and melancholy. He had a round face and some few hairs upon his chin and upper lip. He had a

[1] Strachey, *Travaile into Virginia*, 49.
[2] *William and Mary Coll. Quart.*, X., 2-4.

regular system of finance, and an organized force of tax-gatherers, whom he sent around regularly to make collections. His laws on the subject were rigid and despotic. Every werowance had to pay Powhatan eighty per cent. of all the commodities which his country yielded or the chase afforded; "insomuch that they dared not dress a single deer-skin or put it on until Powhatan had seen and refused it."

To enforce his commands, he kept about him fifty of the choicest men in his kingdom, who were always ready for war. As he knew no mercy or compassion for those who offended

PORTAN BAY.

him, the werowances everywhere groveled before him in abject terror. He had a dozen wives, whose names, as they stood in his affection, were:

Winganuske	Attosomiske	Ortoughnoiske
Ashetoiske	Ponnoiske	Oweroughwough
Amopotoiske	Appomosiscut	Ottermiske
Ottopomtacke	Appimmoiske	Memeoughquiske

In 1612, Powhatan had living twenty sons and twelve daughters including the celebrated Pocahontas, "the nonpareil of her race." The succession of the government, however, was not to his children but to his three brothers and to his sisters, and after them to the heirs male and female of his eldest sister, but never to the heirs of his brothers. So when Powhatan died in April, 1618, he was succeeded by his brother Opitchapan, who, like Powhatan, had several other names: Taughaiten, Itopatin, Istan, Sassapen, etc.; and after the latter's death the chief authority was held by the able and ferocious Opechancanough, whose name meant "the white hair man;" probably from the white robe of fur about his shoulders.[1] He planned the massacres of 1622 and 1644; and when he died in 1646, he was succeeded by Necotowance, probably son of the eldest sister. Then came the Queen of Pamunkey of the "blood royal," who was living in 1676, at which time her authority had shrunk to a command of the Indians in Pamunkey Neck. A fragment of her tribe still exists on a reservation near West Point, and they regularly elect a chieftain.

The religion of these Tide-water Virginia Indians, like that of all the other Indians formerly found on the coast, consisted in a belief in a great number of devils, who were to be warded off by powwows and conjurations. Captain Smith gives an account of a conjuration to which he was subjected at Uttamussick when a captive in December, 1607. At daybreak, they kindled a fire in one of the long houses and by it seated Captain Smith. Soon the chief priest, hideously painted, bedecked with feathers, and hung with skins of snakes and weasels, came skipping in, followed by six others similarly arrayed. Rattling gourds and chanting most dismally, they marched about Captain Smith, the chief priest in the lead and trailing a circle of meal, after which they marched about him again and put down at intervals little heaps of corn of five or six grains each. Next they took some little bunches of sticks and put one between every two heaps of corn. These proceedings, lasting at intervals for three days, were punctuated with violent gesticulations, grunts, and a great rattling of gourds.[2]

The Indian men occupied themselves, for the most part, in hunting and fishing, and the women tended the crops and did the housework, but both sexes were very fond of dancing and

[1] Tooker MS.
[2] Tyler, *England in America*, 45, 46.

revelling. During the visit to Werowocomoco in January, 1609, Captain Smith was witness to a very charming scene, in which Pocahontas was the leading actor. While the English were sitting upon a mat near the fire, they were startled by loud shouts, and a party of Indian girls came out of the woods strangely attired. Their bodies were painted, some red, some white, and some blue. Pocahontas carried a pair of antlers on her head, an otter's skin at her waist and another on her arm, a quiver of arrows at her back, and a bow and arrow in her hand. Another of the band carried a sword, another a club, and another a pot-stick, and all were horned as Pocahontas. Casting themselves in a ring about the fire, they danced and sang for the space of an hour, and then with a shout departed into the woods as suddenly as they came.[1]

The Indians had their love songs, which they sang with some idea of tune, and they had also their angry and scornful songs against the Tassantassees, as they called the English, one of which is given by Strachey.[2] It celebrates an attack upon the English at the Falls of the James River in 1610, when Lord Delaware sent an expedition from Jamestown to search the country above the Falls for gold mines. In this attack Lord Delaware's nephew, Captain William West, was killed and Simon Skore, a sailor, and one Cobb, a boy, were taken prisoners. The song was as follows:

Matanerew shashashewaw erawango pechecoma
Whe Tassantassa inoshashaw yehockan pocosack.
Whe whe yah haha nehe wittowa wittowa.

Matanerew shashashewaw erawango pechecoma
Capt. Newport inoshashaw neir inhoc natian matassan.
Whe whe yah haha nehe wittowa wittowa.

Matanerew shashashewaw erawango pechecoma
Thom Newport inoshashaw neir inhoc natian monacock.
Whe whe yah haha nehe wittowa wittowa.

Matanerew shashashewaw erawango pechecoma
Pochin Simon inoshashaw ningon natian monacock.
Whe whe yah haha nehe wittowa wittowa.

The words of the song boasted that the Indians had killed the English in spite of their guns (pocosack) and copper

[1] Tyler, *England in America*, 48.
[2] Strachey, *Travaile into Virginia*, 79, 80.

(matassun), meaning the copper crown which Captain Newport had presented to Powhatan (hoping thereby to secure his
friendship) ; that Thomas Newport (that is, Thomas Savage,
whom Captain Newport had given to Powhatan, calling him
his son) had not frightened them with his sword (monacock);
and neither had Simon Skore's weapon saved him from
capture. The *whe whe* of the chorus made mock lamentation
over the death of Simon Skore, whom they tortured; and the
words *yah haha nehe wittowa wittowa* conveyed a jeering,
laughing commentary upon the English lack of fortitude under
torment.

In the Powhatan name for Virginia occurs one of the few
instances in which is found an Indian name applied to a
country so extensive. It was called by them "Attanoughkomouck," meaning " land enclosed for producing or growing," and so by free translation " a plantation," in which sense
it was perhaps understood by the Virginia colonists.[1]

[1] Tooker, *The Powhatan name for Virginia,* in *American Anthropologist* (N. S.) VIII. No. I.

AN INDIAN WEROWANCE.

IV.

THE ISLAND OF JAMESTOWN.

Jamestown Island lies on the north side of James River, and is distant about sixty-eight miles from Richmond and thirty miles from the mouth of the river at Newport News. It is about two and a half miles in length, and in width varies from five hundred yards at its western extremity to a mile and a half near its eastern end. The area of the Island, according to a recent survey, is about 1,400 acres, much of which is marsh land. Its soil is very fertile, and produces fine crops of corn and wheat.

It is surrounded on three sides by James River, and on the north side by Back River, which separates it from the mainland. It is traversed by Pitch and Tar Swamp on its northern part and by Passmore's Creek on its southern part.

Pitch and Tar Swamp begins at James River at the west end, winds around the church tower, passes back of the spot where the first state house stood, and, gathering its waters as it goes, empties into Back River, through a creek anciently known as "Kingsmill's Creek." Branches of the swamp penetrate the Island in many directions, forming numerous little ridges; and one of these branches, known as the "Orchard Run," and entering the river about 700 yards below the church tower, was originally the eastern limit of the town.

Passmore's Creek, named after Thomas Passmore, a carpenter, who was living on the Island in 1623, traverses the lower end of the Island. It begins at James River, about a mile below the present church tower, and runs southeasterly, nearly the course of the James, cutting off about one-third of the whole area of the Island.

The upper part of the strip of land between this creek and the river is known as "Goose Hill." It is composed of seven long ridges, about three feet high, made by little slashes of the swamp of Passmore's Creek, and running north and south.

The point at the extreme eastern end is called in the land grants "Black Point."

d Hou
16

ROAD TH

S

LAND

Coleman's Creek

Glebe Land

Archer's Hope

Back River

's Tract

Kingsmill Creek

⚓ 25

Edward Travis' Land
1665

THE ISLAND

Black Point

e Hill

R I V E R

REFERENCES
TO
[ART OF JAMESTOWN ISLAND

—First ridge of the Island, formerly connected with the mainland by a neck.

—Second ridge, formerly patented by John Baldwin.

—Third ridge, site of the third and fourth state houses, 1665-1698.

—Fourth ridge, site of the confederate fort, the brick churches, and the Jaquelin-Ambler house.

a—Probable shore line in 1607.

b b—Present sea wall.

d—Ancient house foundations.

—Sandy Bay.

—Site of blockhouse.

—"Friggett" Landing.

—Present bridge across Back River.

—Lone cypress, 300 feet from the seawall.

—Site of powder magazine, built in 1697.

—Block of houses composed of the country house, Philip Ludwell's three houses, and the State house, 1665-1698.

—Robert Beverley's lot, 1694.

—Richard Lawrence's lot, 1676.

—Confederate fort.

—Island house brick foundations.

—Landing place May 14, 1607, (signified by a cross).

—Brick fort constructed about 1673-1676.

—Confederate fort.

5—Church tower.

6—Dale's "Bridge" or wharf, 1611.

7—First steamboat wharf.

3—Second steamboat wharf.

—Third steamboat wharf.

0—Site of the "old State house" on fourth ridge.

1—Old turf fort, 1663.

2—Ruins of Jaquelin-Ambler house.

3—Old cart way (1624) over Pitch and Tar swamp to the Island house.

4—Confederate fort.

5—Travis graveyard.

6—Present farm house.

7—Confederate fort.

3—Confederate fort.

—Old well.

, 12', 18'—Varying depths of the river channel.

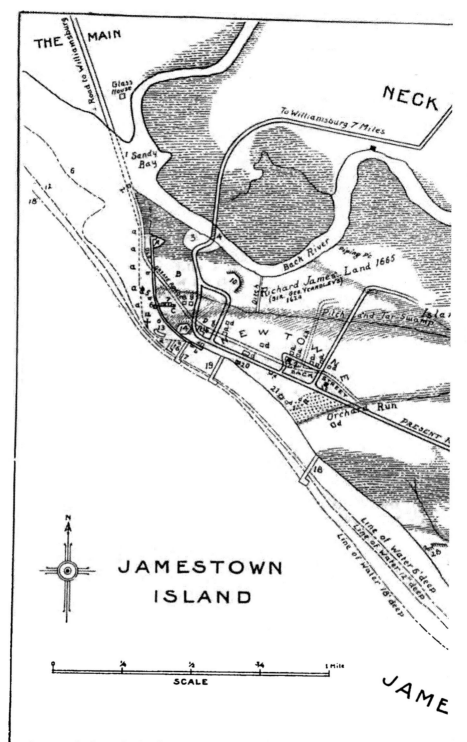

JAMESTOWN
ISLAND

SCALE

Engraved by Christopher Eng. Co., Rich'd, Va. 1906.

The western portion of the Island is composed of four ridges, the highest of which does not rise over fourteen feet above low tide. The first and second ridges are separated by a slash of the Back River; the second and third by a slash of Pitch and Tar Swamp; and the third and fourth by a depression inclining to Pitch and Tar Swamp from the southern point of the Island, which in 1607 projected into the river several hundred feet further than it does at present, forming with the southern shore a beautiful cove. The western shore extended in 1607 about 400 feet beyond the present sea wall, and the low ground between the third and fourth ridges widened at the head of the Island into a valley, in which a brick fort was placed at the close of the century.[1] A "lone cypress," standing about 300 feet in the water, marks the course originally taken by the branch of Pitch and Tar Swamp separating the second and third ridges.

The most important artificial landmarks are the church tower, and the ruins of the Jaquelin-Ambler House. Of the former I shall have much to say in the succeeding pages, but the history of the latter may be conveniently given here. These ruins stand on the fourth ridge of the Island about 350 yards east of the church tower, in the best part of what was once known as New Towne, very near the site of the houses of Sir Francis Wyatt, William Peirce and Richard Kempe. The Back Street ran close in front, and the turf fort of 1663 lay nearly south upon the river. This house was first built by Edward Jaquelin about 1710, and on his death in 1739 passed to Richard Ambler, who married his daughter. It was burnt in the Revolution and was restored by John Ambler, Richard Ambler's grandson. It was burned again in 1862, when the country was in the hands of the Federal troops; and it accidently caught on fire and was burned a third time in 1895. It has not been restored since, but its ragged and massive brick walls attest the dignity of the building.

When the first white settlers came to Virginia in 1607, the tract of land thus described, though called an Island, was in fact a peninsula, because of an isthmus or neck connecting it at the northwest corner with the mainland. The head of

---

[1] Yonge, *Site of Old Jamestowne*, 12. I have in this edition named the ridges after the more exact designation of Mr. Yonge.

Back River was then a creek, called Powhatan Creek, which, flowing from the country beyond, opened at the neck of the Island into a bay called " Sandy Bay." East of this bay, where the present bridge spans the Back River, was a landing called " Friggett Landing," proving by the name that the Back River was navigable for shipping. Further eastward down the Back River was a point called " Pyping Point "[1]— indicating a spot perhaps where the laborers " piped it " (smoked), after meals.

It is interesting to trace the history of the neck since the first settlement, for the rush of the waters and the beating of the tides have made great changes in the whole western shore of the Island.

Strachey described the isthmus in 1610 " as a slender neck no broader than a man will quaite a tileshard."

Mrs. An. Cotton, evidently referring to the middle of the neck, estimated[2] the width across in 1676 as ten paces (fifty feet), but it was probably more, as in 1688 Rev. John Clayton put the width (probably of the middle) at sixty or ninety feet,[3] though he added that during the Spring tides the whole of the neck was usually submerged. On the other hand, the distance from Back River to James River at Block House hill, which was at the beginning of the neck on the Island side, was stated in a grant[4] to William Sherwood in 1694 as " six chains " or 198 feet (" 33 feet to a chain ").

We have no further information till the year 1748, fifty-four years later, when we learn that, long before that time, Richard Ambler, who owned the ferry on the Island, had found it necessary to place over the neck a causeway, which the relentless waves had so affected that the people of James City in the year referred to petitioned the assembly to make Ambler repair the same.[5] Thirty-three years later, as we learn from Tarleton's Campaigns, Jamestown was separated from the mainland by a small gut " not two feet wide at the

---

[1] Patent to Richard James, Va. Land Register, III., 368.
[2] Our Late Troubles in Virginia, written in 1676 by Mrs. An. Cotton of Q. Creeke. (Force, Tracts, I., No. ix.)
[3] A Letter of Mr. John Clayton, rector of Crofton at Wakefield in Yorkshire, May 12, 1688. (Force, Tracts, III., No. xii, p. 23.)
[4] Va. Land Register, VIII., 384.
[5] Council Journal.

reflux of the tide;" but that water was now the prevalent feature of the spot is shown by the fact that the crossing was known at this time as "Jamestown Ford." Nevertheless, according to Louis H. Girardin, formerly professor of modern languages, history and geography in William and Mary College, a bit of connecting land remained as late as 1805, though he spoke of it as "very narrow" and as inundated "at the time of high water," i. e. at each high tide; and further said that the force of the river "threatened soon unless counteracted to form a new channel through the Island, a denomination which Jamestown may shortly assume."[1]

When we next read of the Island in 1837, we learn that the neck "had long since disappeared, having been washed away by the force of the current and the tide." [2]

The Island had passed the year before into the possession of Colonel Goodrich Durfey, and he, feeling the necessity of better communication with the outside world, constructed about 1844 a bridge in the water over the submerged neck, and upon this bridge passed a stage carrying the mail and passengers to the wharf at Jamestown, where the steamer received them.[3]

In 1848, Benson J. Lossing visited the place and found John Coke, father of Richard Coke, late senator from Texas, in possession. Dr. Lossing made a sketch of the Sandy Bay from the opposite shore, then "four hundred yards" distant from the Island, and this view, which is printed, shows the piles only of the bridge. The bridge itself, erected by Colonel Durfey, had been swept away some months before by a tremendous gale and high tide, which submerged a large part of the Island, for three days keeping Mr. Coke and his family, who resided there, close prisoners, and causing them to use for fuel ornamental trees near the house, in the absence of other material.[4]

In October, 1856, Bishop Meade, in company with Dr. Silas Totten, of William and Mary College, and others, visited the Island then owned by Major William Allen, of Clermont. The mainland and the Island were found separated by " a third of

[1] *The Late Jubilee at Jamestown* (1807), p. 8, *note.*
[2] Richard Randolph, in *Southern Literary Messenger*, III., 303.
[3] Mr. J. R. Bacon's Statement, see Appendix A.
[4] Lossing, *Field Book of the American Revolution*, II., 446.

a mile (?) of water," and the only access was by row-boat. A large portion of the most beautiful part of the Island had been engulfed by the waves and the bank was giving away within 150 yards of the old tower to the church.[1]

Now how much land has the Island lost at the upper end since the voyagers landed in 1607? In 1716, Hon. Philip Ludwell, disturbed by the claims that " the Governor's Land " of 3,000 acres belonging to the public took in a part of Greenspring, said that the shore for three miles above Jamestown, along the mainland, where the Governor's Land was situated, had lost by the encroachments of the river 100 acres in a period of thirty years, which showed a recession of the shore line of more than nine feet a year.[2]

VIEW OF JAMESTOWN FROM THE RIVER.
(Sketched in 1857 by Catherine C. Hopley, an English lady.)

In 1805, Professor Girardin declared that " many yards of the palisades erected by the first settlers " were still to be seen at low tide standing at least 150 or 200 paces from the shore. But really Girardin did not know whether the " first settlers " had anything to do with these palisades or not, and he was at best only guessing at their distance.[3]

In 1895, the ladies of the Association for the Preservation of Virginia Antiquities obtained from Congress an appropriation

[1] Meade, Old Churches, &c., I., 111.
[2] Va. Magazine, V., 386.
[3] The Late Jubilee at Jamestown, 7.

of $10,000 for protecting the Island against the encroachment of the waters. Large flat rocks were placed at the west end against the shore bank, but the waves scooped out the sand from behind them and caused them to fall. In five years the shore receded by my measurement some fifteen feet, or on the average about three feet a year, but the recession was doubtless much retarded by the rocks.

April 28, 1900, the author, in company with Mr. H. B. Smith, of Williamsburg, repaired to the western end of Jamestown Island and made some measurements and observations. The distance of the "lone cypress tree" from the shore was measured and found to be about 290 feet. As this cypress tree in 1845 stood at time of low tide at the water's edge, this would suggest, after making allowances for our line of measurement being out of the perpendicular, a recession annually of about five feet.

Supposing then five feet to be the average annual loss of the western shore for 300 years, the diameter of the prism of abrasion if continuous would be as much as 1,500 feet, which would indicate the absorption of over fifty acres of land. But Mr. Yonge points out[1] that as long as the protecting shore along the mainland above the Island stood firm, the abrasion must have been very slight, and that as the protecting shore did not begin to give way till about 1700, twenty acres would be a liberal allowance for erosion. This conjecture is supported by an interesting plat preserved in the Ambler MSS., and made in 1680 by John Soane, surveyor, for William Sherwood. As shown by this plat, the difference in length of two lines — one from the ancient shore line of 1680 to a northerly line running through "Friggett Landing," and the other from the sea wall to the same northerly line does not exceed 400 feet, which is even less than Mr. Yonge's estimate of the diameter of the prism of abrasion (480 ft.). The ravages of the water at first appear to have been directed against the connecting isthmus, and a comparison of the plat with the present topography shows that "Block House hill" stood out in the water 900 feet from the present sea wall. As the "lone cypress," now about 300 feet from the sea wall, was near the shore in 1845, most of the erosion of the Island must have happened after that

[1] Yonge, *Site of Old Jamestown*, 14.

year — a fact attributable, according to Mr. Yonge, to the introduction on the river of side-wheeled steamers.

At the time of my visit to the Island in 1900, the average depth, at low tide, of the water upon the submerged neck was found to be about two feet. From the Island to the mainland, following the line of the piles, the distance was about 1,700 feet or nearly one-third of a mile. On the mainland we found the bed of the old highway to Williamsburg, with large trees growing in its middle. The distance from a tree standing on the first ridge along the river side to the southern shore of the fourth ridge was found to be very nearly 1,500 feet. From the latter point to the middle of the third ridge, it was 300 feet. On the shore at this place were the last relics of a brick building reputed a powder magazine; and along this ridge scattered brick and an old well indicated where some buildings once stood. From the middle of the third ridge to the middle of the branch of Pitch and Tar Swamp separating the second ridge and third ridge, the distance was 361 feet; from the last point to the top of the second ridge, it was 339 feet; and from the top of this ridge to a tree on the first ridge near the submerged neck, it was 500 feet.

As is shown by various land grants, the general direction of the western shore of the Island was approximately the same 250 years ago as it is today — nearly north and south.

The James River varies in width from three and one-fourth to one and one-eighth miles, corresponding, in the widest measurement, to the eastern end of the Island, and, in the narrowest, to the western end. The mean tidal rise and fall is about two feet, and as might be expected the greatest depth of water, eighty-one feet, is in the narrow part of the river, while in the widest part opposite to Goose Hill the channel shallows to about twenty feet.

The varying depth of the channel at Jamestown Island has had remarkable effect upon the history of Virginia. It was because the channel was so deep and approached so near the shore at the upper end that the Island itself, and especially that part of the Island, was selected for settlement; and it was because the water off Goose Hill flats did not afford a sufficient depth to allow the ironclad *Virginia* to pass to Richmond in 1862, that she was blown up by the Confederates off Craney Island.

The map of Virginia, engraved by Frederick Bossler from actual surveys by James Madison, President of William and Mary College (who died in 1812), gives an excellent representation of the topography of Jamestown Island and vicinity, but the scale is too small to admit of many details.

SEA WALL.
Lately erected at the western end of the Island.

THE COUNTRY NEIGHBORING JAMESTOWN ISLAND.

The portion of the country beyond the neck on the west side of Powhatan Creek was called *The Main*.

The portion of the country on the north side of Back River, between Powhatan Creek and Mill Creek, which enters the Back River from the north at the lower end of the Island, was called *Neck of Land*. This should be carefully distinguished from the "neck of land" descriptive of the isthmus formerly connecting Jamestown Peninsula with the mainland.

The country on the north side below the Island, between Coleman's Creek and Archer's Hope Creek, was called *Archer's Hope*.

On the other side of the river a creek known as Gray's Creek cut off *Swann's Point*, opposite to the Point on Jamestown Island above the church. The early settlements in that region were called the *Plantations Across the Water*.

Further up the river on the same side were *Four Mile Tree* and *Pace's Pains*.

And down the river nearly opposite to Archer's Hope was *Hog Island*.

V.

THE ENGLISH AT JAMESTOWN.

May 13, 1607, the *Sarah Constant*, the *Godspeed*. and the *Discovery* came to Jamestown Island, and lay " so neare the shoare that they were moored to the trees in six fathom water." And now the organization of the council was completed by the election of Edward Maria Wingfield as president for one year.[1]

The landing took place the next day, May 14, 1607, at the southwest point of the Island, which projected into the water about 300 feet more southerly and 400 feet more westerly than it does now, forming a cove. As the land there was very low, they selected for their habitation place the rising bank a little east of the ships.[2] The first work undertaken was to clear an opening in the dense growth of trees for a stockade, and while it was building Captain Newport, in the shallop, left Jamestown May 22, with twenty others, to look for a gold mine at the Falls of James River. He was gone only a week, but, before he returned, the Indians assaulted the settlement, and his assistance was necessary in building the palisades. The stockade was completed June 15, was " trianglewise, having three bulwarks (one) at every corner like a halfe Moone," and in each bulwark a piece or two of ordnance was mounted. It enclosed a little more than an acre of land, for the side facing the river was 420 feet long and the other two sides 300 feet each. Through each curtain was a gateway, and each gateway was protected by a piece of ordnance inside.[3]

Within the enclosure, the settlers placed their rude habitations, of which the best consisted of rails covered with sedge and earth, and plastered inside with bitumen or tough clay. Some of the settlers lived in holes in the ground, called on the western plains, "dug-outs," where they are sometimes used. The cabins were very hot in summer and cold in winter. Near the fort, on two little knolls (called " mountains " by George

[1] Smith, *Works* (Arber's ed.), 91.
[2] Yonge, *Site of Old Jamestowne*, 18.
[3] Purchas, *His Pilgrimes*, IV., 1752, 1753.

[30]

Percy), they planted most of their English wheat, and by the time the fort was finished it had sprung "a man's height from the ground." This was the *first essay* at farming on James River.[1]

Newport departed with the ships for England June 22, and after this the sufferings of the colonists were too great to permit any more improvements during the summer. They were besieged by Indians, a small ladle of "ill conditioned" barley meal was the daily ration, the brackish water of the river served them for drink, and dissensions broke out between the president and councillors. In a short time Gosnold died; Kendall, detected in a design to desert the colony, was shot; and Wingfield was deposed from the presidency, and substituted by John Ratcliffe. By September 10, of the one hundred and four men left behind by Newport only forty-six remained alive. September 17, occurred the *two first jury trials* in America, when Jehu Robinson and John Smith sued the deposed president for slander, and recovered verdicts from the jury,— Robinson for 100£ damages, and Smith for 200£.[2]

In September the Indians made peace with the settlers and sent them daily supplies of corn and wild meat; and, the cool weather coming on, the river was full of wild fowl, which supplied the survivors with nourishing food and restored them to health. The settlers purchased[3] the Island from the Paspaheghs, and resumed their work upon the frail habitations;[4] and when in November the Indians declined in their kindly attentions, Smith, as cape merchant, was sent to Kecoughtan and other places on James River to trade for corn, in which business he was very successful. In December, while on an exploring trip up the Chickahominy, he was captured by the Indians, who killed two of his companions and carried him from village to village, and finally to Werowocomoco on York River, where he was saved from death by Pocahontas, Powhatan's daughter. Through her influence he was sent back to Jamestown, where on his arrival January 2 he was promptly arrested by the council and sentenced to death under the Levitical law for the loss of the two men killed by the Indians.

[1] Percy, *Discourse* in Smith, *Works* (Arber's ed.), lxx.
[2] Wingfield, *Discourse* in Smith, *Works* (Arber's ed.), lxxxiii.
[3] *True Declaration*. (Force, *Tracts*, III., No. xvi.)
[4] Smith, *Works* (Arber's ed.), 392.

And he would have been executed the next day, had not that self same evening Newport returned with the " First Supply " of men and provisions and caused his release from custody.[1] Newport found only thirty or forty persons surviving at Jamestown, and he brought about seventy more.

Five days after Newport arrived at Jamestown, the habitations in the fort, together with all the ammunition and provisions, were destroyed by a fire so intense that it burned the palisades though eight or ten yards distant. The result was that as the winter was very severe; many died from exposure while working to restore the town; but with the help of Captain Newport and his mariners the palisades, cabins, church, and storehouse were partially rebuilt before the Winter was out.[2] The provisions brought in this supply were scant, and the mortality would have been even greater, but for the relief afforded by Pocahontas and her Indians, who frequently resorted to the fort.

Nevertheless, to satisfy the expectations of the authorities in England, the settlers, instead of being put to clearing and planting the ground when Spring came, were forced to give all their time to loading the ships with cedar and clapboards and digging for " fool gold."[3]

April 10, 1608, Newport left the colony, and ten days later Captain Francis Nelson arrived in the *Phoenix,* with forty additional settlers. He stayed till June, and during the interval most of the time of the settlers was taken up in providing another load of cedar. So that no improvements were made at Jamestown beyond some slight repairs made by Smith and Scrivener upon the frail habitations in the stockade.[4] Consequently, the second Summer at Jamestown was characterized by misfortunes similar to those of the first. Ratcliffe in his turn was deposed, and after a brief administration by Scrivener, John Smith, who had been absent most of the time exploring Chesapeake Bay, became president, September 10, 1608.

Resuming the work of making repairs, he enlarged the area of the fort by the addition of about three acres and changed

---

[1] Wingfield, *Discourse* in Smith, *Works* (Arber's ed.), lxxxvi.
[2] Ibid.
[3] *A Breife Declaration* in State Senate Doc., extra (1874), 70.
[4] Smith, *Works* (Arber's ed.), 409.

the plan to a "five square forme" (*i. e.* a pentagon). While thus engaged, the Second Supply arrived in October, bringing with it seventy passengers, who added to the fifty persons found at Jamestown raised the population to about 120. Among the new comers were eight Poles and Germans sent over to make glass, pitch and soap ashes, and two women Mrs. Forrest and her maid Ann Burras, who were the first of their sex to settle on James River. The marriage in the church at Jamestown about two months later of this Ann Burras to one of the settlers named John Laydon, a carpenter by trade, was *the first recorded English marriage on the soil of the United States,*[1] and their child, Virginia, born[2] the following year, was the *first child born* in the first permanent English settlement on the Western Continent.

Newport brought a letter from the superior council in England which showed that they were not at all satisfied with the cargoes sent home at the cost of so much labor and suffering, and the colonists were directed to explore the country above the Falls for a gold mine. Compliance with these instructions took them off to such an extent from their necessary labors that, had not Newport and Smith during the Winter following made repeated visits to the Indians, they might all have starved before the Spring.

CAPTAIN JOHN SMITH.

The account which Smith gives of the labor performed by the colonists, from February to May, 1609, speaks much for their endurance. It was by itself a herculean task to cut down forty acres of trees and prepare the land for corn; but besides this, they dug a deep well in the fort, re-covered their church,

[1] Smith, *Works* (Arber's ed.), 130.
[2] Hotten, *Emigrants to America,* 185, 245.

3

erected twenty new cabins, manufactured a supply of glass, set up a block house at the isthmus, and built a new fort up Gray's creek opposite to Jamestown.[1] The misfortunes which interrupted these proceedings are to be attributed not to the colonists, but to the carelessness of Smith, who reigned sole ruler — the other councillors being all dead or gone to England. While they were engaged at the fort across the river, it was suddenly discovered that most of the corn on which the colonists depended was consumed by rats. And as the remainder was " unfit to eat," Smith, in order to save the colony, had to disperse the settlers, sending some to live with the Indians, and others to the oyster banks down the river, where at the end of nine weeks the oyster diet caused all their skins " to peel off from head to foot as if they had been fleade."[2]

While these matters were happening, the reports brought by the ships of the dissensions in the council at Jamestown received the attention of the London Company. In May, 1609, a new charter was issued,[3] extending the company's territory for 400 miles along the coast and inland west and northwest to the South Sea, and giving the stockholders the power to appoint " a sole and absolute governor," for Virginia. Not long afterwards a Third Supply was made ready, and in June, 1609, Sir Thomas Gates took passage as governor with about 500 settlers. But the voyage over was very unfortunate; for an epidemic broke out among the passengers, and there followed a great storm which scattered the fleet and wrecked upon the Bermuda Islands the *Sea Venture,* which bore the governor and one hundred and fifty other passengers; and though the rest of the fleet reached Jamestown in safety, their arrival only added to the troubles already existing there.

The new settlers brought with them the yellow fever and the London plague, and their supplies were all ruined by the rain and sea water. Moreover, Smith received their leaders very unkindly, and after several violent quarrels he took passage for England in October, 1609, with the returning ships, leaving as president, George Percy, brother to the Earl

[1] Smith, *Works* (Arber's ed.), 471.
[2] *A Breife Declaration,* 70.
[3] Hening, *Statutes at Large,* I., 80-98.

of Northumberland. Smith says that at his departure, Jamestown was well protected by ordnance and contained forty or fifty cabins, but it is probable that most of these houses were put up by the new arrivals, about 250 in number.[1]

There succeeded nine months of terrible suffering known as the *Starving Time,* during which most of the settlers died; and when the Spring of 1610 arrived only some sixty wretched survivors were living at Jamestown; and these were saved at the last moment in an almost miraculous manner.

In the month of May, when all hope seemed lost, two ships were discovered one day coming up the river. When they cast anchor, they were found to contain Sir Thomas Gates and the passengers of the *Sea Venture,* whom all at Jamestown considered lost at sea. These ships had been constructed by the castaways out of the cedar that grew in the Bermudas, and bore the names of the *Patience* and *Deliverance* — words of significant import to all the actors in this historic tragedy.

But if the colonists at Jamestown were astonished at the coming of the ships, Gates and his companions were much more so at the strange sights which met their eyes on the sorrow-stricken Island. As stated by Gates himself in a letter[2] written not long after: "Jamestown seemed raither as the ruins of some auntient (fortification), then that any people living might now inhabit it; the palisadoes he found tourne downe, the portes open, the gates from the hinges, the church ruined and unfrequented, empty houses (whose owners untimely death had taken newly from them) rent up and burnt, the living not hable, as they pretended, to step into the woodes to gather other fire-wood; and, it is true, the *Indian as fast killing without as the famine and pestilence within.*"

Gates relieved the immediate distress by the prompt distribution of provisions, and then asserted order by the publication of a code of martial law drawn up in England. Next he called a council of the leading officers, and, on their advice, decided to abandon the settlement, as the provisions brought from the Bermudas were only sufficient to last the company sixteen days longer.

[1] Smith, *Works* (Arber's ed.), 612.
[2] Brown, *Genesis of the United States,* 405.

And now it appeared, indeed, as if another sickening failure would be added to the long list of fruitless endeavors to plant an English colony in America. Sending ahead the pinnace *Virginia*, built on the coast of Maine in 1607, to Point Comfort to take on Captain Davis and the guard there, the company at Jamestown made ready for their own departure. June 7, 1610, Gates ordered all the small arms to be carried aboard, buried the cannon at the fort gate, and commanded every man to repair to the *Patience* and *Deliverance* at the beating of the drum; and while the men were going aboard, lest some one might set fire to the buildings in the town which they were abandoning, he caused his own company, under Captain George Yeardley, to embark after the rest, and was himself the last to leave the shore.[1]

It was in the evening that they left Jamestown, and they halted that night at Hog Island about six miles below the fort. The next morning they resumed their voyage, and had reached Mulberry Island, about eight miles further down, when they saw the white sails of a little vessel coming to meet them. It was the pinnace *Virginia,* and never did vessel bring more important message. Edward Brewster, its commander, informed Gates that Lord Delaware had arrived at Point Comfort with 150 settlers; and, thereupon, the colonists very unwillingly put back to Jamestown, and that evening took possession again of their forlorn habitations. Sunday, June 10, Lord Delaware arrived and went ashore in the afternoon with Sir Ferdinando Wainman. This was a great occasion and one duly appreciated at the time. Sir Thomas Gates caused his company to stand in arms, and William Strachey, the secretary of state, acted as color bearer.

As soon as the Lord Governor arrived near the south gate of the fort opening towards the river, he fell upon his knees, and made a long and silent prayer to God. Then arising, he walked to the entrance of the town, Strachey bowing before him with his colors, and letting them fall in the gateway at his Lordship's feet, who passed on to the church, where Rev. Richard Buck ("Sir Thomas Gates his preacher"), delivered an impressive sermon.

[1] Brown, *Genesis of the United States,* 406.

After this, Lord Delaware caused his ensign, Anthony Scott, to read his commission, which entitled him " Lord Governor and Captain General," during his life, of the colony and plantation in Virginia (" Sir Thomas Gates our Governor hitherto, being now styled therein Lieutenant General "), upon which Sir Thomas Gates delivered up to his Lordship " his owne commission, both patents, and the Counsell seale." Delaware next made the crowd a speech, in which he mingled words of reproach, warning, advice and cheer. He set the men to cleaning the town, and rehabilitating the houses, after a much more substantial manner. Boards were hewed and placed upon the roofs, and the sides of some of the houses were protected with Indian mats, which rendered them much more defensive against heat and cold. The chimneys were made of wattles daubed with clay and were wide and large, permitting great fires in the winter. Strachey accurately describes the new houses in the following quaint verses:

THOMAS WEST (Lord Delaware).

"We dwell not here to build vs Bowers
And Hals for pleasure and good cheere,
But Hals we build for vs and ours
To dwell in them whilst we live here."

The settlement of four acres was defended by new palisades, and everything was made safe and comfortable for the time being.[1]

Delaware next proceeded to settle matters with the Indians, and, in retaliation for the killing of Humphrey Blunt opposite to Blunt Point, he ordered Gates to attack and drive Powha-

[1] Purchas, *His Pilgrimes*, iv., 1753.

tan's son Pochins and his tribe from Kecoughtan; and when this was done, he erected two forts at the mouth of Hampton River, called Charles and Henry, about three miles from Point Comfort.   In the Autumn he sent out an expedition to the Falls of James River to search for gold mines, but, like its predecessors, the expedition proved a failure and many of the men perished by the Indians.   In a short time Delaware himself fell sick, and to save his life he departed the colony March 28, 1611,[1] leaving George Percy again in charge.

The houses in Jamestown having been built of unseasoned timber did not last long in the changeable climate of Virginia; and it is not surprising that Sir Thomas Dale, who arrived at Jamestown as deputy governor, May 21, 1611, found it necessary to make repairs on most of the buildings which Strachey had praised.[2] He also started some additional improvements, which were completed by Sir Thomas Gates, who came as lieutenant governor August 1. Besides repairing the church and storehouse they erected a stable, munition house, and a sturgeon dressing house; brick was made; and, as the water of the old well was contaminated, a new well was dug in the fort. "A bridge" (that is a wharf), "the first in the country," was built out to the channel about 200 feet distant "to land our goods dry and safe upon;" and a block house was put up on the Back River. Then a new platform for ordnance in the fort was raised and three storehouses joined together were constructed; making a block forty feet wide and 120 feet long. By the care and providence of Sir Thomas Gates, there were at Jamestown in 1614, when Ralph Hamor, Strachey's successor as secretary of state, wrote an account of Jamestown, "two rows of faire houses, all of framed timber, two stories and an upper garret or corn-loft high, besides some other houses without the town."[3] Among the houses referred to by Hamor was one built by Gates for a governor's house,[4] which was probably outside of the stockade, and in the section of the Island afterward known as

[1] Brown, *Genesis of the United States*, I., 490.
[2] Ibid., 492.
[3] Hamor, *True Discourse*, 33.
[4] *A Breife Declaration*, in Va. State Senate Doc. (extra), 1874, p. 80.

" New Towne." Gates stayed in Virginia till February, 1614, and after his departure the government was administered by Dale, marshal of the colony, till May, 1616. They subjected the colonists to the strictest martial law, and under the severe system of labor instituted "many young men of Auncyent Houses and born to estates of £1,000 by the year," perished[1] at Jamestown and at the new settlements up the river — Henrico, Bermuda Hundred and Charles Hundred.

During this period, however, there were interesting dealings with the Spanish, Indians and French. In 1611, a Spanish ship, sent to spy on the English colonists, came to Point Comfort where three of the officers — alcayde Don Diego de Molina, ensign Marco Antonio Perez, and pilot Francis Limbrye — going ashore, were arrested and remained prisoners at Jamestown for several years. Two years after this incident, succeeding some heavy punishments inflicted upon the Indians by Dale, Pocahontas was captured by Argall, and brought also to Jamestown. Not long afterwards, Gates and Dale, hearing that the French in Nova Scotia and Maine were preparing to settle New England, sent Argall with an armed vessel, who dispossessed the intruders and brought fifteen of them to Virginia, where they were added to the list of captives at Jamestown.

The colonists must have been much excited over this interesting collection, but if any of them were given to writing, Dale did not give him the time or opportunity to print his account. Most of the colonists during this period were engaged up the river, building Henrico, Bermuda Hundred and Charles City, where they were subjected by Dale to a more than " Scythian cruelty." At Jamestown, according to the report[2] of John Rolfe, who succeeded Hamor as secretary, there were in 1615 under the command of Lt. Sharpe, " in the absence of Captain Francis West," about sixty persons only, " whereof thirtie one are farmers;" who all maintained themselves with " food and rayment." The " farmers " referred to were of the fortunate class to whom Governor Dale gave three acres of land to be

. [1] *The Tragical Relation*, in Neill, *Virginia Company*, 407–411.
[2] Rolfe, *Relation* in *Southern Lit. Messenger*, V., 401.

cultivated in their own way, on condition of their paying two and one-half barrels of corn, and giving one month's service in every year to the public.

These were really dark days, and emigration from England entirely ceased. When Dale left in 1616, there were only 351 persons in the colony, and the enterprise might have been given over entirely had not, in the cultivation of tobacco begun by John Rolfe in 1612, a fresh hope been found. Dale frowned upon the new occupation, but after his departure Captain George Yeardley, who acted as deputy-governor for a year, gave the "weed" every encouragement, with the result that emigration set in again with force. Private companies were formed, who sent colonies of their own to Virginia; and, despite martial law which slew its hundreds and climatic disease which slew its thousands, the colony slowly increased in population. Three years after Dale's departure for Virginia the number of inhabitants had risen from 351 to 1,000.[1]

In the meantime, important changes ensued in England in the constitution of the London Company. Till 1612 all power had been invested in the treasurer, Sir Thomas Smith, and his council, but in that year the stockholders applied for and obtained a third charter limiting all important business to a quarterly meeting of the members. On the question of governing the colony, they soon divided into two parties, the "court party" in favor of continuing martial law, headed by Sir Robert Rich, afterwards Earl of Warwick, and the country or "patriot party" led by Sir Thomas Smith, Sir Edwin Sandys, the Earl of Southampton, Sir John Danvers, and John and Nicholas Ferrar. Of the two, the "country party" was the more numerous, and when the joint stock partnership expired November 30, 1616, they appointed Captain Samuel Argall, a kinsman of Treasurer Smith, to be deputy-governor of Virginia, with instructions to give every settler a dividend of fifty acres, and to permit him to visit England if he chose,[2] a privilege hitherto denied.

[1] Va. Company *Proceedings* (Va. Hist. Soc. Coll., new series, VII., pt. I., 65).

[2] Brown, *Genesis of the United States*, II., 775–779, 797–799, 1015.

Argall sailed to Virginia about the first part of April, 1617, and was received at Jamestown by Yeardley in military style, "his right hand file being led by an Indian." According to his own statement he found Jamestown in a very neglected condition. Only five or six of the "farm houses" described by Hamor were habitable, the palisades were rotten and broken, the wharf was in pieces, and even the well dug in 1611 was polluted and not fit to drink from. Argall attributes the evil to the rage for tobacco, and says that the market place, the margin of the streets and all other spare places were set with the plant.[1] He was partially correct, but the decay was really more truly attributable to the sappy timbers of which the works of the colony were constructed, and the deadening influences of martial law, which deprived labor of its natural stimulus of pride or self interest. But Argall, though he had been very useful in a subordinate capacity, proved wholly unscrupulous as deputy-governor. Instead of obeying his instructions, he continued the common slavery under one pretense or another, and even plundered the company of all the servants and live stock belonging to the

SIR EDWIN SANDYS,
Second treasurer, or president, of the London Company.

"common garden." Beyond patching up the houses he constructed no new buildings at Jamestown, except a wing to the governor's house erected by Gates, and a church, which was, however, paid for by the inhabitants.[2] In April, 1618, the company incensed at his behavior dispatched the Lord Governor Delaware to arrest him, but Delaware died on the way over, and Argall continued his tyrannical government one year longer.

[1] Smith, *Works* (Arber's ed.), 535.
[2] *A Breife Declaration*, in State Senate Documents (extra), 1874, p. 80.

During this interval, Sandys was associated with Sir Thomas Smith in preparing a paper which gave America its first experience of a written constitution for internal affairs. It abolished martial law and communism, assured to every settler a dividend of land, and authorized the people of the colony to elect representatives, who should share with the company in making laws. To put the constitution into effect Sir George Yeardley was sent in January, 1619, as "Governor and Captain General," and he arrived at Jamestown April 19, and made known the intentions of the London Company. At nearly the same time the supervision of Virginia affairs in England fortunately passed into the hands of Sir Edwin Sandys and his noble friend, the Earl of Southampton, assisted especially by the sincere and pure-hearted brothers John and Nicholas Ferrar, sons of Nicholas Ferrar, Sen.

Under the orders to Yeardley, Jamestown was made the capital of one of the four new corporations, comprising the settlements, and called "James Citty," which continued afterwards its official designation. Other events render the year memorable — the meeting of the first legislative assembly on July 30, the introduction in August of the first negro slaves, and the arrival from England of a ship with twenty young maidens "pure and undefiled," sold to the settlers for wives at the cost of their transportation, viz: one hundred and twenty pounds of tobacco, equivalent to $500, in present currency. Despite martial law, the culture of tobacco, which brought sometimes as much as $12 a pound in the London market, had already effected a great change. This is seen from an act of this earliest assembly which taxed every man according to the apparel worn by him or his wife,[1] and from a letter[2] of John Pory, written two months after the assembly adjourned, containing this paragraph: "Now that your lordship may know that we are not the veriest beggars in the world, our cow-keeper here of James citty on Sundays goes accowtered all in freshe flaming silke; and a wife of one that in England had professed the black arte, not of a schollar, but of a collier of Croyden, weares her rough bever hatt with a faire perle hatband, and a silken suite thereto correspondent."

[1] Va. State Senate Doc. (extra), 1874, 20.
[2] Massachusetts Hist. Soc., *Collections*, 4th series, IX., 11-13.

Soon, in place of the old log cabins, there rose at Jamestown and elsewhere framed buildings "better than many in England," and for three years this prosperous condition kept up, notwithstanding an appalling mortality among the swarms of settlers sent over by the vigorous managers of the London Company. One thousand people were in Virginia at Easter, 1619, and to this number 3,560 were added during the next three years; yet only 1,240 were resident in the colony on Good Friday, March 22, 1622, a day when the horrors of an Indian massacre reduced the number to 893.

Since 1614, when Pocahontas, during her captivity with the English, married John Rolfe, peace with the Indians prevailed with some slight interruptions. But in April, 1618, Powhatan died and the chief power was wielded by his brother Opechancanough, who secretly formed a plot for exterminating the English. In November, 1621, Sir Francis Wyatt arrived as governor, and soon after the blow was struck. Jamestown was fortunate enough to receive notice, and repelled the savages when they appeared before the fort in four canoes.

The scattered and dispersed mode of living in Virginia had enabled the savages to attack with deadly result, and after the massacre the colonists determined to abandon the weaker plantations and concentrate the surviving population in five or six well fortified places. Jamestown peninsula was one of these, and as the old quarters were overcrowded, William Claiborne, who, as surveyor general, came with Wyatt, laid out in 1623 a new section for habitation on the fourth ridge, eastward of the old stockade. The addition was called " New Towne," and commanded a beautiful view of the river, and here probably was already established the governor's house built by Gates in 1610, enlarged by Argall in 1617, and granted by the company in 1618 to the use of Governor Yeardley and his successors.[1]

[1] Instructions to Yeardley in *Va. Magazine*, II., 158.

THE MASSACRE IN 1622.

(From a cut in the Scheeps-Togt van Anthony Chester Na Virginia gedaan in het jaar, 1620. Printed in Leyden by Peter Vander, 1707. A pamphlet, 12 mo.)

According to the census of 1624, the number of inhabitants living at Jamestown and in the immediate neighborhood amounted in all to 353, distributed as follows: Jamestown, 182 persons, including three negroes; the Island outside, 39; the Main, 88; Neck of Land, 25; the Glass-house 5, and Archer's Hope 14. There were at this time in Jamestown four pieces of ordnance, twenty-two dwellings, one church, one merchant's store, three storehouses, and one large court-of-guard (guard house).

The new houses at Jamestown were framed buildings, and being made of seasoned lumber they were necessarily a great improvement over the sappy edifices hitherto constructed. In reference to the houses generally in Virginia Rev. William Mease told[1] the Londoners that " throughout his majesty's dominions here (in England) all labouringe men's houses (wch wee chiefly pfess ourselves to be) are in no wise generally for goodness to be compared unto

NICHOLAS FERRAR, JR.

them. And for the howses of men of better ranke and quallity they are so much better and convenyent yt noe man of quallity without blushinge can make exception against them."

The leading men resident in Jamestown were Sir Francis Wyatt, the governor; Sir George Yeardley, the ex-governor; Dr. John Pott, appointed in 1621 physician to the colony, on the recommendation of the distinguished physician Gulstone, who spoke of him as " a Master of Arts and well practised in Chirurgerie and physique;" Captain Ralph Hamor, Jr., formerly Dale's secretary of state; Captain William Peirce, father of John Rolfe's third wife Jane, and successor to Captain William Powell as captain of the fort; Captain Roger Smith, whose wife Jane in 1624 was probably widow of John Rolfe,

[1] Neill, *London Company*, 402.

as she had Elizabeth Rolfe, daughter of Jane Rolfe, living with her, and came to the colony in 1609 in the same vessel *The Blessing;* Edward Blaney, who came in 1621 in charge of a magazine of goods sent by the company in England, and who married the widow of Captain William Powell; Captain Richard Stephens, noted as party to the *first duel fought in an English colony,* wounding his antagonist George Harrison so severely that he died in a few days; Captain John Harvey of Lyme Regis, Dorset, England, afterwards governor; John Chew, a great merchant, who about 1649 removed to Maryland and was ancestor of Chief Justice Benjamin Chew, of Germantown, Pennsylvania; Captain George Menifie, who in 1635 took a leading part in the deposition of Sir John Harvey, resided afterwards at "Littletown" in James City County, and died about 1647 at "Buckland" in Charles City County.

All these lived in the "New Towne," and the following will perhaps give some idea of the Island as it appeared in 1624–1628.

There was a highway, called in later land grants the "Old Great Roade," and sometimes the "Maine Roade," which ran from the block house at the Isthmus, first near the river shore and then over the second and third ridges, past the old quarter of the town, and on by the northeast corner of the churchyard, till it connected with the Back Street in the "New Towne," and the road that passed along the river side.

"New Towne" began at Orchard Run, a branch of "Pitch and Tar Swamp," and on the first lot westward of this branch lived Captain John Harvey.[1] This lot, which contained six and one-half acres, lay between Back Street and the river bank; and as its west side was twenty-six poles or 143 yards, this approximately represented the distance of Back Street from the river at that point. Next to Harvey's lot was George Menifie's tract[2] of three roods and twenty poles, bounded as the patent states "northward upon the bounds over along to the ground belonging to Back Streete." Separated from Menifie by a cross street was Captain Ralph Hamor's[3] town lot

---

[1] *Va. Land Register,* I., 7.
[2] Ibid., I., 6.
[3] Ibid., I., 5.

of an acre and a half, which "abutted southward upon the highway along the banke of the Maine River and northward upon the Back Streete." Its breadth "alwayes" was eleven poles, and its eastern side was twenty-two and its western nineteen poles in length.

Next to Hamor was Captain Richard Stephens, whose wife Elizabeth was daughter of Abraham Peirsey, cape merchant of the colony, and married secondly Captain John Harvey. His lot[1] contained sixty rods, and reached back to the lot[2] of John Chew, which contained one rood and nine poles and faced north upon the Back Street. Next to Captain Richard Stephens, was a lot belonging to one Jackson (probably John Jackson), which lay nearly south of the present ruined Jaquelin-Ambler house.

On the north of Back Street, opposite to Captain John Harvey's lot, and fronting upon the street twenty-five poles, was Dr. John Pott's lot[3] of three acres, which he enlarged in 1628 by adding nine acres in the rear. On his west was a small tract belonging in 1624 to Captain William Peirce, whose house was pronounced by George Sandys, the poet and brother of Sir Edwin Sandys, the "fairest in Virginia." Sandys had a room there, in which he raised silkworms and turned into English the Latin of Ovid's Metamorphoses. Next to Peirce, was the lot of Governor Sir Francis Wyatt, not far from the site of the ruins of the Jaquelin-Ambler house; and north of Wyatt's lot were the four acres of Captain Roger Smith described in the patent as bounding "South upon the pale of the Governor's Garden, north upon the ground of Sir George Yeardley divided by the highway, eastward upon the bridge in the said highway leading into the Island," (i. e. the part of the Island north of Pitch and Tar Swamp) "and also upon the yard of Captain William Peirce, and west upon the highway leading into the Parke."[4] A cartway passed from Back Street through Captain William Peirce's lot over the Bridge across the swamp to the "Island House" of Richard Kingsmill.

[1] *Va. Land Register.*, I., 1.
[2] Ibid., I., 7.
[3] Ibid., I., 8.
[4] The leaf in the record book containing this grant was torn out a few years ago, when the agents of West Virginia copied the books in the Land Office; but I had previously made a careful copy of the descriptive part, as above.

Finally, in the rear of Smith on the third ridge was Sir George Yeardley's lot[1] of seven acres and one rood, and it abutted "northerly upon the Back River, southerly upon the ground of Captain Roger Smith, easterly upon the railes and fence which pteth the same from the land of the Maine Island and westerly upon the Parke." Of an ancient English family, Yeardley came to Virginia a poor man, but from the culture of tobacco amassed so much money that at his appointment as governor in 1619 he was able to spend £3,000 in providing an outfit.[2] In 1625, he was the richest man in Virginia, and had, at his residence in Jamestown, his wife, Lady Temperance Yeardley, his three children, sixteen white employees, and eight negro slaves.[3]

The parts of the Back Street located by the patents extended from Orchard Run to the ruins of the Jaquelin-Ambler mansion, a distance of about 400 yards. The "street" was sixty feet wide, and had the same general direction east and west as the highway referred to in the patents as the "way along the Greate River" or "the Maine River," which constituted the front street of the New Towne. "The Back Street," says[4] Mr. Yonge, "could not have been a street in the modern signification of the word, with sidewalks and pavements, for paving before the doors of houses, even in 'London Towne,' was not introduced until 1614. It seems to have merged into the 'old Greate Road,' which led to the head of the Island and passed near the northeast corner of the old churchyard, a few rods from the same corner of the present one, near which there appear to be traces of a road.

"Traces of the highway along the river-bank, bordered by

---

1 William Claiborne, who surveyed this lot, adds a note in the records: "This ground by measure conteyneth as said seaven acres and a quarter on that side towards the back river it conteynenth thirtie two poles there lying a little marsh between the same and the back river, the aforesaid towards Capt. Smith's ground is little more than thirtie fower poles." This patent was lost from the records at the same time as Roger Smith's, but it was copied by Dr. E. D. Neill, who published it in the *Macallester Historical Contributions* (1st series), No. 1, 32.

2 John Pory's letter in Mass. Hist. Soc. *Collections* (4th series), IX., 14–16.

3 Hotten, *Emigrants to America*, 173, 222.

4 Yonge, *Site of Old Jamestowne*, 34–35.

its gnarled and riven mulberries, lineal descendants, no doubt, of some cited in several patents as reference trees, are still to be seen. The planting of mulberry trees for feeding silk-worms was initiated in 1621, and made compulsory by statute. Silk culture received attention as early as 1614, but the enterprise was never a commercial success. Foreign workmen were imported to teach silk making, and a present of silk was sent Charles II. by Sir William Berkeley in 1668.

"New Towne after 1624 was the most thickly inhabited part of James City, and the grants for land show that the location has not been encroached upon to any considerable extent by the waters of James River."

In the section of the Island, north of "New Towne," we know of only one person at this time — Richard Kingsmill, and he owned eighty acres called the "Island House" Tract, situated between Back River and Pitch and Tar Swamp.

In the section of the Island east of James City, Ensign William Spencer had some land[1] near Black Point, and adjoining him on the west was John Johnson, yeoman, with fifteen acres.[2] West of Johnson were twelve acres, between Back River and "the highway leading to Black Point," belonging to John Southern, gent.;[3] and, separated by a marsh called Tucker's Hole, were twelve acres south of Kingsmill's Creek,[4] patented February 20, 1620, by William Fairfax, and sold by him December 18, 1620, to Rev. Richard Buck who died in 1623. A "green thicket" parted this tract from Mary Bailey's tract of ten acres which lay still further west.

Adjoining his tract already mentioned and bounding south on the land[5] of Mary Holland, widow of Gabriel Holland, and west on that of Thomas Passmore, carpenter, John Southern had another tract of twelve acres. Mary Holland's land referred to amounted to twelve acres "lately in the tenure of her former husband William Pinke, alias William Jones," and Thomas Passmore's land[6] also comprised twelve acres, which lay "south upon the highway running close to

[1] *Va. Land Register,* I., 15.
[2] Ibid.
[3] Ibid., I., 55.
[4] Ibid., I., 648.
[5] Ibid., I., 11.
[6] Ibid., I., 10.

Goose Hill Marsh," and extended east and west forty-eight poles and north and south forty poles. Near by, and "south of the highway leading to Black Point," were eight acres[1] of Richard Tree, carpenter, "who came as a freeman in the *George,* with Captain Abraham Peirsey, cape merchant." His neighbor on the south was Edward Grindall.

Abutting on the " Maine River," at Goose Hill, three ridges of land, containing eight acres each,[2] belonged respectively to Sir Thomas Dale, William Spencer, yeoman, "an antient planter," and John Lightfoot, also "an old planter," who came in the *Sea Venture* in 1610 with Sir Thomas Gates and Sir George Somers.

HENRY WRIOTHESLEY,
Earl of Southampton.
Third treasurer, or president, of
the London Company.

Finally, as appears from the above account, there was a road which connected Black Point with the river street of " New Towne " at the head of Passmore's Creek.

Probably, at the building of " New Towne," some were sanguine enough to hope that a real city would rise at Jamestown, but these hopes, if entertained, received a severe shock by the order, not long after, permitting the re-establishment of the old plantations. The colonists carried fire and sword among the Indian villages along James River, and soon drove the Indians far back into the forests. Jamestown Island, therefore, instead of becoming a town with a steadily increasing population, served the bulk of the colonists chiefly as a safety place for their hogs and cattle, which found

---

[1] *Va. Land Register,* I., 19.
[2] Ibid., II., 9, 10.

good feeding in the rich marsh land of Passmore's Creek and Pitch and Tar Swamp.[1]

In the meantime, the attention of the people of Virginia was directed to a danger in England which threatened their rights as freemen. The Spanish government regarded English possession of Virginia as an intrusion on Spanish territory, and the Virginia tobacco trade, coming in competition with the West India product, excited their jealousy. As force was out of question, Count Gondomar, the Spanish ambassador at London, tried to poison the king against the company; and in this work he was aided by a faction in the company itself headed by Sir Thomas Smith and Alderman Johnson. The king was already jealous of Sandys and Southampton, who opposed him in Parliament; and, as the massacre and amazing mortality in Virginia afforded him an excuse, he was now easily persuaded to take action. In 1623, he sent several commissioners to Virginia, and on their one-sided report of the condition of things had the charter declared null and void in the court of the king's bench, May 24, 1624.

Thus fell the great London Company, which in settling Virginia expended upward of £200,000 (equal to $5,000,000 in present currency), and sent more than eight thousand emigrants. In this service the company did not escape the troubles incident to the mercenary purpose of a joint stock corporation, yet under Sandys and Southampton it assumed a national and patriotic character, which entitles it to be considered the greatest and noblest association ever organized by the English people. The heavy cost of the settlement was not a loss, for it secured to England a fifth kingdom and planted in the new world the germs of civil liberty. The change proved to the advantage of the colony, which had outgrown the management of a distant corporation.[2]

At Jamestown, sympathy with the company was so openly expressed that Wyatt and his council ordered their clerk, Edward Sharpless, to lose his ears for giving to the king's commissioners copies of some of their papers; and in January, 1624, a protest called the *Tragical Relation* was addressed to the king, denouncing the administration of Sir Thomas

[1] Smith, *Works* (Arber's ed.), 887.
[2] Tyler, *England in America*, 88.

Smith, and extolling that of Sandys and Southampton. Although Wyatt cordially joined in this protest, and was a most popular governor, the general assembly in the same year passed an act[1] which inhibited the governor from laying any taxes or impositions upon the colony except with the consent of the assembly. By this act Virginia first asserted on the American continent the *indissoluble connection of taxation with representation*.

After the dissolution of the London Company, affairs were very much depressed in the colony on account of the death of James I., the uncertainty attending land titles, and even the form of government. Yet emigration continued, and while Jamestown served chiefly as a landing place for colonists who settled elsewhere, the wealth and population of the colony increased. In June, 1627, the following action took place[2] at Jamestown:

A court held 25th. June, 1627, S[r] George Yeardley, K[nt], Governor &c., Capt. Smyth and M[r] Claybourne: whereas M[r] William Barnes and Robt. Paramor did on Thursday last behave themselves very negligently on their watch, it is, therefore, ordered that they shall pay 3 days work apiece in cuting downe and clearing off all shrubs and lowe wood as are before the town in the fields, & likewise that Goodman Osborne[3] for the like offence give one day's work.

This order was doubtless entered to guard against the savages, who still carried on a desultory war with the English.

November 13, 1627, Sir George Yeardley died at Jamestown, and was interred either in the church or churchyard. This good man was one of the greatest benefactors of Virginia, and with Sir Edwin Sandys deserves a monument at the hands of the people of the United States. If Sandys instituted the move for a representative government on this continent, Yeardley executed the orders and proved himself always the sympathetic friend of liberty.

After Yeardley's death Charles I. sent directions to acting Governor Francis West to summon a general assembly, and March 26, 1628, after an interval of four years, the regular

[1] Hening, *Statutes at Large*, I., 124.
[2] *Va. Magazine*, IV., 160.
[3] John Osborne.

law-making body again assembled at Jamestown — an event second only in importance to the original meeting in 1619.

Jamestown Island was now pretty well freed from trees, and was, for the most part, "pasture and gardens." The soil was rich, and in 1629 "Mrs. Pearce" (wife of Captain William Peirce), "an honest and industrious woman," who "had been there (in Virginia) neere twentie years and now returned to England" reported[1] that she had gathered from her garden "neere an hundred bushels of figges," and that "of her own provision she could keepe a better house in Virginia than here in London for 3 or 400 pounds a yeare, yet went thither with little or nothing." The population of the colony at large chiefly under the stimulus of tobacco had risen from 893 after the massacre in 1622 to about 3,000 in 1629.

In October of this year (1629) George Calvert, Lord Baltimore, who planned to obtain a large grant of land in Virginia, visited Jamestown with his wife and children. Dr. John Pott had succeeded West as acting governor; and now Pott and his council suspecting Baltimore's motives tendered him the oath of supremacy, which the various instructions of the king strictly enjoined upon them to require of all new comers. This oath, Baltimore, as a Catholic, refused to take, and he soon after sailed away to press his suit in person at court. During his stay at Jamestown, Baltimore was treated coldly; but, when one Thomas Tindall "gave him the lie and threatened to knock him down," the council vindicated Virginia hospitality by putting the offender in the pillory for two hours.[2] As Baltimore was unable to take his wife and children with him back to England, they were hospitably cared for at Jamestown for some months. Baltimore obtained a charter in England, which resulted in the first spoliation of Virginia territory under the charter of 1609 by the establishment of Maryland as an independent colony.

[1] Smith, *Works* (Arber's ed.), 887.
[2] Hening, *Statutes at Large*, I., 552.

These were exciting days at Jamestown, and Col. William Claiborne, the surveyor of " New Towne," who had settled a colony at Kent Island in the limits of Maryland, became the central figure in the colony. John Harvey, who succeeded Pott as governor in 1630, courted the favor of Lord Baltimore, and in 1635 Claiborne's friends in the council and assembly arrested Harvey and shipped him off to England. However,

Charles I. pronounced the deposition of Harvey as an act of " regal authority;" and, fearing the precedent, gave an order for his reinstatement. He did not return, however, until about eighteen months after his deposition; and in the meantime Captain John West, brother of Lord Delaware, acted as governor.

Harvey reached Virginia the second time in January, 1637, and the assembly which met him at Jamestown, February 20, 1637, made a special effort to promote the growth of the place. They passed an act[1] confirmed at a subsequent session February 20, 1638, offering " a convenient proportion of ground for house and garden " to every person who should build thereon within two years. Harvey joined his endeavors with the rest, and in January, 1639, he wrote[2] home as follows: " there are twelve houses and stores since built in the

---

[1] *Va. Land Register,* I., 689.
[2] *Calendar of State Papers,* colonial, 1574-1660, p. 288.

town, one of brick by the secretary (Richard Kempe, Esq.), the fairest ever known in this country for substance and uniformity, by whose example others have undertaken to build framed houses and beautify the place."

Harvey stated also that he and the council, as well as the masters of ships and the ablest planters, had liberally subscribed for a brick church, and that a levy had been laid for a state house, but that the recent instructions permitting ships

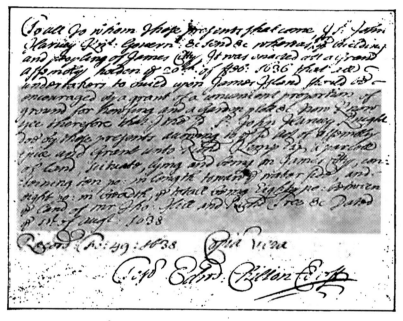

RICHARD KEMPE'S GRANT OF AN HALF ACRE IN NEW TOWNE IN 1638.
A copy about 1683.

to land goods elsewhere than at Jamestown had disheartened the investors. Till that order "there was not one foot of ground for half a mile together by the river side that was not taken up and undertaken to be built upon."

Several of those who obtained lots at this time — such as Richard Kempe, Arthur Bayley, Captain Thomas Hill, Richard Tree and George Menifie — located them in New

Towne. Rev. Thomas Hampton secured a tract on a ridge
"behind the church," presumed to be the old framed church
erected in 1617–1619 at the site of the subsequent brick
churches. And Alexander Stonar, "brickmaker," obtained a
small tract "near the brick kiln," which the description shows
to have been near the neck of the Island.[1] It was doubtless
from this brick kiln that the bricks for Kempe's house referred

COURT ORDER OF LAND FOR SIR FRANCIS WYATT IN 1641.
A copy about 1683.

to by Harvey, and for the other brick buildings now erected,
were obtained.

Richard Kempe's brick house stood in a half acre lot[2] on
the Back Street, very near the site of the present Jaquelin-
Ambler House; and when the liberal Sir Francis Wyatt, once
governor before, superseded Harvey in November, 1639, this

[1] Va. Land Register, I., 67.
[2] Ibid., I., 587.

property was sold by Kempe to him; and in October, 1641, the general court gave Wyatt three acres more, covering the site of his old lot in 1624.

Wyatt was succeeded by Sir William Berkeley, whose instructions dated August 1, 1641, directed him, by way of encouraging the building of substantial dwelling houses in the colony, to give 500 acres to every person who should build a brick house twenty-four feet long and sixteen feet broad, with a cellar to it; and, "because the buildings at Jamestown were for the most part decayed and the place found to be unhealthy and inconvenient in many respects," he was, with the advice of his council and of the general assembly, permitted to change the chief town to another place, " retaining the ancient name of Jamestown."[1] Nevertheless, the general assembly preferred to keep the old site, and, March 2, 1643, passed an act[2] that all persons who had built upon deserted lots since January, 1641, or should hereafter do so, should be protected in their occupation against the original proprietors, who might have an equal quantity of ground in some other places conveniently near.

Under this act, Richard Sanders, Edward Challis and Radulf Spraggon each obtained an acre on the river at the west end, beginning near the block house and Thomas Paule and Richard Clarke secured land at " Friggett Landing," where the bridge now crosses Back River. There were also grants to Rev. Thomas Hampton, Captain Robert Huchinson and John White, which are useful in locating the church and state house.

In 1639, and again in 1640, levies were laid for a state house, and April 17, 1641, the general assembly purchased two houses formerly belonging to Sir John Harvey in which the public business had been transacted. These appear to have been built tenement wise; and they were transferred to Sir William Berkeley, who erected a third house against the west wall, and thus made a block of houses 120 feet long by 20 feet wide. The buildings were situated on the shore east of the church tower, and the middle building continued to be " the

[1] *Va. Magazine*, II., 284.
[2] Hening, *Statutes at Large*, I., 252.

state house" under Berkeley, as it had been under Harvey, until its destruction by fire in 1656.

The civil war was raging in England, and the Indians, under Opechancanough, made another attempt to exterminate the colony; and April 27, 1644, the day before Good Friday, they attacked the plantations and killed 300 settlers. But the colony, which had now a population of about 12,000, hardly felt the shock, and after the first surprise the current of Virginia life flowed on as usual. The settlers accepted the gauntlet thrown down by the Indians, and waged a vigorous war upon them, till, in a resolute march in 1646 by Sir William Berkeley in person, the grim chief Opechancanough, aged and blind, was captured, and brought to Jamestown. However, we are told that he retained his usual haughty spirit, for hearing one day foot-steps in his room he requested his eyelids to be raised, when, perceiving about him a crowd of curious persons, he called loudly for the governor, and, upon his appearance, exclaimed: " Had it been my fortune to take Sir William Berkeley prisoner, I would have disdained to make a show of him." About a fortnight later, one of his guards shot him in his prison house, and, languishing awhile of the wound, he died at Jamestown, and was probably buried there.[1] Necotowance, his successor, made peace with the white people soon after.

In March, 1646, to discourage the sale of liquor on the Island, the general assembly confined[2] the privilege of "retailing wines, or strong waters" (whiskey), to licensed ordinary keepers, which was the first temperance legislation attempted in Virginia.

In October, 1646, the general assembly, to encourage the manufacture of linen, decided[3] upon the erection of two houses at Jamestown, which were to be forty feet in length, twenty in width, and eight in pitch; and to have roofs of boards and a brick chimney placed in the center of each. Governor Berkeley undertook the contract of building, for 10,000 pounds of tobacco, " to be paid him the next crop," and the different counties were respectively required to furnish

[1] Beverley, *Virginia*, 49–50.
[2] Hening, *Statutes at Large*, I., 319.
[3] Ibid., I., 336.

two poor children, male or female, of the age of seven or eight years at least, to be instructed in the art of carding, knitting and spinning. This act, and others like it, in the colonial records, give reason to believe that there was more manufacturing done in Virginia than has been generally supposed.

In 1649, the general assembly established[1] a market at Jamestown on every Wednesday and Saturday; and the market place was bounded "from the Sandy Gutt, commonly called and knowne by the name of Peter Knight's storehouse westward, and soe to the gutt next beyond the house of Lancelot Elay eastward, and bounded on the north side with the Back River." "Sandy Gutt" mentioned here was probably "Orchard Run;" for in 1656 Lancelot Elay had land there, and in a deed[2] dated 1736 the market is referred to as "adjoining a ditch" which opened upon the River six and one fourth chains (about 206 feet) south 31° west of "the garden pales" of the Jaquelin-Ambler house. Within the area of land designated in the act, stretching across the Island, all bonds, bills or other writing attested by the market clerk for anything sold in the market on a market day, were to have the force of a judgment.

Near the market was probably the ferry between the Island and Crouch's Creek and Swann's Point on the Surry side; for, besides the natural connection of the two, a deed[3] in 1755 shows that the Island ferry then was at Orchard Run. At least, that is what I infer from the location of an acre of land described as "bounded on the east by the *slash* which separates it from the *ferry-house land,* on the *south* by James River, on the north by the Main Roade, and on the *west* by the acre of land lately conveyed to John Smith."

These were turbulent days in the mother country between roundheads and cavaliers, and after the battles of Marston Moore and Naseby there was a large emigration of the latter class to Virginia. As the culture of tobacco by reason of its low price no longer held out much inducement, these new settlers came not so much to make tobacco as to make homes.

[1] Hening, *Statutes at Large*, I., 362.
[2] Ambler MSS. in Library of Congress.
[3] Ibid.

The health of Virginia was generally improved by the opening of the forests, and though of the new emigrants " many
were landed men in England and have good estates there,"
few, we are told, ever desired to return.[1] This accession was
to some extent offset by Berkeley's expulsion of the Puritans
on Elizabeth and Nansemond rivers, who to the number of
1,000 left Virginia in 1649, and settled in Maryland. Nevertheless, by 1652 the population of Virginia had certainly
reached upwards of 20,000.

The execution of Charles I., in 1649, created much indig-
nation at Jamestown, and the assembly, largely influenced by
the newcomers, denounced the act as murder and proclaimed
Charles II. as king. This brought the colony into direct
collision with Parliament, and in 1651 a fleet was dispatched
to reduce it to terms, whereupon, Governor Berkeley called
out the train bands and prepared to resist. But the council
and assembly meeting at Jamestown in March, 1652, con-
vinced of the hopelessness of the king's cause, overruled the
governor and made an honorable accommodation. The
Virginians, for their part, recognized[2] the authority of the
commonwealth of England, and promised to pass no statute
contrary to the laws of Parliament; while the commissioners
accepted the submission of Virginia, " as a voluntary act not
enforced nor constrained by a conquest upon the countrey;"
and conceded her right " to be free from all taxes, customs,
and impositions whatever, not enforced by the General
Assembly." In particular, it was stipulated that " Virginia
should have and enjoy the antient bounds and lymitts granted
by the charters of the former kings." Berkeley retired to his
country residence " Greenspring," distant three miles from
Jamestown; and Richard Bennett succeeded him at the head
of affairs and was governor for three years.

March 30, 1655, Sir William Berkeley sold[3] to Bennett the
westermost brick house of the state house block, but the
next year all three tenements were burned, and after this,
for several years, the assembly occupied, it is believed, near

[1] *Leah and Rachel* (Force, *Tracts,* III., No. xiv).
[2] Hening, *Statutes at Large,* I., 363–367.
[3] Ibid., I., 407.

the ruined structures, a rented or purchased house, which, in 1660, fell a victim also to the flames.

March 31, 1655, Edward Digges, of " Bellfield," on York River, fourth son of Sir Dudley Digges, master of the rolls to King Charles I., succeeded Bennett as governor, and chiefly distinguished himself in silk culture, employing two Armenians in the work; but Digges, like his predecessors, failed to turn the inhabitants away from their favorite occupation of tobacco raising.

While Digges was governor, a ship landed in Virginia the first two Quaker preachers, Josiah Cole and Thomas Thurston, whose bold harangues calling on men to repent, as John the Baptist did in the wilderness, incurred for them the vigorous opposition of the authorities. They were arrested and confined in a prison at Jamestown, which is described[1] as " a dirty

Samuel Mathews

dungeon where we have not the benefit to do what nature requireth, nor so much as air to blow in at a window, but close made up with brick and lime."

Digges was succeeded in March, 1658, by Samuel Mathews of " Denbigh," who died in January, 1660, during the time of anarchy in England following the resignation of Richard Cromwell from his office as lord high protector. The burgesses assumed the supreme power in Virginia, and in March, 1660, recalled Sir William Berkeley to the government. Two months later, General Monk proclaimed Charles II. in London, and the example was followed at Jamestown by Sir William Berkeley, September 20, when the following proclamation[2] was issued:

By his Matyes Govern^r and Captain Generall of Virginia:
Itt is thought fitt & accordingly ordered for the speedy & better dispatch of all Affaires tending to the peace and welfare of this collony and the Inhabitantes yereof that all officers whatever within this Countrey doe remaine & continue wiyin their severall offices until furyer Order to ye contrary.

[1] Neill, *Virginia Carolorum*, 285.
[2] Published for the first time from York County records in *William and Mary Coll. Quarterly*, I., 196.

And, forasmuch as it hay pleased Almighty God to Invest our most Gratious Soveraigne, Charles the Second, King of England, Scotland, ffrance, & Ireland in the dominions & Just Rights of his Royall ffayer of Ever Sacred Memory. These are, therefore, ln his Matyes Name strictly to chardge and comand you and every of you fforthwiy to cause the said King to be proclaimed in every of y^r respective Counties, and that all Writts and warrants from henceforth Issue in his Majestyes name. Hereof faile not as you will answer ye contrary at yor uttermost perile. Given at James City under my hand this 20th of Septemb^r, sixteen hundred and sixty.

William Berkeley.

As Virginia had been the asylum of many fugitive loyalists, the joy produced by the Restoration was great. Throughout the colony music, drinking, and the firing of guns were the order of the day, and this is evidenced by entries in the York County levy[1] in 1661 :

YORK COUNTY LEVY 1661.

	Lbs. tobacco.
At ye proclaiming of his sacred Maiesty	
To ye Honble Govn.^r ℔ a barrell powd^r 112 lbs..., ...	00996.
To Capt. ffox six cases of drams........................	00900.
To Capt. ffox for his great Gunnes.....................	00500.
To M^r. Philip Malory	00500.
To ye trumpeters	00800.
To M^r. Hansford 176 gallons Syd^r. at 15, and 35 gall at 20: caske 264	03604.

Among the cavaliers living in Virginia at the Restoration, or shortly before it, were Sir Thomas Lunsford, lieutenant of the Tower of London; Rev. Alexander Murray, former companion of Charles II., in his wanderings, and afterwards in 1673 minister of Ware parish in Gloucester Co.; Col. Mainwaring Hammond; Sir Philip Honeywood; Col. Guy Molesworth, who had received twenty-five wounds while battling for the king; Francis Moryson, Richard Moryson, and Robert Moryson, brothers-in-law of Lucius Cary, Lord Falkland; John Woodward, assay-master of the mint, and Thomas, his son, afterwards surveyor general of North Carolina; Anthony Langston, ensign in Prince Maurice's regiment; Major Richard Fox; Major John Brodnax; Nicholas Dunn, chief clerk of the king's kitchen; Alexander Culpeper, brother of Lady Berkeley, whose father "lost all his estate, life and liberty" for the king; Dr. Jeremiah Harri-

1 *William and Mary Coll. Quart.*, I., 196.

son and his wife Frances Whitgreave, whose father, Thomas Whitgreave, saved the life of Charles II. at the battle of Worcester; Peter Jenings "who faithfully served his Majesty's father;" Sir Dudley Wyatt, an officer in the royal army, who died at Jamestown in 1650; Sir Gray Skipwith, baronet, son of Sir Henry Skipwith of Prestwould in Leicestershire; Sir Henry Chicheley, brother to Sir Thomas Chicheley of Charles II.'s privy council; and Sir Henry Moody, who died about 1662 at Col. Francis Moryson's house in Virginia. In token of the loyalty as well as importance of the colony, King Charles gave Virginia a new seal, which recognized her in the number of his kingdoms by the words *En dat Virginia Quintum*. England, France, Scotland and Ireland were four kingdoms to which he laid claim, and Virginia made the fifth (Quintum Regnum).

SEAL OF VIRGINIA 1661.

After the Restoration, Berkeley visited King Charles in England, leaving Francis Moryson as acting governor, and on his return, a year later, brought with him instructions to induce the planters in Virginia to make silk, flax, hemp, pitch and potashes and build a city on every river. Accordingly, the general assembly in December, 1662, passed an elaborate law,[1] for building James City, and the terms were a significant commentary upon the attempt so long persisted in. The place had been occupied for fifty years, and yet the provisions of the act proceeded as if the foundations of the place had yet to be laid.

The act provided that the town to be built should consist of thirty two brick houses, each "forty foot long and twenty foot wide" within the walls, and "eighteen foot" high with a slate or tile roof "fifteen foot" pitch. The bricks were to be statute bricks, and to cost, per thousand, 150 pounds of tobacco, and brickmakers were to receive — in addition to their diet, wood

[1] Hening, *Statutes at Large*, II., 172.

for burning the bricks, and the help of six laborers — forty pounds of tobacco for every thousand of bricks " moulded and burned."

To expedite the work, each of the seventeen counties was required to build a house, and to every county or private contractor the promise was made of 10,000 pounds of tobacco gratis, to be paid out of a levy of thirty pounds per poll laid throughout the country. The erection of any more wooden houses, or even the repair of any already standing, was strictly forbidden; and to encourage merchants and storekeepers, the town was made the sole mart of the three counties of James City, Charles City and Surry, and the sole place of shipment for their tobacco.

Danger from an Indian attack was now deemed so remote that on September 17, 1663, it was debated[1] in the general assembly " whether it was not fit to order the townsmen to pull up all the stakes of the old wars about Jamestown and to build no new ones in the face of the town." But we are told by Professor L. H. Girardin, in his *Amœnitates Graphicæ* that in 1803 " many yards of the palisades erected by the first settlers were still to be seen at low tide standing at least 150 or 200 paces from the present shore."

If Col. Francis Moryson, the agent for Virginia, is to be believed, " only four or five buildings " were the result up to 1665 of our " poore assaye of building " under the act of 1662,[2] but among these buildings was doubtless a new state house; since Thomas Ludwell, the secretary of state, writing during the same year, declared[3] that in obedience to the king's instructions " they had begun a town of brick, and already built enough to accommodate the affairs of the country."

The best built part of the town was east of the present

1 Hening, *Statutes at Large*, II., 205.
2 Neill, *Va. Carolorum*, 205.
3 Yonge, *The Site of Old Jamestowne*, 64.

Jaquelin-Ambler house, and there on the Back Street were the most substantial houses — among them Richard Kempe's house, and a brick house called the "Country House," formerly belonging to the colony, and sold by the general assembly to Major Richard Webster, who assigned it to Richard Rix, whose widow Elizabeth, with her second husband, Edward Shipdam in behalf of John Rix, the heir-at-law, sold it to John Phipps, from whom it came to Captain John Knowles, the owner in 1665.[1] This "Country House" was like some of the houses in James City a block of three buildings,[2]

which is shown on a plat made for Knowles by Captain John Underhill, surveyor. Nearly opposite to the "Country House" was Mr. William May's house, and a short distance to the east was a house formerly belonging to Mr. John Phipps — then the property also of Captain John Knowles. On the west of the country house was Richard Kempe's old brick house, enlarged by a brick addition of thirty-seven feet in width, made by Walter Chiles, Jr., who inherited it from his father, Col. Walter Chiles, to whom Sir William Berkeley had sold it in 1650. Southwestward of William May was John Fitchett's house, and on the river bank to the south of May was, it is believed, the turf fort erected a year or two before as the result of a scare springing from a conspiracy of the servants.[3]

A list of those who obtained patents in "New Towne" from 1654 to 1665 would include John Barber, Robert Castle, Thomas Woodhouse, Thomas Hunt, John Phipps, John Fitchett, John Knowles, and William Harris.

Outside of "New Towne" the Island was chiefly held as follows: (1) John Bauldwin had a tract near the block house

---

[1] Deed in *Ambler MSS.* in Congressional Library. "Country house" meant a house belonging to the country, i. e., the Colony.
[2] Houses were built in this way in order to save two walls in six.
[3] Hartwell, Blair and Chilton, *Present State of Virginia*, 56.

5

reputed at first to be fifteen acres and sixty-nine poles, but subsequently found by a new survey to be twenty-eight and one-half acres, (2) Richard James had 150 acres east of Bauldwin and north of Pitch and Tar Swamp; (3) Nicholas Meriwether had the "Island House" Tract of eighty acres, purchased in 1656 from Nathaniel Bacon and Elizabeth, his wife, daughter and heiress of Richard Kingsmill. This was situated, as already stated, east of Richard James between Back River and Kingsmill's Creek; (4) John Knowles had about 133 acres south of Richard James and north of "New Towne," where besides the "Country House," he owned Dr. John Pott's old tract of twelve acres and other property; (5) John Senior had 150 acres in the eastern section of the Island near Passmore's Creek; (6) Edward Travis, son of Edward Travis and Ann Johnson, daughter of John Johnson, an early settler in the east end, had 326 acres beginning at Black Point; (7) Walter Chiles had seventy acres south of Edward Travis; and (8) William May had 100 acres at Goose Hill.

The new state house stood at the west end of the Island on the third ridge.

On March 12, 1673, the following action[1] took place at Jamestown:

Present: Sir William Berkeley, Governor; Thomas Ludwell, Secretary, Edward Digges and Col. Nathaniel Bacon, Esquires:
Upon the Peticon of the several inhabitants of James City Island, it is ordered that all marsh lands unpatented in James City Island forever hereafter be and remain in common for a pasture to the use of those who now, or shall hereafter, live in the said Island or towne.

It appears from this order that there was no town government in Jamestown, but that, like our present city of Washington, the authorities were the general authorities of the whole country.

For the year 1676, famous as the year of Bacon's Rebellion, there are descriptions of the town from two different sources. According to one description found in the report of the commissioners sent over to enquire into the causes of the outbreak, Jamestown "consisted of twelve new brick houses and a considerable number of framed houses with brick chimneys, besides a brick church and state house."

[1] Randolph MSS.

Then in Mrs. An. Cotton's "*Bacon's Proseedings,*"[1] the Island is described as follows:

The place on which the towne is built is a perfect Peninsulla or tract of land allmost wholly incompasst with water: haveing on the sowth side the river (formerly Powhetan, now called James River) 3 miles brode incompasst on the North, from the Easte pointe with a deep creek rangeing in a cemicircle, to the west, within 10 paces (50 ft.) of the River; and there by a small Istmos tackt to the Continent. This Iseland (for so it is denominate) hath for Longitude (East and West) nere upon two miles, and for Latitude about halfe so much, bearing in the wholl compass about 5 miles, littlle more or less. It is low ground, full of Marches and Swomps, which make the Aire especially in the summer insalubritious and unhelthy. It is not at all replenished with springs of fresh water, and that which they have in their wells, brackish, illsented, penurious and not gratefull to the stomack which render the place improper to endure the commencement of a seige. The Town is built much about the midle of the sowth line close upon the River, extending east and west about 3 quarters of a mile; in which is comprehended some 16 or 18 houses, most as is the church built of brick, faire and large: *and in them about a dozen familees (for all their howses are not inhabited) getting their liveings by keeping of ordnaries, at extreordnary rates.*

From this latter account it appears that the ambitious design of the thirty-two new brick houses contemplated by the act of 1663 was never fully realized. The people did not care for towns, and regarded the work at Jamestown as a mere excuse for taxes. Doubtless, the prominent men of the colony fully realized the impracticability of town building in Virginia, but their anxiety to please the English authorities induced the general assembly not only to favor town building, but to acquiesce in the extensive projects proposed by Berkeley about the same time for building courthouses, prisons, churches, public roads, forts, warehouses, etc.; and the burdens which these improvements imposed created widespread discontent, which was heard from later on.

At the time of Bacon's Rebellion, there lived at Jamestown two particular friends of the rebel leader, Richard Lawrence, a "thoughtful gentleman," who had been a student at Oxford University, and William Drummond, a Scotchman, who acted under Sir William Berkeley's appointment as first governor of North Carolina. Elizabeth Lawrence, wife of the former, had been a rich widow, and kept one of the ordinaries referred to by Mrs. An. Cotton, being very popular with persons of the "best quality" in the colony. Her home was

[1] Force, *Tracts*, I., No. xi, p. 25.

situated[1] on the third ridge near the new state house; and west of the churchyard was a half acre lot[2] belonging to Sarah Drummond (wife of William Drummond) to whom it was given in 1661 by Edward Prescott (probably her father).

Bacon's Rebellion is probably the most dramatic episode to be found in the history of the English colonies. Tobacco had been steadily declining in price, and the operation of the navigation act passed first in 1651 caused a continuous further reduction. Then titles to lands were rendered very uncertain by extensive grants to court favorites, and there was a heavy burden of taxation due to the extravagance of officials in Virginia. The same assembly continued for fourteen years, and by it taxes were imposed, as we have seen, for towns that never flourished, and for public utilities that exceeded the needs of the people and cost three times as much as they were worth. To all these things were added invasions, in 1667 and

AUTOGRAPH OF NATHANIEL BACON, THE REBEL.

1673, by Dutch fleets, which destroyed the shipping in the river, and the ravages of a great storm in the former year, which blew down 15,000 houses, principally tobacco barns, in Virginia and Maryland. At length, in 1676, matters were brought to a crisis by troubles with the Indians, who committed many murders on the frontiers of the settlements, which stretched at that time to the falls of the different rivers. The people begged Nathaniel Bacon, Jr., of Curls, in Henrico County, to protect them; and he, after petitioning Governor Berkeley in vain for a commission, went out against the Indians on his own authority. He won a great victory over the Occaneeches on an island in the Roanoke River; and on his return home was elected to the new assembly which convened at Jamestown June 5, 1676. Berkeley resented Bacon's fighting without his authority, and, when the latter came to the

[1] Va. Land Register, VIII., 400.
[2] Ibid., V., 634.

assembly, he had him arrested for high treason; but as Bacon's friends were very numerous, Bérkeley soon let him go, and restored him to his seat in council.

The conciliation was not cordial, and after a few days Bacon, fearing that his life was in danger, secretly left Jamestown and hurried home to Henrico. Here his neighbors thronged around him, and begged him to lead them down to Jamestown. Bacon consented, and on June 23, he was again at the Island, this time with 500 men at his back. Yielding to force, the governor gave him a commission, and the legislature passed some very wholesome laws, correcting many long standing abuses; and among them was one making the bounds of " James Citty " include the whole Island as far as Sandy Bay, and giving the people within those limits the right for the first time of making their own local ordinances.

Bacon returned to Henrico, and was on the eve of going out a second time against the Indians, when news arrived that Berkeley was over in Gloucester Co., endeavoring to raise forces to surprise and capture him. This caused him to give up his expedition, and to direct his march to Gloucester, where, being arrived, he found that the governor had fled to Accomac. Bacon thus left supreme summoned the leading men of the colony to Middle Plantation, and there on August 1 made them swear to stand by him, even as against soldiers sent from England, saying " 500 Virginians might beat 2,000 red coats."[1] After this his next move was to lead his troops against the Pamunkeys, whom he discovered and defeated in the recesses of the Dragon Swamp,[2] somewhere in King and Queen County. But his troubles did not end, and when he returned to the settlement, he found the governor once more established at Jamestown.

Bacon made straight for his antagonist, and, having arrived on September 13 in " Paspahegh Old Fields," across from the Island, found that Berkeley had fortified the isthmus on the Island side. He caused his men to throw up some earthworks;

---

[1] Bacon's conversation with John Goode, in Fiske, *Old Virginia and her Neighbours*, II., 71–75. The author remembers, as a boy, that the boast was frequently made on his father's plantation in 1861 that " one Virginian could whip four Yankees " (!), the exact proportion represented in Bacon's remarks.

[2] *William and Mary Coll. Quart.*, XIII., 194.

and in an engagement on the neck soon after killed some of
Berkeley's soldiers, which so disheartened the rest that they
took ship and abandoned Jamestown. Bacon, thereupon,
entered the town, and, supposing that Berkeley would soon
return, gave orders for its destruction, setting the example by
applying a torch to the church, while Lawrence and Drummond, his two most important supporters, fired their own

William Berkeley

houses. In the general conflagration, the state house and
church perished with the other buildings, but Drummond did
a good deed in saving the public records.

Berkeley, driven from Jamestown, made the house of Col.
John Custis in Northampton County his headquarters, while

Bacon after pillaging Greenspring marched to Gloucester and encamped at Major Pate's house, near Poropotank Creek. Here he was taken sick, and died October 26, 1676, and the Rebellion being without a real leader soon collapsed. It continued, however, for a few months longer under Ingram and Walklate, but they soon made haste to ensure their own safety by surrendering West Point in January, 1677. Lawrence who was at the "Brick House" opposite, informed of the treachery, fled to the forest, and was never heard of again; but Drummond was taken and presented to Berkeley at King's Creek, January 19, 1677, the day he first set foot on the western shore after the flight from Jamestown in September previous. When Drummond was brought before him, Berkeley said with mock politeness: "Mr. Drummond, I am more glad to see you than any man in Virginia. You shall hang in half an hour." And he was true to his word, for the next day he caused Drummond to be hanged at the Middle Plantation, seven miles distant. Berkeley called an assembly to meet at Greenspring, February 20, at which time all the laws passed by the previous June assembly were repealed. At this assembly a petition was presented from York County for making Middle Plantation the seat of government, but the assembly gave their preference to Tindall's Point (Gloucester Point).[1]

In the meantime, a new authority had established itself in Virginia. When the news of Bacon's Rebellion reached England, the king sent over a commission, composed of Col. Herbert Jeffreys, Col. Francis Moryson and Sir John Berry, authorized to enquire and report regarding the causes of the disturbances. They arrived in James River February 2, 1677, and were accompanied by a thousand troops, who were conveyed to Jamestown and encamped there during the rest of the Winter and most of the ensuing Spring. Jeffreys had a commission to succeed Berkeley, but coming as he did after hostilities had ceased, neither he nor his troops had any occasion to exercise their courage. Jamestown being in ruins, the commissioners made the residence of Col. Thomas Swann at Swann's Point over against Jamestown their headquarters, but when Berkeley left for England, Jeffreys, now governor, marched the soldiers to Middle Plantation, where they took

---

[1] Hening, *Statutes at Large*, II., 405.

part in celebrating a peace with the Indian chiefs on his Majesty's birthday May 14, 1677.

While the soldiers were in camp at Jamestown, some of them had a curious experience, which may be worth narrating. Among the plants of native growth was a weed named after the town itself—the well-known Jamestown ("Jimson") weed, which sprang up in the early Spring in the rich ground under the shadow of the burned walls. Some of the soldiers boiled the new sprouted leaves for salad and ate of it plenti-

FRANCES CULPEPER, LADY BERKELEY.

fully, and it turned them "natural fools." One soldier would blow a feather up in the air, and a second would rush furiously forward and tire himself out darting straws at it. A third stripped himself naked, sat in a corner, and made faces at all who passed; while a fourth, taking an amorous turn, kissed and caressed his companions, and leared in their faces. The fit lasted for eleven days, and during a part of the time these soldiers were confined to prevent their doing themselves injury. Such is the story as told by Beverley,[1] but it is more than likely the soldiers were playing a joke, as the Jamestown weed, while it has remarkable cooling powers which are useful in reducing inflammation, is not believed to have any dangerous characteristics such as Beverley describes.

The following persons[2] were reported to Jeffreys and the other two commissioners as the heaviest losers by the burning of Jamestown: "Col. Thomas Swanne who had a house burned and ye Goods in it; Major Theophilus Hone, who had also a house and goods destroyed by the fire; Mr. Will Sherwood and the orphan of one Mr. James, whose house was burnt downe by the rebell Lawrence, and the losse estimated at least at 1,000 £ sterling. There are Divers other poor Inhabitants whose pticular names and losses wee cannot give in, that were great sufferers by this calamity that befell James Citty after the Governor and his party left it." The total value of all private property destroyed in the town was estimated at " 1,500,-000 pounds of tobacco" (about £30,000 sterling in present value.)

In December, 1678, Jeffreys died, and was succeeded by Sir Henry Chicheley, and in March, 1679, the privy council of England, on the recommendation of the commissioners, ordered that Jamestown be rebuilt and be the metropolis of Virginia, "as the most ancient and convenient place." Accordingly, when Lord Culpeper was appointed to the head of affairs in Virginia, he brought with him instructions to rebuild Jamestown, and the members of the council were requested to erect houses and dwell there. The need of ports of entry in other rivers induced the further recommendation that a town be built in the valley of each of the principal water courses.[3]

Culpeper arrived in the colony in May, 1680, and the general assembly which met him at Jamestown passed an act[4] to condemn fifty acres for a town in every county in the colony. The purchase price of the land in each place was to be

[1] Beverley, *Virginia*, 110.
[2] *Va. Magazine*, V., 68.
[3] Bruce, *Economic History of Virginia*, II., 547.
[4] Hening, *Statutes at Large*, II., 471.

10,000 pounds of tobacco; and, as an encouragement to settlers, the towns were made the sole places of import and export for the respective counties. Half an acre of land was offered to every person building a residence and warehouse and paying down 100 pounds of tobacco; and all brickmakers and other laborers were declared free from arrest for debt.

As this act would have operated as a great hardship upon Jamestown, the inhabitants through William Sherwood, Thomas Clayton, and William Harrison presented a petition against it, a rude copy of which, as preserved in the Ambler MSS., reads as follows:

To the Honble [   ] embly of Virga:

The Inhabts & freeholders of James Citty:

Humbly prsent

That ye sd. Citty accordi[n]g to Capt Smiths discovery of Virga: was dated in ye yeare [1]607 & hath ever since beene **Md this** ye seate [o]f ye cheife Corts of Judicature, & metropolis of **Act was** this his Matles Colony Country & dominion yett y[ts] **drawne vp** certaine limittes & boundes, hath not b[y] any publiq A[c]t **& Passed** or Instrument beene ascert[a]in'd, although b[y] report of **ye howse** ye ancient Inhabts: itt be[g]ins att ye Sandy Bay & soe **Apll 1682** includes all ye Land Island, betwene River & Creeke from **All ye** thence to ye run or slusb by Wm Briscoe ye Smiths & soe **Island** to ye back Creeke. We humbly pray yt y[e] said bounds may be ascertain'd by Act of Assembly.

And [w]hereas by one A[c]t of ye last Sessions, of Assbly itt was enioyned yt 50 acres of land should be laid out for a Town in James Citty att ye rate of 10000 ll tobco: We humbly inform yor honrs: yt ye land in Ja the sd. Citty is of considerable value & not an acre there but cost above 5ll sterl besides our great charg in building. And therefore we humbly ppoase, yt we & ye owners of the land in ye sd. Citty may have libty to build store howses there (in case itt be enioyned & if we fayle, that then any others may have **land for** land assigned ym: by ye County Cort: vpon paymt of soe **Mills is to** much as ye land so valued att shall be valued att, by an able **be valued** Jury, according to ye Law & presidentes of Engld in ye like **by a** cases. And yt ye whole Islande may be assigned to build **Jury: &c:** on.

And for yt itt is our desyer yt all Nusances & corrupcons of ye Air may be hereafter removed: & ye Citty for ye future kept clean & del decent wch can not well be don without a Law [   ]se, & ye pticuler ways and means to effect ye same [   ]o tedious & troublesome for th yor honrs to direct & sett d[ow]n, We humbly pray yt as Liberty is given to ye seurall Countys of this Colony to make by laws: soe authority may be given to ye sd. Citty to make such By laws as shall be agreed on by ye major pt of ye freeholders & howsekeeps thereof, for ye better governing & conueniency of ye sd Citty & Inhabitant[s] thereof: A wh And whereas there is a Marsh in James Citty Island not hitherto taken vp or pattented by any, wᶜʰ by ordʳ of the Rᵗ: honᵇˡᵉ: yᵉ Governʳ & Councill, was & is to lye in Comon for all yᵉ Inhabtˢ: of James Citty, we humbly pra[y] that the said order of yᵉ Genˡˡ Court may be confirmed by Act of Assembly:

Wᵐ Sherwood, Tho Claton, Wᵐ Harrison
Copᵃ: pet Ja: Citt: 1682.

It will be noticed that this petition before erasure made the limits of the town — James River, Back Creek and Orchard Run.

The suspension of the act by the king, in 1684, relieved the inhabitants of Jamestown of the hardships complained of; and, by the marginal notation on the paper above, it appears also that their prayer for self-government was granted in April, 1682, though there is no record preserved of any town meetings at Jamestown or of any ordinances passed by local authority. In 1683, Lord Culpeper wrote that he had given all the encouragement possible for the rebuilding of Jamestown, and though his own residence was at Greenspring, the auditor, Nathaniel Bacon, Sr., had lately built two very good dwellings there, and Col. Joseph Bridger and Mr. William Sherwood " were going about severall wᶜʰ will bee finished this or the next yeare, and there are severall others marked out for building." That he had, however, no great hopes was shown by a remark which slipped from his pen in the same paper: " nothing but profitt and advantage " can make a city of Jamestown.[1] As to markets in the colony he said: " there were none except a most sad one at James Citty."

Culpeper left the colony in May, 1684, and was succeeded by Lord Howard, of Effingham, under whom the state house was restored; and then followed Col. Francis Nicholson in 1690 and Sir Edmund Andros in 1692, which last remained governor till 1698. House building at Jamestown continued during all these different administrations, and the result in 1697 was

[1] Culpeper's Report in *McDonald Papers,* Vol. VI., 165.

reported by Dr. Blair to the Lords of Trade, when he said there was about "twenty or thirty houses at Jamestown." The new state house and the new church included in this number were respectively the fourth and fifth in time of construction.

As shown by the land patents, the ownership of the Island, in 1697, was as follows:

In the west end William Sherwood had all the land between James River, Back River, Pitch and Tar Swamp and Kingsmill's Creek, amounting to about 378 acres secured from time to time as follows: 120 acres lying north and east of " New Towne," purchased in 1677 from David Newell, brother and heir of Jonathan Newell who got it from John Knowles; twenty-eight and one-half acres near the block-house formerly John Bauldwin's, purchased the same year from John Fulcher; 150 acres formerly Richard James's, lying between Pitch and Tar Swamp and Back River, which escheated on the death of Richard James, Jr., and was patented by Sherwood in 1690; and 80 acres known as " the Island House " tract, purchased in 1695 from Francis Meriwether, the son of Nicholas Meriwether, who obtained it as already noticed from Nathaniel Bacon and his wife Elizabeth, daughter of Richard Kingsmill.[1] Pitch and Tar Swamp, which was included in William Sherwood's land, contained 150 acres and was described in the following language[2] by Rev. John Clayton, who was minister of Jamestown from 1684 to 1686:

Even in Jamestown Island, which is much-what of an oval Figure, there is a Swamp runs diagonal-wise over the Island, whereby is lost at least 150 Acres of Land, which would be Meadow, and would turn to as good account as if it were in England. Besides it is the great Annoyance of the Town, and no doubt but makes it more unhealthy. If, therefore, they but scoured the Channel, and made a pretty ordinary Trench all along the middle of the Swamp, placed a Sluce at the mouth, where it opens into the Back Creek; for the mouth of the Channel there is narrow, has a good hard Bottom, and is not past two Yards deep when the Flood is out; as if Nature had designed it beforehand: they might thus drain all the Swamp absolutely dry, or lay it under Water at their pleasure. I have talked several times hereof to Mr. Sherwood, the Owner of the Swamp, yet nothing is essayed in order thereto.

On the third ridge, in 1697, near the river was the powder magazine recently erected, and near it was the " Country

[1] See *Ambler MSS.* in Library of Congress; *Virginia Land Register.*
[2] *Letter of John Clayton,* Force, *Tracts,* III., xii, 23.

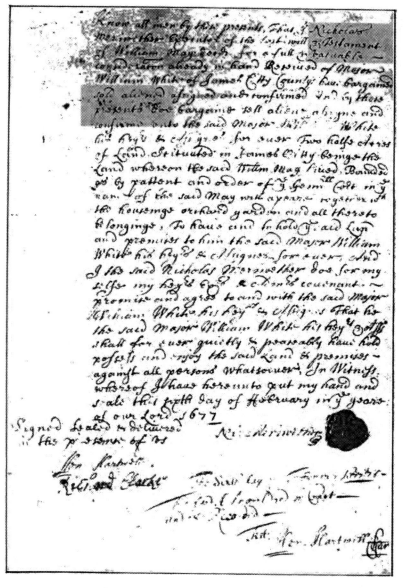

MERIWETHER'S DEED FOR WILLIAM MAY'S HOUSE AND LOT TO
MAJOR WILLIAM WHITE.

House," joining which last were the ruins of three brick houses, belonging to Philip Ludwell, jun., standing in a lot of one and one-half acres.[1]   West of these ruined houses (burned probably in Bacon's Rebellion) was the state house, which was separated by the main road from a lot of three acres, one rood, and three poles patented[2] in 1694 by Robert Beverley. Then east of Beverley's property was a lot, patented[3] in 1683 by Col. Nathaniel Bacon, Sen., first cousin once removed of Nathaniel Bacon, Jr., "the Rebel."   It comprised three and three-eighths acres, and was a part of a lot formerly belonging to Richard Lawrence, who, "being guilty of high treason against his Majestry, not daring to abide his trial, fled for the same, whereby all his goods, chattels, lands and tenements are forfeited to his Majesty."

Lawrence's or Bacon's lot thus referred to stretched across the low ground between the third and fourth ridges to a lot on the latter elevation, also belonging to Col. Bacon and covering most of the eastern part of the present Confederate fort.

Wm Edwards   Eliz^a Edwards

On the fourth ridge, at the southwest point of the Island, adjoining the brick fort, were two acres and seventeen chains formerly patented[4] in 1683 by Edward Chilton, then clerk of the council, and in 1697, attorney general.   Adjoining westerly were seventy and one-half perches of land patented[5] in 1690 by William Edwards, Sen., whose western line corresponded with the eastern line of the Chilton tract.   Next was Col. Bacon's land in the Confederate fort already referred to, and then a tract adjoining the churchyard of one hundred and seventy-two poles patented[6] in 1690 by John Howard.

In that part of the town east of the church tower, first called "New Towne," the land on Orchard Run had come into the hands of James Chudleigh, who was the second husband of Ann Holder.   She obtained it partly by gift from her first

---

[1] *Va. Land Register,* VIII., 315.
[2] Ibid., VIII., 400.
[3] Ibid., VII., 300.
[4] Ibid., VII., 292.
[5] Ibid., VIII., 42.
[6] Ibid., VIII., 82.

husband's father, William Briscoe, Sen., a blacksmith, and partly by inheritance from her own father, Richard Holder. James Chudleigh's neighbor was William Edwards, Jr., son of William Edwards, clerk of the council, who had purchased from Chudleigh an acre of land on the river.[1] Thomas Holliday had property adjoining Edwards, and next to him was Henry Hartwell, Esq., one of the council, whose western line was about 550 feet from Orchard Run and passed along the angular points of a trench which embraced two of the eastern bastions of "an old ruined turf fort" (the fort of 1663), Hartwell's house was the former residence of William May, who in 1670 left it by will to Nicholas Meriwether, by whom it was deeded in 1677 to Major William White; and when the latter died without issue about 1686, the land escheated and was patented[2] in 1689 by Henry Hartwell, who married White's widow, Jane Meriwether, sister of Nicholas Meriwether. At this time William Sherwood owned the lots on the north side of the old Back Street on which formerly stood the house known as Richard Kempe's and the "Country House," both burned in Bacon's Rebellion. He had bought the "Country House" lot in 1677 from David Newell, with the land already mentioned north and east of "New Towne," which Newell's brother bought from John Knowles; and the three and one-half acres, containing the ruins of Squire Kempe's old brick building, he had obtained the same year from John Page, who in 1673 purchased them from Rev. James Wadding and his wife Susannah, widow of Walter Chiles, Jr.[2] William Sherwood resided on the country house lot, where as early as 1681 he is described as having built[4] "a faire house and app(ur)t(enan)ces."

[1] *Ambler MSS.* in Library of Congress.
[2] *Virginia Land Register*, VII., 701.
[3] *Ambler MSS.*
[4] *Va. Land Register*, VII., 98.

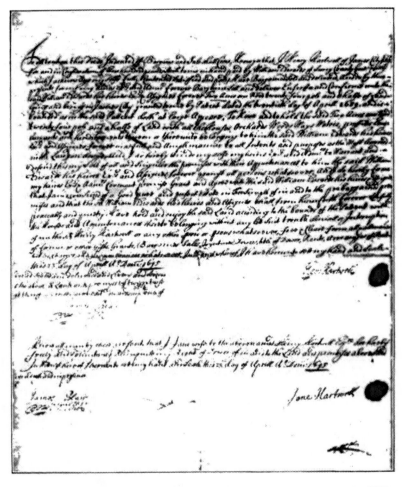

HENRY HARTWELL'S DEED TO WILLIAM EDWARDS FOR A LOT ON THE BANK
OF THE RIVER ADJOINING THE TURF FORT.

Thus the town had been pretty well restored by 1697, but
the evil genius of misfortune still pursued it. In September,
1698, King William superseded Sir Edmund Andros with
Col. Francis Nicholson, and the instructions given him contained the usual orders " to rebuild and enlarge Jamestown ;"

but before he arrived in the colony a fire occurred October 31, 1698, by which the state house, the prison, and probably all other buildings on the third ridge, except the magazine, which stood apart, were destroyed. In announcing the calamity to the Lords of Trade Governor Andros congratulated himself that the records and papers had again been saved.

In February, 1699, Nicholson wrote that it would require about £2,000 "to build a new court house where the house of burgesses also sat;" but, ambitious to be the founder of a city, he selected Middle Plantation as the site of the proposed building. The last meeting of the assembly at James City was held in the house of Mrs. Sarah Lee, alias Smith,[1] and an act was passed[2] for removing the seat of government to Middle Plantation, which Nicholson named Williamsburg in honor of William III., king of England. This abandonment of the ancient seat of government must have produced with many a

COL. JOHN PAGE.

spirit of sadness, but Jamestown had performed its mission, and could afford to be neglected. How totally unlike the feeble colony of 1607 was the Virginia of 1699 with its population of 80,000, stretching to the foot of the mountains. And not Virginia alone was the exhibit, but all the other English colonies along the Atlantic coast, for they also owed the authority and inspiration of their existence to the heroic residents of the little hamlet of Jamestown.

[1] *Council Journal* in Library of Congress.
[2] Hening, *Statutes at Large*, III., 197, 213, 471.
6

The extinction of Jamestown as the capital of the colony was almost coincident with the deaths of the two largest landed proprietors on the Island — William Sherwood, and Edward Travis (third of that name). William Sherwood was born in the parish of White Chapel, London, was bred to the law and served in the office of Sir Joseph Williamson, England's secretary of state. As the result of some youthful indiscretion committed against his patron, he came to Virginia in 1668, where he conducted himself in such a manner as to win the good will, not only of Williamson, but of all who knew him. His first five years in the colony were spent as deputy sheriff of Surry County, and there is on record a declaration of the court testifying highly to his "discretion and integrity."[1]

He removed to Jamestown, where he practiced law in the general court, and married Rachel James, widow of Richard James, one of the early land proprietors. He was present at Jamestown, when Bacon forced a commission from Berkeley, and wrote to Sir Joseph Williamson an interesting account of the affair. In March, 1678, he was appointed attorney general and served about two years, when he was succeeded by Edmund Jenings, Esq. He was coroner and justice of James City Co.; and in 1684 and again in 1696 represented Jamestown in the house of burgesses. He died in 1697, and was buried in the churchyard at Jamestown, where a broken tombstone refers to him as "a great sinner waiting for a glorious resurrection"— words inscribed by the express direction of his will.

The other proprietor, Edward Travis (son of Edward Travis and Elizabeth Champion, his wife, and grandson of Edward Travis and Ann Johnson), died November 12, 1700, and was buried in a graveyard at the east end of the Island, where his

---

[1] For William Sherwood see *William and Mary Coll. Quart.*, **V.,** 51-53; X., 166.

tombstone may yet be seen. By his wife, Rebecca (born in 1677), he had issue a son, Edward, who was fourth of the name from the original Travis emigrant. The rights of these two proprietors — Sherwood and Travis — were represented after their death by two new comers — Edward Jaquelin and William Brodnax, who married their respective widows, and by Edward Travis referred to above as son of Edward Travis and Rebecca, his wife.

Jamestown, however, did not lose its historic character, and it is a noteworthy fact that in his address of welcome to the general assembly in Williamsburg delivered April 21, 1704, Governor Nicholson declared that three years hence he designed to celebrate a jubilee in honor of the centennial of the settlement at Jamestown — a suggestion, the consummation of which he never witnessed, because of his recall to England in 1705.

Nor did Jamestown lose at once its public character; for after the removal of the seat of government it retained its representation in the assembly, and had a fort, county court house (made in 1706 out of the bricks of the old state house), a church and public ferry; but they all gradually passed away in the course of years, till after 1776 only the ferry remained. The fort went first, for, in 1716, the place was visited by John Fontaine,[1] who reported as standing at Jamestown only "a church, a court house, and three or four brick houses." There was also "a small rampart with embrasures," but it was deserted and gone to ruin. A year or two later, Williamsburg was made the site of a new court house for the county, and in 1722 Jamestown was described[2] by Rev. Hugh Jones as "an abundance of rubbish with three or four inhabited houses." The church continued in use for many years longer, till in 1751–1758 it was also abandoned for one "newly built" on the Main,[3] and in 1781 Thacher in his "Military Journal" reports only two houses as standing by the river side; one of which must have been the manor house of Mr. John Ambler (great-grandson of Edward Jaquelin, pro-

[1] Maury, *Huguenot Family*, 271.
[2] Jones, *Present State of Virginia*, 25.
[3] *Va. Magazine*, V., 246.

prietor of the western end.)   Before this, through the action
of the state convention of 1776, the Island lost its representation in the general assembly.

By the time of the Revolution, most of the land on the
Island had been consolidated into the hands of the Amblers
and Travises, as shown by the following history.   William Sherwood, having no children, by his will, left all
his land, with the exception
of twenty-eight and one-half
acres at Block House hill
(which he gave by deed to
his nephew, John Jarrett),
to his widow Rachel for
life, and after her death to
Sir Jeffrey Jeffreys, of
London.   Rachel Sherwood
(previously Rachel, widow
of Richard James), mar-
ried Edward Jaquelin, son
of John Jaquelin, of Kent
Co., England, and Elizabeth
Craddock his wife; and in
1 7 0 4 , Jeffreys
surrendered all
his title to Ra-
chel's new hus-
band, estimating
the area at 400 acres.

Jaquelin built a house near the site of the house of Sir
Francis Wyatt, and, surviving his first wife Rachel (who was
old enough to be his mother), married secondly, in 1707,
Martha Cary, daughter of William Cary, of Warwick Co., by
whom he had three daughters to survive him viz.: (1) Martha,
born January, 1711, died in 1804, aged ninety-three years, who
remained single and was known as "Lady Jaquelin," on ac-

---

[1] Jaquelin was born in 1668, but it seems from the *Ambler MSS.* that
Rachel, his first wife, had by Richard James, her first husband "Richard
born the 14th day of December, 1660." She afterwards married William
Sherwood, and thirdly Edward Jaquelin, about 1697. Jaquelin was
then about 29, while Rachel his wife must have been about 57.

count of her high aristocratic ideas; for it is said she waited for a duke or count to come over and address her. (2) Mary, born in 1714, and died October, 4, 1764; married John Smith, of "Shooter's Hill," Middlesex Co., and had eight children among whom was Gen. John Smith, of "Hackwood." (3) Elizabeth, born October, 1709, died 1756, married Richard Ambler, collector of the port at Yorktown, son of John Ambler, of County York, England, and Elizabeth Bickadike, his wife. Jaquelin died at Jamestown in 1739, aged seventy-one years, and under his will

MARTHA (CARY) JAQUELIN.

Richard Ambler, his son-in-law, succeeded to his lands at the old metropolis.

Six years later Ambler largely increased his estate by a purchase from Christopher Perkins of land. the history of which is as follows: About 1700 there came to the Island a gentleman named William Brodnax, who was son of Robert Brodnax, a goldsmith of Godmersham in Kent Co., England, and a great nephew of Major John Brodnax, a cavalier officer, who in 1657 died in York County, Virginia. William Brodnax, who was born February 28, 1675, married, soon after his arrival in Virginia, the widow Rebecca Travis, and afterwards, from time to time acquired an extent of interest in the Island represented by about 280 acres. This comprised the Howard lot of 172 poles by the church, the Beverley tract of three acres, one rood and six poles on the third ridge, the old Bauldwin tract of twenty-eight and one-half acres near the connecting neck (given by Sherwood to his nephew, John Jarrett), twelve acres called " Thorny Ridge," the ferry formerly owned by Lt. Edward Ross, and two large tracts containing 107 and 127 7/10 acres respectively. The western boundary of the last named tract began " at a Ditch adjoining the market place in Jamestown," and ran thence north thirty-one degrees east six and one-quarter chains to the " Garden pales of Richard Ambler, Esquire, formerly of Edward Jaquelin." [1] Brodnax died in February, 1726, and after his death, the property above mentioned fell to his son William Brodnax, Jr., who in about ten years removed to Prince George County, where he married Ann Hall. In 1744, William Brodnax and Ann, his wife, sold their interest

at Jamestown to Christopher Perkins, of Norfolk County, and a year later Christopher Perkins and Elizabeth, his wife, sold all the lands thus devised to Richard Ambler.

To the property thus acquired further additions of land were afterwards made by said Ambler — the most interesting of which was a half acre, portion of the three and one-half acres on which formerly stood Squire Kempe's old historic brick house, sold by John Page to William Sherwood in 1677. This lot was purchased[2] in 1753 by Ambler from Edward Champion Travis, who bought it of William Drummond, to whom it was given by his father, William Drummond, Sr.,[3]

[1] Deed in *Ambler MSS.* For Brodnax family, see *William and Mary Coll. Quart.*, XIV., 52–58.
[2] Deed in *Ambler MSS.*
[3] Son of William Drummond, of Bacon's Rebellion.

and the last named bought it in 1701 from John Harris, to whom William Sherwood sold it in 1696, describing it as the property "late in the occupation of Secretary (Ralph) Wormeley," and as "beginning at a stake in the line of Omoone's land, formerly Fitchett's, and running along the south side of the mulberry trees 90 foot, thence northwardly toward the main road 40 foot, thence northwest near the main road to the corner of Omoone's land 100 foot, and

AUTOGRAPH AND SEAL OF WILLIAM DRUMMOND, SR.

so along the line of Omoone's land to the place or stake it first began."

Richard Ambler died at Yorktown in 1766, and his three sons, Edward, John and Jaquelin, shared his large estate between them. To Edward was given his Yorktown property and extensive interests in Caroline, Hanover and Warwick counties, and to John the ferry at Jamestown and the negroes there, as well as all the land and houses on the Island except the land "between the Fort Hill and the churchyard and the houses erected thereon," which were willed to Jaquelin Ambler, who was also presented with £1,000 sterling in the hands of Samuel Athawes and company in London.[1]

John Ambler, who received most of his father's property at Jamestown, was born in Yorktown December 31, 1735, and was educated at Leeds Academy, near Wakefield, in Yorkshire, and at the university of Cambridge and the Middle Temple, from which last he graduated as barrister of law. After his return to America he was considered one of the most accomplished scholars in the

[1] Will of Richard Ambler in *William and Mary Coll. Quart.*, XIV., 126.

colony, and represented Jamestown in the general assembly in 1760 and 1765. Attacked by consumption, he went to Barbadoes for his health, but died there unmarried, May 27, 1766. His body was brought to Jamestown and deposited in the old graveyard at the church, and over his remains a splendid marble monument was placed, of which hardly any vestige now remains.

After John Ambler's death, Edward Ambler inherited his brother's interests at Jamestown, and was one of the wealthiest men in Virginia. He was born in 1733, was schooled like his brother at Wakefield and at Cambridge, and finished his education by a " grand tour " of Europe. Returning to Virginia,

MARY CARY.

he was made collector of York River, and married Mary Cary (daughter of Wilson Miles Cary, of Ceeley's in Elizabeth City Co.), who is said to have been " a sweetheart " of George Washington, her elder sister marrying George William Fairfax, Washington's intimate friend. Edward Ambler settled at Yorktown, but upon the death of his brother John, in 1766, he went to Jamestown to live, where he died October 30, 1768, in the thirtieth year of his age, leaving his Jamestown estate to his wife Mary Ambler, during her widowhood. She remained there with her young children till 1777, when for greater safety she removed to " The Cottage " in Hanover, and continued there till her death in 1781.[1] After this time the Ambler interests on Jamestown Island, which comprised nearly all the western portion as far as Passmore's Creek, fell to John Ambler, Edward Ambler's only surviving son, who was born September 25, 1762, and

[1] For Ambler family see *William and Mary Coll. Quart.*, IV., 49; V., 54; Meade, *Old Churches*, etc., I., 95–110; Richmond *Standard*, Jan 20, 1889; Call, *Reports*, IV., 605.

married three times, viz.: (1) Frances Armistead, daughter of Gill Armistead of New Kent; (2) Lucy Marshall, sister of Chief Justice John Marshall; (3) Catherine, widow of John Hatley Norton, and daughter of Philip Bush, of Winchester. He was a member of the house of delegates, and Lt.-Col. of State troops during the War of 1812. Removing from Jamestown, he lived first in Hanover County and then in Richmond, where he died April 8, 1836, and was buried in Shockoe Hill cemetery.

JOHN AMBLER,
Last proprietor of the name.

The Travis family, in the meantime, was represented at Jamestown during the first part of the eighteenth century by Edward Travis, already referred to as the fourth of that name. His son was Col. Edward Champion Travis, who was born in 1721, and married Susanna Hutchings, daughter of Col. Joseph Hutchings, of Norfolk. Col. Travis represented Jamestown in the house of burgesses in 1752, and other years, and died in 1779. Champion Travis, the latter's son, was a member of the first state convention, and married Elizabeth Boush, daughter of Capt. Francis Boush, of Norfolk. As John Ambler was the last Ambler, so Champion Travis was the last Travis to live on the Island.[1]

July 4, 1781, Lord Cornwallis moved, at the head of his army, from Williamsburg, where he had his headquarters in the president's house at the college,[2] towards Jamestown

[1] For Travis family see *William and Mary Coll. Quart.*, V., 16.
[2] Hunt, *Fragments of Revolutionary History*, 45.

with a view of crossing James River and retiring to Portsmouth. La Fayette, who commanded an American army, hastened to fall on his rear, when Cornwallis should have passed over the river the greater part of his soldiers; but Cornwallis, suspecting the intention of his adversary, hid his main army in a dense pine wood near the "church on the Main," three miles from Jamestown and made a show of posting a few troops on the Island and at Jamestown Ford, where they could be seen. While making this disposition, he employed himself in transporting over the river his baggage of every description, which were mistaken by the American scouts for the army itself. La Fayette reached Greenspring in the morning of July 6, and, supposing that he had only Cornwallis's rear guard to deal with, left General Steuben with the main body of the militia at Greenspring, and marched to attack with the Continental troops under General Wayne. The Americans crossed the causeway leading through the swamp from Greenspring to the Williamsburg road, and very soon came into collision with the main body of the British. Probably only the lateness of the evening saved them from a great defeat; they were repulsed, with a loss of 118 men killed and wounded, and Cornwallis taking advantage of his victory, marched to Jamestown Island, and safely crossed the river with his army three days later. Some part of the earthworks cast up by him to protect the army in the woods may yet be seen on the right bank of Powhatan Creek on the Williamsburg road. Fifteen weeks later, Cornwallis, who had in the meantime moved over from Portsmouth, surrendered at Yorktown; and thus Amercian Independence was won within twenty miles of the spot where English civilization was first permanently planted in America by the mother country.

In the year 1807, the second centennial anniversary of the landing of the colonists was celebrated at Jamestown by the citizens of Williamsburg, Norfolk, Portsmouth, Hampton, Petersburg, and the surrounding country. There was present from Norfolk Captain Peter Nestell with his volunteer State artillery; James O'Connor, editor of the Norfolk and Portsmouth *Herald;* the talented Thomas Blanchard and his son C. K. Blanchard; Major John Saunders, of the United States army, stationed at Fort Nelson. From Petersburg came John D. Burk, the historian; from Williamsburg Chancellor Samuel Tyler, Bishop James Madison and many others. Conspicuous among the older people were Colonel Thomas Newton, of Norfolk, Colonel Champion Travis, of Jamestown, and Colonel Wilson Miles Cary, of Ceeley's, Elizabeth City County — surviving members of the Virginia Convention of 1776, which had been the first to declare for State independence and to recommend to congress and the other States similar action.

The dawn of the 13th day of May, 1807, was ushered in by a salute from cannon, and the eye rested on an attractive picture at Jamestown. There were thirty-two vessels in the "crescent cove" of the Island, and the crowd numbered about 2,000, among whom were over 400 ladies. A procession was formed and the visitors marched in dignified manner to the graveyard of the old church, then represented as now by its solitary brick tower; and

BRISCOE G. BALDWIN,
Orator at Jamestown in 1807.

there Bishop Madison, standing on a tombstone, delivered an eloquent prayer. After this, the procession returned to the ground in front of Colonel Travis's house, where orations were delivered by Briscoe G. Baldwin and John Madison, and odes by C. K. Blanchard and Leroy Anderson — all four students of William and Mary College. When these exercises were ended the ladies dined in the spacious apartments of the Travis mansion house,[1] and in the evening and night there were dances in the long room by the water side.

[1] From the reference to the location of the house it would appear that Col. Travis was then living near the churchyard.

The morning of the 14th, like that of the 13th, was ushered in by cannon, and at eleven o'clock the visitors attended the funeral of a young man at the graveyard, who had fallen a victim to the heat and " the too free use of ice in cider." Next a meeting was held at which Thomas Newton presided, and several resolutions were adopted looking to making the 13th of May an annual holiday for the State.

On the 15th, the pilgrims assembled at Williamsburg in the very room of the Raleigh Tavern, where exactly thirty-one years before the " Declaration of Independence " had been drafted by the committee of the Virginia convention. Samuel Tyler, chancellor of the Williamsburg District, acted as president, and James Semple as vice-president; and among the toasts drank at the dinner was " The virtuous and en-lightened, the patriotic convention of the State of Virginia, that body which with one voice dared to declare themselves independent, and to propose a similar declaration to their sister States." And after dinner a procession commenced, at the head of which were borne in triumph Colonels Cary, Newton and Travis, surviving members of the Virginia convention.[1]

In 1816, the *Powhatan*, the first steamer to navigate the waters of the James, arrived from New York, and began to make regular trips between Norfolk and Richmond. The trip one way took about twenty-two hours and cost the pas-senger $10.[2]

In 1822, another celebration was held at Jamestown Island, the orators being, as on the former occasion, students of Wil-liam and Mary, William Barton Rogers, Robert Saunders and Mr. McCreary, the first two of whom were afterwards distinguished professors at their *Alma Mater;* and William Barton Rogers became founder and first president of the Massachusetts Institute of Technology and Robert Saunders became president of William and Mary College.[3]

---

[1] *Proceedings of the Late Jubilee at Jamestown* in 1807.
[2] James. *Lower Norfolk County Antiquary.* IV., 49.
[3] *Richmond Enquirer,* May 14, 1822.

In 1837, Mr. Richard Randolph, of Williamsburg, called the antiquary, published a description of the Island in the Southern Literary Messenger of which the following is a synopsis.[1]

There was then only one residence on the Island — the Ambler house (with its outhouses and negro quarters), where the brick ruins are now seen. At the west end some portions of the brick fort were visible, but most of it had been washed away by the encroaching tides. To the right of the fort, a few hundred yards distant, was a small brick building called a powder magazine. Near this house were the remains (consisting of bricks, plaster, &c.) of a large building, which Mr. Randolph correctly conjectured had been the state house. All that existed of the church above ground was the tower, but in the graveyard there was quite a number of old tombstones, among which now missing were the monuments to John Ambler (first of the name) and William Lee. The Island was intersected by a great number of ditches, indicative of lots which once existed, on some

WILLIAM BARTON ROGERS,
Orator at Jamestown, 1822.

of which were to be found the foundations of brick buildings; and on one there was an old well, "the brick walls of which were quite perfect and sound." Skeletons might be found in many places near the site of the town, showing that the churchyard was not the only graveyard. The Island was in a high state of cultivation and was esteemed a most valuable estate. "The soil," concludes Mr. Randolph, "is well adapted to the growth of corn, wheat, oats, and *palma christi,* and the Island and surrounding country abound in game of almost every

[1] *Southern Literary Messenger,* III., 303.

description — partridges, pheasants, wild turkeys, waterfowl and deer."

In 1831, the Amblers and Travises parted with their interest on the Island to David Bullock, of Richmond, who then became the first sole proprietor. Five years later it was assessed to Colonel Goodrich Durfey, and in 1846 to John Coke, father of Hon. Richard Coke, late U. S. senator from Texas. Then in 1848, it was assessed to Martha Allen Orgain, daughter of Colonel William Allen, of Clermont on James River, from

THE AMBLER BRICK HOUSE, BEFORE IT WAS BURNED.

whom it came in 1851 to William Allen Orgain, her son, who by legislative enactment took the name of William Allen and was the owner of the Island during the war between the States.

May 13, 1857, the 250th anniversary was celebrated under the auspices of the Jamestown Society, organized in 1854 by Virginia residents in Washington.[1] As the then owner of

[1] See account of the celebration in the *Southern Literary Messenger*, Vol. XXIV.

Jamestown had devoted the land surrounding the old church to agricultural purposes, the ceremonies were held at the east end, two miles back, near the burial ground of the Travis family. The crowd included the governor, Henry A. Wise, and upwards of 8,000 people; and the orator was Ex-President John Tyler, and poet was James Barron Hope. The weather was intensely dry and warm, and at night there was a great fall of rain.

One sentence in Ex-President Tyler's speech has more than ordinary interest. Referring to his early recollections of the houses, he said that, when he was a student at William and Mary College in 1802–1807, a line of ruined houses stood " in a connected street running east and west from the present dwelling house (Jaquelin-Ambler House) to the ruins of the church." " The connected street " was undoubtedly the Back Street of old ". New Towne," and the ruined houses indicated where the business part of the Island once existed.

MAJOR WILLIAM ALLEN.

May 13, 1859, a pilgrimage was made to the Island by Edward Everett, the great orator of Massachusetts, in company with the poet, John R. Thompson editor of the *Southern Literary Messenger* and some fourteen other persons. The Virginia creeper which had covered the tower of the church had died out, and the object of the visit was to plant ivy at the base of the old ruin. Mr. Everett made some very happy remarks, and referred to the tower " as marking the spot, where the first germs of this mighty republic, now almost coextensive with the continent, were planted in 1607."

In 1861, the Island was occupied by about 500 Confederate soldiers consisting of companies from Petersburg, and James

City, Bedford and Hanover counties, and near the church was thrown up an earth fort called "Jamestown battery." About the same time earthworks were constructed on the second ridge commanding the Back River, and at other points of the Island, notably near Passmore's Creek and at Black Point.[1] These works were raised by the late E. D. T. Meyers, as military en-

JOHN TYLER,
Orator at Jamestown, 1857.

gineer, acting under Lt. Catesby ap R. Jones, afterwards famed as captain of the iron clad *Virginia* in her battle with the monitor *Ericsson*. The battery at Jamestown had five faces, and was intended to have sixteen guns, though it does not appear to have ever had this number. When General Johnston withdrew his army to Richmond, the defences at Jamestown and

---

[1] *Official Records of the Union and Confederate Navies* (**Series 1**), Vol. VI., 699; Vol. VII., 473. 566.

Archer's Hope were abandoned by the Confederates, and they soon after fell into the hands of the Federals, who found in the works nine eight inch army columbiads, and four navy thirty-two pounders.

In a letter dated December 28, 1900, Major E. D. T. Meyers wrote as follows:

There was no bridge across the creek in 1861, nor any causeway across the marsh on the north side of the creek, nor do I recall any evidence of the former existence of either. I built the bridge and causeway for military purposes soon after I went there.

I do not distinctly recall any houses, other than the mansion itself, then not in very good repair, but entirely habitable, and the ruins of the old church. There may have been, and probably were, some small frame buildings at the shore end of the wharf. The Island was in a very good state of cultivation, and I recollect General Lee bemoaning the sacrifice of a promising wheat field to a square redoubt. The Island at that time belonged to William Allen.

The battery, which was built just above the old tower, was not far from the brink of the river bank, which I understand (for I have not been there since the war) has been heavily encroached upon by the river. During the course of the war the Ambler house was burned to the ground.

Travel by steamboat necessitated the establishment of wharves for the public convenience at intervals on James River, and the first wharf at Jamestown was placed just above the Confederate fort, very near where stood in 1611 "the bridge" of Sir Thomas Dale. This was done to save expense, as it only required a short wharf to reach the channel. After some years, however, the site was abandoned, because the point of the Island above made it inconvenient and even dangerous to effect a landing. The wharf was then built (about 1850) down the Island below Orchard Run, but after the war of 1861-'65, this site was also abandoned, because of the expense of maintenance; and the present location, being a

JAMES BARRON HOPE,
Poet at Jamestown, 1857.

compromise between the two old positions, was selected. The respective sites of the old wharves may still be exactly determined by the lines of piles standing out in the water in the vicinities mentioned.

The rest of the history of the place is familiar to many. When the college of William and Mary was reorganized in 1888, the earliest celebration attempted by the faculty and students was held in the very shadow of the old tower.[1] Then followed the munificent act of Mr. and Mrs. Edward Barney, who presented twenty-two and one-half acres of land including the churchyard, to the Association for the Preservation of Virginia Antiquities, consisting of representative ladies of Virginia.

Among the most notable events since was the gathering upon the Island, May 13, 1901, of the bishops of the Episcopal church, representing the different States of the American Union.

Under the auspices of the Association for the Preservation of Virginia Antiquities now having charge, the United States government has erected, in the last few years, a substantial sea wall at the western end of the Island; and recent excavations have unearthed both in the churchyard and other places many relics of old buildings and tombstones.

The Island is a beautiful spot, and is one of the best plantations on the James River. There is now a fine artesian well affording very pure and palatable water. Many of the swampy places have been drained, and its health under present conditions is excellent.

Preparations are now making for a suitable celebration of the foundation of the colony at Jamestown, on the Tercentennary, May 13, 1907, of the arrival of the settlers. In the senate of Virginia, Hon. D. Gardiner Tyler was the first to offer a bill calling upon the president of the United States and congress to make a national commemoration of the event. It was duly passed, and the ringing proclamation of President Theodore Roosevelt sets forth the significance of the settlement and the purposes and intention of the government, and deserves a closing place in this historic compendium.

[1] In 1895, an address was delivered by the president of the college, and in other years addresses were made by J. Lesslie Hall, professor of history in the college.

A PROCLAMATION

BY THE

PRESIDENT OF THE UNITED STATES OF AMERICA.

WHEREAS the congress of the United States has passed an act approved March 3, 1905, and entitled "An act to provide for celebrating the birth of the American nation, the first permanent settlement of English speaking people on the Western Hemisphere, by the holding of an international naval, marine and military celebration in the vicinity of Jamestown, on the waters of Hampton Roads, in the State of Virginia, to provide for the suitable and permanent commemoration of said event and to authorize an appropriation in aid therefor and for other purposes."

And whereas section 3 of the said act reads as follows:
"Section 3. The President of the United States is hereby authorized to make proclamation of said celebration, setting forth the event to be commemorated, inviting foreign nations to participate by the sending of their naval vessels and such representation of their military organizations as may be proper;"

Now, therefore, I, Theodore Roosevelt, President of the United States, by virtue of the authority vested in me by said act, do hereby declare and proclaim that there shall be inaugurated in the year 1907, at and near the waters of Hampton Roads, in the State of Virginia, an international naval, marine and military celebration, beginning May 13 and ending not later than November 1, 1907, for the purpose of commemorating in a fitting and appropriate manner the birth of the American nation; the first permanent settlement of English speaking people on the American continent made at Jamestown, Virginia, on the 13th day of May, 1607, and in order that the great events of the American history which have resulted therefrom may be accentuated to the present and future generations of American citizens.

And in the name of the government and people of the United States, I do therefore invite all the nations of the earth to take part in the commemoration of the event which has had a far-reaching effect on the course of human history, by sending their naval vessels to the said celebration and by making such representations of their military organizations as may be proper.

In testimony thereof, I have now set my hand and caused the seal of the United States to be affixed.

Done in the city of Washington this twenty-ninth day of March, one thousand nine hundred and five, and in the independence of the United States the one hundred and twenty-ninth.

By the President: Alvey A. Adse,
    Acting Secretary of State.

                THEODORE ROOSEVELT.

CENSUS OF INHABITANTS.

Names of the first settlers at Jamestown, 1607.

(From Smith, *Works*, [Arber's ed.] p. 389).

Council.

Master Edward Maria Wingfield
Captaine Bartholomew Gosnoll
Captaine John Smith
Captaine John Ratcliffe
Captaine John Martin
Captaine George Kendall

Gentlemen

Master Robert Hunt, Preacher
Master George Percie
Anthony Gosnoll
George Flower
Captaine Gabriell Archer
Robert Fenton
Robert Ford
William Bruster
Edward Harrington
Dru(e) Pickhouse
Thomas Jacob
John Brookes
Ellis Kingston
Thomas Sands
Benjamin Beast
Jehu Robinson
Thomas Mouton
Eustace Clovill
Stephen Halthrop
Kellam Throgmorton
Edward Morish
Nathaniell Powell
Edward Browne
Robert Behethland
John Pennington
Jeremy Alicock
George Walker
Thomas Studley
Richard Crofts
Nicholas Houlgraue
Thomas Webbe
John Waller
John Short
William Tankard
William Smethes

Francis Snarsbrough
Richard Simons
Edward Brookes
Richard Dixon
John Martin
Roger Cooke
Anthony Gosnold
Thomas Wotton, *Chirurg.*
John Stevenson
Thomas Gore
Henry Adling
Francis Midwinter
Richard Frith

Carpenters

William Laxon
Edward Pising
Thomas Emry
Robert Small

Labourers

John Laydon
William Cassen
George Cassen
Thomas Cassen
William Rodes
William White
Old Edward
Henry Tavin
George Goulding
John Dods
William Johnson
William Vnger
Jam: Read, *Blacksmith*
Jonas Profit, *Sailer*
Thomas Cowper, *Barber*
Wil Garret, *Bricklayer*
Edward Brinto, *Mason*
William Loue, *Taylor*
Nic: Scott, *Drum*
Wil: Wilkinson, *Chirurg.*
Samuel Collier, *boy*
Nat Pecock, *boy*
James Brumfield, *boy*
Richard Mutton, *boy*

With divers others to the number of one hundred. (The **total** number left at the Island on June 22, 1607, was 104.)

Names of those who came in the First Supply:

(From Smith, *Works*, [Arber's ed.] p. 411).

Mathew Scrivener appointed to be one of the Councell.

Gentlemen.

Michaell Phittiplace.
William Phittiplace.
Ralph Morton.
Richard Wyffing.
John Taverner.
William Cantrell.
Robert Barnes.
Richard Featherstone.
George Hill.
George Pretty.
Nathaniell Causy.
Peter Pory.
Robert Cutler.
Michaell Sicklemore.
William Bentley.
Thomas Coe.
Doctor Russell.
Ieffrey Abbot.
Edward Gurgana.
Richard Worley.
Timothy Leeds.
Richard Killingbeck.
William Spence.
Richard Prodger.
Richard Pots.
Richard Mullinax.
William Bayley.
Francis Perkins.
Iohn Harper.
George Forest.
Iohn Nichols.
William Griuell.

Laboroures.

Raymond Goodison.
William Simons.
Iohn Spearman.
Richard Bristow.
William Perce.

Iames Watkins.
Iohn Bouth.
Christopher Rods.
Richard Burket.
Iames Burre.
Nicholas Ven.
Francis Perkins.
Richard Gradon.
Rawland Nelstrop.
Richard Savage.
Thomas Savage.
Richard Milmer.
William May.
Vere.
Michaell.
Bishop Wiles.

Taylers.

Thomas Hope.
William Ward.
Iohn Powell.
William Yonge.
William Beckwith.
La(w)rence Towtales.

Apothecaries.

Thomas Field.
Iohn Harford.

Dani: Stallings, Jeweller.
Will. Dawson, a refiner.
Abram Ransack, a refiner.
Wil. Johnson, a Goldsmith.
Peter Keffer, a gunsmith.
Rob: Alberton, a perfumer.
Richard Belfield, a Goldsmith.
Post Ginnat, a Chirurg(ion).
Iohn Lewes, a Cooper.
Robert Cotton, a Tobacco-pipe-maker.
Richard Dole, a Blacksmith.
And divers others to the number of 120.

Names of those who came in the Second Supply:

(From Smith, *Works*, [Arber's ed.] p. 445).

Captaine Peter Winne } were appointed to be of the
Captaine Richard Waldo } Councell.
Master Francis VVest, brother to the Lord Le VVarre.

Gent.

Thomas Graues.
Raleigh Croshaw.

Gabriel Beadle.
Iohn Beadle.
Iohn Russell.

William Russell.
Iohn Cuderington.
William Sambage.
Henry Leigh.
Henry Philpot.
Harmon Harrison.
Daniel Tucker.
Henry Collings.
Hugh Wolleston.
Iohn Hoult.
Thomas Norton.
George Yarington.
George Burton.
Thomas Abbay.
William Dowman.
Thomas Maxes.
Michael Lowick.
Master Hunt.
Thomas Forrest.
Iohn Dauxe.

Tradesmen (i. e., *Artizans*).

Thomas Phelps.
Iohn Prat.
Iohn Clarke.
Ieffrey Shortridge.
Dionis Oconor.

Hugh Winne.
Dauid ap Hugh.
Thomas Bradley.
Iohn Burras.
Thomas Lavander.
Henry Bell.
Master Powell.
David Ellis.
Thomas Gibson.

Labourers.

Thomas Dawse.
Thomas Mallard.
William Tayler.
Thomas Fox.
Nicholas Hancock.
Walker.
Williams.
Floud.
Morley.
Rose.
Scot.
Hardwyn.

Boyes.

Milman.
Hilliard.

Mistresse Forrest, and Anne Burras her maide; eight Dutch men and *Poles,* with some others, to the number of seaventie persons, &c.

Names of inhabitants of Jamestown in 1624:

(From Hotten, *Lists of Emigrants to America,* 173–178.)

Sir Francis Wyatt, Governor,
Margaret, Lady Wyatt
Hawt Wyatt, Minister
Kathren Spencer
Thomas Hooker
John Gather
John Matheman
Edward Cooke
George Nelson
George Hall
Jane Burtt
Elizabeth Pomell
Mary Woodward
———
Sir George Yeardley, Knight
Temperance, Lady Yeardly
Argall Yardley
Frances Yeardley
Elizabeth Yeardley
Kilibett Hichcocke
Austen Combes
John Foster
Richard Arrundell

Susan Hall
Ann Grimes
Elizabeth Lyon
——— Younge
——— Negroe } Women
——— Negroe }

Alice Davison—vid
Edward Sharples
Jone Davies
George Sands, Treasurer
Captain William Perce
Jone Perce
Robert Hedges
Hugh Wms. (Williams)
Thomas Moulston
Henry Farmor
John Lightfoote
Thomas Smith
Roger Ruese
Alexander Gill
John Cartwright,
Robert Austine
Edward Bricke

William Ravenett
Jocomb Andrews
vx Andrews
Richard Alder
Ester Evere
Angello A Negar

Doct. John Pott
Elizabeth Pott
Richard Townsend
Thomas Leister
John Kullaway
Randall Howlett
Jane Dickenson
Fortune Taylor

Capt. Roger Smith
Mrs. Smith
Elizabeth Salter
Sarah Macocke
Elizabeth Rolfe
Chri Lawson
vxor eius Lawson
Francis Fouler
Charles Waller
Henry Booth

Capt. Ralph Hamor
Mrs. Hamor
Jereme Clement
Elizabeth Clement
Sarah Langley
Sisley Greene
Ann Addams
Elkinton Ratcliffe
Frances Gibson
James Yemanson

John Pontes
Christopher Best
Thomas Clarke
Mr. Reignolds
Mr. Hickmore
vx Hickmore
Sarah Riddall

Edward Blaney
Edward Hudson
vx Hudson
William Hartley
John Shelley
Robert Bew
William Ward
Thomas Mentis
Robert Whitmore
Robert Chauntree
Robert Sheppard
William Sawier
Lanslott Damport

Math. Loyd
Thomas Ottway
Thomas Crouch
Elizabeth Starkey
Elinor

Mrs. Perry
Infans Perry
Frances Chapman
George Graues (Graves)
vx Graues
Rebecca Snowe
Sarah Snowe
John Isgraw (Isgrave)
Mary Ascombe vid
Banamy Bucke
Gercyon Bucke
Peleg Bucke
Mara Bucke
Abram Porter
Bridget Clarke
Abigall Ascombe
John Jackson
vx Jackson
Ephraim Jackson

Mr. John Burrows
Mrs. Burrows
Anthony Burrows
John Cooke
Nicholas Gouldsmith
Elias Gaill
Andrew Howell
An Ashley

John Southern
Thomas Pasmore
Andrew Ralye

Nath. Jefferys
vx. Jefferys
Thomas Hebbs

Clement Dilke
Mrs. Dilke
John Hinton

Richard Stephens
Wassell Rayner
vx. Rayner
John Jackson
Edward Price
Osten Smith
Thomas Spilman
Bryan Cawt

George Menify
Moyes Ston

Capt. Holmes
Mr. Calcker
Mrs. Calcker
infans Calcker
Peceable Sherwood
Anthony West
Henry Barker
Henry Scott
Margery Dawse

———

Mr. Cann
Capt. Hartt
Edward Spalding
vx. Spalding
Puer Spalding
Puella Spalding
John Helin
vx. Helin

puer Helin
infans Helin
Thomas Graye et vx.
Jone Graye
William Graye
Richard Younge
vx. Younge
Jone Younge
Randall Smalwood
John Greene
William Mudge

———

Mrs. Southey
Ann Southey
Elin Painter

———

Goodman Webb

IN JAMES ISLAND.

John Osbourn
vx. Osbovrn (Osbourn)
George Pope
Robert Constable

———

William Jones
vx. Jones
John Johnson
vx. Johnson
infans
Johnson
Johnson
John Hall
vx. Hall
William Cooksey
vx. Cooksey
infans Cooksey
Alice Kean

———

Robert Fitts
vx. Fitts
John Reddish

John Grevett.
vx. Grevett
John West
Rhomas West
Henry Glover

———

Goodman Stoiks
vx. Stoiks
infans Stoiks
Mr. Adams
Mr. Leet
William Spence
vx. Spence
infans Spence
James Tooke
James Roberts
Anthony Harlow

———

Sarah Spence
George Shurke
John Booth
Robert Bennett.

MEMBERS OF THE HOUSE OF BURGESSES, 1619–1776. ·

(Partial List.)

July 30, 1619.— Capt. William Powell, Ensign William Spence.
March 5, 1624.— Richard Kingsmill, Edward Blaney.
October 16, 1629.— Richard Kingsmill, George Menifie.
March 24, 1630.— John Southerne, Robert Barrington.
February 21, 1632.— John Southerne, Lieutenant Thomas Crumpe.
September 4, 1632.— John Jackson.
February 1, 1633.[1]— John Corker, Gent.
June 5, 1666.— Major Theophilus Hone.
June 7, 1676.— Richard Lawrence.
Nov. 10, 1683.— Thomas Clayton.
April 16, 1684.— Henry Hartwell.
April 25, 1688.— William Sherwood.
March 2, 1693.— Capt. Miles Cary.
September 24, 1696.— William Sherwood.
1697.— Philip Ludwell.
December 5, 1702.— Robert Beverley.
November 16, 1714.— Edward Jaquelin
April 23, 1718.— Archibald Blair.
May 9, 1722.— William Brodnax.
May 12, 1726.— William Brodnax.
August 13, 1736.— Lewis Burwell.
May 22, 1740.— Lewis Burwell.
May 6, 1742.— Philip Ludwell.
Sept. 4, 1744.— Philip Ludwell.
July 11, 1746.— Philip Ludwell.
March 30, 1747.— Philip Ludwell.
Nov. 3, 1748.— Philip Ludwell.
April 10, 1749.— Philip Ludwell.
Feb. 5, 1752.— Edward Champion Travis.
Nov. 1, 1753.— Edward Travis.
Feb. 14, 1754.— Edward Champion Travis.
Aug. 22, 1754.— Edward Champion Travis.
Oct. 17, 1754.— Edward Champion Travis.
May 1, 1755.— Edward Champion Travis.
Oct. 27, 1755.— Edward Champion Travis.
March 25, 1756.— Edward Champion Travis.
April 3, 1757.— Edward Champion Travis.
Feb. 22, 1759.— Edward Champion Travis.
Nov. 1, 1759.— John Ambler.
1760.— John Ambler.
Nov. 3, 1761.— Edward C. Travis.
Jan. 14, 1762.— Edward C. Travis.
March 30, 1762.— Edward C. Travis.
Nov. 2, 1762.— Edward C. Travis.
May 19, 1763.— Edward C. Travis.
Jan. 12, 1764.— Edward C. Travis.
Oct. 30, 1764.— Edward C. Travis.

---

[1] In 1634, the plantations were formed into counties, and Jamestown appears after that to have had no representative apart from James City County until 1661. But in March, 1661, the general assembly gave Jamestown the right to elect one of itself. And this privilege was exercised down to the adoption of the State constitution, in 1776.

May 1, 1765.— Edward C. Travis.
Oct., 1765.— John Ambler.
Nov. 5, 1766.— Edward Ambler.
March, 1767.— Edward Ambler.
March 31, 1768.— Edward Ambler.
May 8, 1769.— Champion Travis.
Nov. 7, 1769.— Champion Travis.
May 21, 1770.— Champion Travis.
July 11, 1771.— Champion Travis.
Feb. 10, 1772.— Champion Travis.
March 4, 1773.— Champion Travis.
May 5, 1774.— Champion Travis.
June 1, 1775.— Champion Travis.

MEMBERS OF CONVENTIONS.

March 20, 1775, February 17, 1775, December 1, 1775, May 6, 1776.—
Champion Travis.

HISTORICAL SUMMARY.

*From the landing of the first colony sent by the London Company to
the abandonment of Jamestown in 1699.*

FIRST CHARTER, APRIL 10, 1606.

May   14, 1607.— Landing of the colonists at Jamestown.
June   22, 1607.— Capt. Christopher Newport leaves for England.
Sept. 10, 1607.— Wingfield deposed, and Capt. John Ratcliffe president.
Jan.   2, 1608.— Capt. Newport arrives with the "First Supply" of
                  men and provisions.
April 10, 1608.— Newport leaves for England.
April 20, 1608.— Arrival of Capt. Francis Nelson from the West Indies
                  (a belated part of the First Supply).
Sept. 10, 1608.— Ratcliffe's year expires and John Smith becomes
                  president.
Oct.,   1608.— Arrival of the Second Supply.
Dec.,   1608.— First marriage in Virginia — John Laydon and Ann
                  Burras.
Dec.,   1608.— Return of Newport to England.
Aug.,   1609.— Arrival of the Third Supply.
Sept. 10, 1609.— Capt. Smith's presidency expires and Capt. George
                  Percy made president.
———,   1609.— Virginia Laydon, the first English child born in
                  Virginia.
Oct.   5, 1609.— Capt. Smith returns to England.

SECOND CHARTER, MAY 23, 1609; THIRD CHARTER, MARCH 12, 1612.

May   23, 1610.— Arrival of Sir Thomas Gates, first governor, with that
                  portion of the Third Supply which was wrecked in
                  the Bermudas.
June   7, 1610.— The colonists abandon Jamestown.
June   10, 1610.— Lord Delaware arrives at Jamestown.
March 28, 1611.— Lord Delaware sails for England, **leaving Capt.**
                  George Percy deputy-governor.
May   21, 1611.— Sir Thomas Dale arrives.
Aug.   1, 1611.— Sir Thomas Gates arrives.
Sept.,   1611.— Henrico founded.

————, 1612.— John Rolfe introduces the culture of tobacco.

Christmas,1613.— Bermuda Hundred founded.

March, 1614.— Sir Thomas Gates returns to England, and Sir Thomas Dale acts as deputy-governor.

About April 5, 1614.— Pocahontas marries John Rolfe.

May, 1616.— Sir Thomas Dale returns to England, and Capt. George Yeardley made deputy-governor.

March 21, 1617.— Pocahontas buried in the Parish Church at Gravesend, England.

May, 1617.— Capt. Samuel Argall arrives as deputy-governor.

April, 1618.— Powhatan dies.

April 10, 1619.— Capt. Argall leaves Jamestown and Capt. Nathaniel Powell becomes deputy-governor.

April 19, 1619.— Sir George Yeardley arrives as governor and captain-general of Virginia.

July 30, 1619.— First legislative assembly.

Aug., 1619.— First negroes landed; African slavery introduced.

Nov. 18, 1621.— Sir Francis Wyatt becomes governor.

March 22, 1622.— Indian massacre; 347 whites slain out of a population of 1,258.

ROYAL GOVERNMENT.

May 24, 1624.— Chief-Justice Ley declares the charter null and void.

May 17, 1626.— Sir Francis Wyatt sails for England, and Sir George Yeardley becomes governor, the second time.

Nov. 13, 1627.— Sir George Yeardley buried at Jamestown, and the next day Capt. Francis West becomes deputy-governor by the council's election.

March 5, 1629.— Capt. West goes to England, and Dr. John Pott elected deputy-governor by the council.

March 24, 1630.— Sir John Harvey arrives as governor and captain-general of Virginia.

April 28, 1635.— Harvey deposed, and Capt. John West elected by the council deputy-governor.

Jan. 18, 1637.— Sir John Harvey reads his commission at Elizabeth City to be governor a second time.

Nov., 1639.— Sir Francis Wyatt arrives governor.

Feb., 1642.— Sir William Berkeley becomes governor.

April 17, 1644.— Second Indian massacre; 300 English killed in a population of 8,000.

June, 1644.— Richard Kempe elected by the council deputy-governor in the absence of Governor Berkeley.

June, 1645.— Sir William Berkeley returns to Virginia.

1646.— Opechancanough dies at Jamestown.

March 12, 1652.— Surrender of the colony to the Parliament.

April 30, 1652.— Richard Bennett elected governor by the assembly.

March 31, 1655.— Edward Digges elected governor.

March 13, 1658.— Samuel Mathews elected governor.

Jan., 1660.— Death of Mathews.

March 13, 1660.— Sir William Berkeley re-elected governor by the assembly.

May 8, 1660.— Charles II. proclaimed in London.

Sept. 20, 1660.— Charles II. proclaimed in Virginia.

April 30, 1661.— Col. Francis Moryson deputy-governor in the absence of Sir William Berkeley in Europe.

Sept.–Nov.,1662.— Berkeley returns to Jamestown from Europe.

Sept. 19, 1676.— Jamestown burned by Bacon.

Oct. 26, 1676.— Nathaniel Bacon, Jr, dies.

May   5, 1677.—Berkeley leaves the country, and Col. Herbert Jeffryes
          becomes lieutenant-governor.
Dec.   17, 1678.— Col. Jeffryes dies, and Sir Henry Chicheley succeeds
          as deputy-governor.
May   2, 1680.—Lord Culpeper arrives governor of Virginia.
Aug.,   1680.—Lord Culpeper visits England, and Sir Henry Chich-
          eley acts as deputy-governor.
Dec.   17, 1682.— Lord Culpeper arrives the second time in Virginia.
May   28, 1683.— Lord Culpeper goes back to England, and Nicholas
          Spencer, Esq., president of the council, acts as
          deputy-governor.
April   15, 1684.— Francis, Lord Howard of Effingham, governor.
Oct.,   1688.— Nathaniel Bacon, president of the council, deputy gov-
          ernor.
May   16, 1690.— Francis Nicholson lieutenant-governor.
Sept.   11, 1692.— Sir Edmond Andros lieutenant-governor.
Oct.   9, 1698.—Col. Francis Nicholson lieutenant-governor till August
          15, 1705.
Oct.   31, 1698.— State house at Jamestown destroyed by fire.
April,   1699.— Act of the general assembly for building the capitol
          at Williamsburg.

SEAL OF VIRGINIA DURING THE REIGN OF GEORGE III.

VI

THE FORT.

There were at different periods in the history of Jamestown three forts erected by the settlers. The *first fort* was a triangular stockade made of poles of oak and poplar about fourteen feet high, and set four ,feet in the ground, each of the poles forming a load for three or four men.[1] As stated elsewhere, the side facing the river was 120 yards in length, and the other two sides were 100 yards each, making the fort include a little more than an acre. In each corner was a platform on which a piece or two of cannon were mounted, and there was an entrance or port through each side commanded by a piece of ordnance stationed within.[2] George Percy and Gabriel Archer described[3] the difficulties incurred from the savages, while the fort was building, in the following language :

May 14, 1607, "We landed all our men ; which were set to work about the fortification, and others some to watch and ward as it was convenient." About midnight some savages came close to the fort, but ran away when the alarm was given.

The Island lay in the territory of Wowinchopunck, werowance of the Paspaheghs, and a day or two later messengers "bravely dressed with crownes of coloured hair upon their heads," came to announce the werowance's speedy arrival.

May 18. This day Wowinchopunck arrived attended by 100 savages armed with bows and arrows. As the savages thronged into the fort, one of them stole a hatchet from one of the soldiers, who struck him on the arm and took it from him. Thereupon, another savage came up with a wooden sword fiercely raised. The settlers then rushed to their arms, and Wowinchopunck and his company departed in great anger.

[1] Smith, *Works* (Arber's ed.), 612.
[2] Strachey in Purchas, *His Pilgrims*, IV., 1752. 1753.
[3] Smith, *Works* (Arber's ed.), lii–lv., lxvi–lxviii.

May 20, Wowinchopunck sent forty Indians with the present of a deer, who asked to sleep in the fort at night, but were refused. "One of our Gentlemen hauing a Target which hee trusted in, thinking it would beare out a slight shot, hee set it vp against a tree, willing one of the Sauages to shoot: who tooke from his backe an Arrow of an elle long, drew it strongly in his Bowe, shoots the Target a foote thorow, or better: which was strange, seeing that a Pistoll could not pierce it. Wee seeing the force of his Bowe, afterwards set him vp a steele Target: he shot again, and burst his arrow all to pieces. He presently pulled out another Arrow, and bit it in his teeth, and seemed to bee in a great rage: so hee went away in great anger. Their Bowes are made of tough Hasell, their strings of Leather, their Arrowes of Canes or Hasell, headed with very sharpe stones, and are made artificially like a broad Arrow: other some of their Arrowes are headed with the ends of Deeres hornes, and are feathered very artificially."

May 26. While the fort was yet unfinished, the Indians of Paspahegh made a fierce assault. There came above 200 Indians with their werowance. They came up almost into the fort, shot through the tents, and killed a boy and wounded eleven men, whereof one died after. "We killed dyvers of them." The council stood in front, and four out of the five present were wounded (Gosnold, Ratcliffe, Martin and Kendall), and "our President, Mr. Wingfield (who shewed himselfe a valiant gentleman), had an arrow cleane through his bearde, yet escaped hurte."

May 28. "We laboured pallozadoing our fort." Captain Newport, who had now returned from a trip up the river, caused his sailors to assist in the work.

May 29. The savages made a second attack, and shot more than forty arrows into and about the fort, but did no harm beyond killing a dog.

May 30. All was quiet.

May 31. The Indians came lurking among the thickets and long grass, and shot six arrows into a gentleman named Eustace Clovell, who had left the fort unarmed.

June 1. Some twenty Indians appeared, but their arrows fell short of the fort.

June 2 and 3. All was quiet and the settlers worked upon their fort and cut clapboard for the ships to take back to England.

June 4. Three savages crawled unperceived through the long grass under one of the bulwarks and shot arrows through the clothes of one of the emigrants, " but missed the skynne."

June 8. Master Clovell, who was shot on May 31, died of his wounds.

June 13. " Eight salvages lay close amonge the weedes and long grasse: and spying one or two of our Maryners Master Ihon Cotson and Master Mathew ffitch by themselves, shott Mathew ffytch in the (?) somewhat dangerously, and so rann away this Morning."

June 14. Two friendly savages visited the fort and informed the emigrants that the war was not the act of all the tribes, but of the Paspaheghs, Tapahanas, Weyanokes, Apamatecohs and Chiskiacks.

June 15. " We had built and finished our Fort, * * *." The cabins of the settlers were within the fort, in three lines parallel to the sides of the stockade, and separated from them by a street twenty-four to thirty feet wide, and in the middle of the open space were the church, the storehouse, and the guardhouse. As already noticed, the stockade, with all the cabins, was burned[1] January 7, 1608; and when restored, being made up of sappy timber, it required frequent repairing from year to year.

In the fall of 1608, three acres adjoining the fort were palisaded so as to form, with the original stockade, a pentagon, or " five-square." At this time " a plain " by the west bulwark was used for drilling the men, which was called " Smithfield " (after Sir Thomas Smith); where sometimes more than a hundred savages would stand in amazement to witness a file of soldiers shoot at a mark on a tree.[2]

In October, 1609, there were, according to Captain Smith,[3] at his departure from Virginia, twenty-four cannon of different calibers in the fort, culverins, demi-culverins, sakers and falcons, " most well mounted upon convenient platforms."

[1] Smith, *Works* (Arber's ed.), 407.
[2] Ibid., 434.
[3] Ibid.

In 1613, Don Molina, a Spanish prisoner at Jamestown, reported[1] that the fort at Jamestown had six guns; and a little later Count Gondomar, the Spanish ambassador, declared[2] to his king that there were five forts in Virginia — James, Henerique (Henrico), Charles, Point Comfort and Henry, " which were surrounded with earthworks on which they plant their artillery."

In 1610, the captain of the fort was George Webb. In 1611, the captain was George Percy; in 1615, Francis West, in whose absence Lt. John Sharpe commanded; in 1617, William Powell; and when he was killed by the Indians, in 1622, Captain William Peirce succeeded him.

The site of the stockade is supposed to be, in part, covered by the Confederate fort, but most of it lies under the water west of this fort. When the Confederate fort was constructed in 1861, pieces of armor, sword hilts, gold, silver and copper coin were discovered, a good evidence of an earlier occupation.

The second fort was an earth fort, described by the Rev. John Clayton in 1688 as " a sort of tetragone with something like bastions at the four corners." It was probably erected after the Birkenhead conspiracy, in 1663, in obedience to the orders of the king, to be a curb " upon all such traitorous attemptes for the future." [3] In a grant[4] to Henry Hartwell in 1689 the western line of his tract is described as " passing along by the angular points of ye trench which faceth two of ye eastern bastions of an old ruined turf fort." In a deed dated November 6, 1710, the remains of this fort referred to as " the old ffort," is described as near the bank of the river, not far from the house of Edward Jaquelin.

In 1667, Virginia was invaded by a Dutch fleet of four ships, and as the fort of Point Comfort was out of repair, they burned an English frigate-of-war and a number of merchant ships at the mouth of the river. After this we learn that the fort at James City had fourteen old guns, to which ten more, rescued from the burned frigate, were added.[5]

---

[1] Brown, *Genesis of the United States*, 651.
[2] Ibid., 660.
[3] Hartwell, Blair and Chilton, *Present State of Virginia.*
[4] *Va. Land Register.* VII., 701.
[5] *Cal. of State Paps. Col.*, 1661–1668, p. 474.

The third fort grew out of the wars with the Dutch. Despite the king's orders, the colonists were averse to relying upon the fort at Point Comfort, and a law was passed in 1667 by the assembly for five forts on the principal rivers — that for the protection of James River to be built at Jamestown Island, at the charge of the counties of James City, Surry, Charles City and Henrico. Each of the new forts was to be capable of holding eight great guns, and to have walls " ten foote high, and towards the river or shipping ten foote thick, at least." The forts were built; but, as the material was not substantial or lasting, an act passed in 1671 directed that they should be constructed of brick; and, thereupon, William Drummond, Theophilus Hone and Matthew Page contracted to do the work at Jamestown.

The contractors were in no hurry, and a fresh invasion of the Dutch in 1673 caused a complaint to be lodged with the governor and council that the fort was not yet erected, and " only some brick had been made." Thereupon, Drummond and Hone, Page being dead, were peremptorily ordered to complete the work.[1]

On April 6, 1674, Matthew Swann and his associates, engaged in a mutiny in Surry, were fined, and the fines given to the fort; but on their due submission these fines were remitted. Mr. Hubert Farrell, of James City County, and Mr. Richard Lawrence, of Jamestown, did not fare so well. The former, on April 7, was fined, to the use of the fort, 10,000 pounds of tobacco for scandalizing Mrs. Tabitha Bowler at the house of Mr. White; and the latter, on April 9, was fined, to the same use, 500 pounds of tobacco and cask, " for entertaining the Hon'ble the Governor's servants."

The fort was probably completed before June, 1676, when Bacon sent a squad of troops to hold it. It had the shape of a half moon, and lay at the head of Pitch and Tar Swamp, in a vale near the original landing place, where the river channel ran close to the shore. This fort was criticised by the minister, John Clayton, in the following language:

Jamestown Island is rather a peninsula, being joyned to the continent by a small neck of land, not past twenty or thirty yards over, and which at spring tides is overflowed and is then an absolute Island.

[1] *General Court Records* (1670–1676).

Now they have built a silly sort of a fort, that is a brick wall in the shape of a half moon, at the beginning of the swamp, because the channel of the river lies very nigh the shoar; but it is the same as if a fort were built at Chelsea to secure London from being taken by shipping. Besides, ships passing up the river are secured from the guns of the fort, till they come directly over against the fort, by reason the fort stands in a vale, and all the guns directed down the river, that should play on the ships, as they are coming up the river, will lodge their shot within ten, twenty or forty yards in the rising bank,[1] which is much above the level of the fort; so that if a ship gave but a good broadside, just when she comes to bear upon the fort, she might put the fort into that confusion, as to have free passage enough. There was indeed an old fort of earth in the town, being a sort of a tetragone, with something like bastions at the four corners, as I remember; but the channel lying further off to the middle of the river there, they let it be demolished, and built that new one spoken of, of brick, which seems little better than a blind wall, to shoot wild ducks or geese.

In 1697, Sir Edmund Andros took a notion to strengthen the fort, and in the council book for December 9, 1698, there is an order for paying Edward Ross, gunner of the fort at "James Citty," his salary of £10 sterling. This Ross dwelt not far off in a house near the head of Pitch and Tar Swamp, on a lot of 5 roods and 7 perches, now under water beyond the "Lone Cypress." As the result of Andros's activity, the fort in 1701 contained 20 guns, but the removal of the capital to Williamsburg, in 1699, was fatal; and in 1716, it is mentioned[2] as deserted and gone to ruin.

In 1837, Mr. Richard Randolph wrote[3] that some of the walls and mounds of the fort were then to be seen, and he added that the fort evidently extended some distance beyond "its present termination," having been gradually washed away by the encroaching tides. When Lossing visited the Island in 1848, some portion of the fort was still to be seen at low water, several yards from the shore.[4] Nothing now is visible; but the site of the fort may still be identified by masses of brick under water at the head of the Island.

Powder Magazine.

When the brick fort at the head of the Island was repaired in 1697, there was erected on the third ridge, several hundred yards distant, a powder magazine, concerning which Dr. James

[1] A grant to Edward Chilton April 16, 1683, describes the shore of James River near the fort as a hill. *Va. Land Register*, VII., 292.
[2] Maury, *Memoirs of a Huguenot Family*, 270, 271.
[3] *Southern Literary Messenger*, III., 303.
[4] Lossing, *Field Book of the American Revolution*, 446, note 2.

Blair, in a memorial[1] against Sir Edmund Andros, commented in the following language: "He (Andros) has thrown away a great deal of money in raising an old fort at Jamestown, & in building a powder house, and in making a platform for 16 great guns there, and another platform at Tindall's Point in York River. I never heard one man that pretended to understand anything of Fortifications that, upon sight of these works, did not ridicule & condemn them as good for nothing but to spend money. The Guns at Jamestown are so placed that they are no defence to the town, which being *much lower in the river*, might be taken by the Enemies' shipping, without receiving any the least assistance from those Guns. The powder house stands all alone without any Garrison to defend it, and is a ready prey for any foreign or domestic Enemy."

President Tyler, in his address[2] at Jamestown in 1857, mentioned "a tradition" that this building had been used for a jail to confine Opechancanough — which only shows that traditions are interesting, but not of much historic value. When Col. Goodrich Durfey owned the Island (1836–1846), the magazine was still in good condition, and was used as a residence for white carpenters. In 1837, it was referred to by Mr. Randolph as follows: "A few hundred yards to the right of the fort stands a small building, which tradition says was a powder magazine. Underneath this there is a cellar, arched and paved with brick, in which in all probability the ammunition was deposited." He further said that on the north side of the house were numerous impressions in the walls, "evidently made by balls fired against the building by Bacon's party or the Indians"!

The magazine stood on the third ridge, about 100 yards inland, in 1837, but the waves advanced, and in 1891 all that remained was the eastern foundation wall, which was then located and found to be about thirty-two feet long. In 1900, the powder magazine was visited by the editor in company with Mr. John Gilliam, whose father had resided in the magazine. At that visit only one corner of the wall was to be seen; and when the present sea wall was built, all the remaining bricks, being in the way, were removed.

[1] Perry, *Papers Relating to Hist. of the Church in Va.*, 14.
[2] Tyler, *Letters and Times of the Tylers*, I., 1–34.

VII

THE CHURCH.

The beginning is thus stated[1] by John Smith: "When I went first to Virginia, I well remember wee did hang an awning (which is an old saile) to three or foure·trees, to shadow us from the Sunne, our walles were railes of wood, our seates unhewed trees, till we cut plankes; our Pulpit a bar of wood nailed to two neighbouring trees; in foule weather we shifted into an old rotten tent; for we had few better, and this came by way of adventure for new. This was our Church till we built a homely thing like a barne, set upon cratchetts, covered with raftes, sedge and earth; so was also the walls: The best of our houses (were) of the like curiosity, but, the most part, farre much worse workmanship, that neither could well defend wind nor rain; yet wee had daily Common Prayer morning and evening, every Sunday two Sermons, and every three months the holy communion, till our minister died (the Rev. Mr. Hunt): but our prayers daily, with an homily on Sundaies, we continued two or three years after, till more Preachers came."

The First Church. The first church was within the fort, and was, as Smith states, fashioned like "a barn set upon cratchetts," and covered with "raftes, sedge and earth." It was consumed[2] by fire January 7, 1608, five days after the arrival of the "First Supply," when Mr. Hunt lost his library, and nearly all the houses in the fort were burned.

The Second Church. The second church was also in the fort, and was not much superior to the first. It was built[3] by Captain Newport and his sailors, and Smith and Scrivener made repairs[4] in the Spring of 1608, and again in the Spring of 1609.

In this church was doubtless performed, by Rev. Robert Hunt, the first marriage in Virginia. When the "Second

---

[1] Smith, *Works* (Arber's ed.), 958.
[2] Brown, *Genesis of the United States*, 175.
[3] Smith, *Works* (Arber's ed.), lxxxvi.
[4] Ibid., 105, 154.

Supply " arrived, in October, 1608, it brought the first gentlewoman, Mrs. Forrest; and her woman servant, Anne Burras,
about two months later, married John Laydon, a carpenter.[1]

THE OLD CHURCH TOWER AT JAMESTOWN.

In the same church was doubtless baptized a year later the
fir̃st child of this marriage — Virginia Laydon (or Layton),

[1] Smith, *Works* (Arber's ed.), 130.

who was the first fruit of the first English Protestant marriage in the New World.[1] The parents and child survived the " Starving Time," and the Virginia Council of 1632 recognized officially the birth by a gift to John Laydon of 500 acres of land, situated in Elizabeth City County. In 1625, there were living at Elizabeth City John and Anne Laydon and their children, Virginia, Alice, Katherine and Margaret Laydon — all born in Virginia.[2]

Some future genealogist may be able to trace the descendants of these children in Virginia, when perhaps the fortunate representative of this first Virginia marriage may receive special recognition!

Sir Thomas Gates, who came May 23, 1610, during the horrors of the " Starving Time," found the church in a " ruinous " condition, and Lord Delaware, who by his timely arrival prevented the desertion of the colony, had the church overhauled and reconstructed. The church was made of timber, and was sixty feet long by twenty-four feet wide, and it was fitted with a chancel of cedar and a communion table of black walnut.

All the pews and pulpit were of cedar, with fair, broad windows, also of cedar, to shut and open as the weather should occasion. The font was hewn hollow like a canoe, and there were two bells in the steeple at the west end. " The church was so cast as to be very light within, and the Lord Governour caused it to be kept passing sweet, trimmed up with divers flowers." There was a sexton in charge of the church, and every morning at the ringing of a bell by him, about ten o'clock, each man addressed himself to prayers, and so at four o'clock before supper. There was a sermon every Thursday, and two sermons every Sunday, the two preachers (Rev. Mr. Buck and the preacher brought by Lord Delaware) taking their weekly turns.

Every Sunday, when the Lord Governor went to church, he was accompanied by all the councillors, captains, other officers, and all the gentlemen, and with a guard of fifty halberdiers in his lordship's livery, fair red cloaks on each

1 Brown, *First Republic,* 113.
2 Hotten, *Emigrants to America,* 185. 245.

side and behind him. The lord governor sat in the choir on a green velvet chair, with a velvet cushion before him, on which he knelt, and the councillors, captains, and officers sat on each side of him, each in their place, and when the lord governor returned home, he was waited on in the same mannor to his house.[1]

The most noted event supposed to be connected with this church was the marriage of Pocahontas to John Rolfe, about April 5, 1614, celebrated by Rev. Richard Buck. Her father, Powhatan, approved the match, and her old uncle, Apaschisco, attended as the deputy for Powhatan, and gave her away; two of her brothers were also present, and a general peace ensued which lasted as long as Pocahontas lived.[2]

The distinction of this couple warrants some further statement. John Rolfe, the bridegroom, came of an ancient family of Heacham, County Norfolk, England, and was the son of John Rolfe and Dorothea Mason. He was baptized in the church at Heacham, May 6, 1585, and in 1609 went to Bermuda, in the Third Supply, with Sir Thomas Gates. While there, a wife married in England bore him a daughter, who was christened Bermuda by Rev. Richard Buck, but soon died. The parents reached Virginia in May, 1610, where the mother died. In 1612, John Rolfe was the first Englishman to introduce the cultivation of tobacco in Virginia. He succeeded Ralph Hamor as secretary of state in 1614, and went to England with his Indian bride in 1616, where he wrote an account of Virginia for King James and Sir Robert Rich. After the death of Pocahontas he married, thirdly, Jane, daughter of Captain William Peirce, by whom he had several children. He was a member of the council of Virginia in 1619, and met his death, it is believed, in the massacre of 1622 at the hands of the Indians, whose spiritual welfare he had hoped to elevate by his marriage with Pocahontas. His widow, Jane, married, secondly, Captain Roger Smith; and in 1625 Elizabeth Rolfe, her daughter by John Rolfe, is mentioned as living with them at Jamestown.

The bride was the daughter of Powhatan, head-war-chief of all the Indians in Tide-water Virginia, and was born in

---

[1] Purchas, *His Pilgrimes*, IX., 1752.
[2] Hamor, *True Discourse*, 11.

1595. Pocahontas, the name by which she is usually known, was a pet name for "Little Wanton," for her true name was Matoaka. During the infancy of the colony at Jamestown she was often the means of providing the settlers with provisions, and, by her influence with her father, saved the lives of two men prominent in colonial annals — Captain John Smith and Captain Henry Spellman. In April, 1613, while on a visit to the Potomac Indians, she was captured by Captain Samuel Argall, and brought to Jamestown, where she was converted to Christianity and baptized under the name of Rebecca. About April 5, 1614, she married John Rolfe, and is supposed to have lived at Varina with her husband till she accompanied him to England in 1616. There she attracted much atten-

POCAHONTAS.

tion, and her portrait was engraved by the celebrated artist, Simon de Passe, and Lord and Lady Delaware introduced her at court. While in England she met Captain John Smith; and when Smith saluted her as princess, Pocahontas insisted on calling him father, and having him call her his child. When Argall sailed to Virginia, about the first part of April, 1617, he took with him Pocahontas' husband, John Rolfe. Pocahontas was to have gone with him, but she sickened and died, and was buried at Gravesend, March 21, 1617. She left one son, named Thomas, who was educated in England by his uncle, Henry Rolfe, and afterwards resided in Virginia. He married a Miss Poythress, and had a son, Anthony, of England, and a daughter, Jane, who married Robert Bolling, of Virginia; and the most distinguished descendant in Virginia was John Randolph, of Roanoke.

Pocahontas was the *first of her race,* within the limits of the original English colonies, to be converted to Christianity and baptized. Her union with John Rolfe was the *first recorded lawful marriage* between Indian and white man in the limits of the present United States.

The Third Church. When Captain Argall arrived in 1617 as deputy-governor under Lord Delaware, the colonists were so absorbed in the culture of tobacco that Jamestown was much neglected. The church was " down," and a storehouse was used instead. Captain Argall enlarged the governor's house, and a new church of timbers was built " 50 foote in length by· twenty foote in breadth," wholly at the charge of the inhabitants of Jamestown.[1]

On the arrival of Sir George Yeardley in 1619, he called a general assembly of the plantations to meet at Jamestown on Friday, July 30, of that year.[2] This was an epoch in the history of not only Virginia, but the United States. This first American popular legislative body sat in the choir of the church: "Where Sir George Yeardley, the Governor, being sett downe *in his accustomed place,* those of the Counsel of Estate sate next to him on both handes, except onely the Secretary (John Pory), then appointed Speaker, who sate right before him; John Twine, clerke of the General assembly, being placed next the Speaker; and Thomas Peirse, the Sergeant, standing at the barre, to be ready for any service the Assembly should comand him.

" But forasmuche as men's affaires doe little prosper where God's service is neglected, all the Burgesses took their places in the Quire till a prayer was said by Mr. (Richard) Bucke, the minister, that it would please God to guard and sanctifie all our proceedings to his owne glory and the good of this Plantation.

" Prayer being ended, to the intente that as we had begun at God Almighty, so we might proceed with awful and due respecte towards the Lieutenant, our most gratious and dread Soveraigne (James I.), all the Burgesses were intreatted to retyre themselves into the body of the Churche, wch being done, before they were fully admitted, they were called in order and by name, and so every man (none staggering at it) took the oathe of Supremacy, and then entred the Assembly."

[1] *A Breife Declaration,* in Virginia State Senate Doc. (extra), 1874, p. 80.

[2] " The General Assembly convented at James Citty in Virginia July 30, 1619," in Va. State Senate Doc. (extra), 1874, 9–32.

The general assembly consisted of the governor, six councillors and twenty burgesses, two from each of ten plantations. It sat six days, and did a great deal of work in a very intelligent manner.

There is reason to believe that the church building, thus made famous, was not in the same place as its predecessors, but lower down the river shore. The recent excavations made at Jamestown disclosed, in addition to the foundations of two brick churches, the side walls of a narrower building having an inside width of about twenty feet, and consisting of a footing of cobble-stones one foot thick capped by a one-brick wall. The length of the superstructure could not be ascertained, as only the western ends of the foundations of the two walls remained, but the slenderness of the foundations indicate that they supported a building of timber. Now the width of a building matching the foundations would be the same as that given for the church built during Argall's term as deputy-governor, a good indication that they were the same. Moreover, in making the before-mentioned excavations, the workmen disclosed three distinct sets of floor tiles lying at slightly different levels across the east end of the building formerly belonging to a chancel five and one-half feet by twenty-two feet. The lowest layer of tiles probably belonged to the third church at Jamestown, the next lowest to the fourth church, and the highest layer to the fifth and last church. In case its end walls were enclosed in the same manner as its side walls, which seems quite likely, the length of the third church would have been about fifty feet — the extent of the Argall church of 1617–1619.[1]

The land grants afford additional evidence regarding the location of the third church. November 4, 1639, the Rev. Thomas Hampton received a grant[2] for land described as "on a ridge behinde the church," running east and west eighty-two poles, and north and south thirty-six paces. June 12, 1644, he received a second grant[3] of land on the same ridge, "containing from the easternmost bounds westerly one hundred and

[1] Yonge. *The Site of Old Jamestowne*, 47.
[2] *Virginia Land Register*, I., 689.
[3] Ibid., II., 105.

twelve paces (five foote to the pace), and running the same breadth northerly to the Back River."

A grant[1] of one acre to John White, August 28, 1644, was " bounded west upon the Church Yard, East upon the land appertaining to the State house, North toward the land of Mr. Thomas Hampton and South upon James River; the Length (of the lot) being 23 poles and the breadth seven poles almost." Then there is another grant[2]—one to Radulph Spraggon, August 18, 1644 — for an acre of land at the west end of the Island situated south of the " way Leading towards the Mayne " and " east towards the land of Mr. Hampton." Mr. Hampton's land must have been on the second ridge, and the natural position of a church to satisfy these references could have been no other than the site of the later churches.

The Fourth Church (First Brick Church). In January, 1639, Sir John Harvey reported[3] that the council and himself, as well as the ship-captains and ablest planters, " had largely contributed to the building of a brick church." Building did not proceed very fast in those days, and the inclosure of the foundations of the third church by the fourth suggests that, while the later church of brick was being constructed around the earlier one of timber, the latter was used for service. This brick church was still unfinished in November, 1647, at which time Southwark Parish in Surry (then part of James City County) was made into a separate parish, and it was provided[4] by the general assembly that the inhabitants of Southwark " pay and satisfie unto the minister of James Citty all customary tithes and dues, and all rates and taxes already assessed, and to be assessed, *for and toward the finishing and repairing of* the church at James Citty."

Last to be completed was probably the tower situated at the western end of the church, which is interestingly described by Mr. Yonge in the "Site of Old Jamestown." As it stands to-day it is a dignified old pile of sombre detail and lasting workmanship, approximately eighteen feet square in the plan, with walls three feet thick at the base, diminished by offsets in the inner

[1] *Va. Land Register,* II., 10.
[2] Ibid., II., 11.
[3] *Va. Magazine,* III., 30.
[4] Hening, *Statutes at Large,* I., 347.

faces at each story to about seventeen inches thick at the belfry. "The brick work is in the so called English bond quaintly embellished after the fashion of the period with glazed headers."[1] The present height of the church tower is about thirty-six feet, but from the ground to the peak of the wooden steeple that surmounted it, the original height was about forty-six feet. The tower itself was divided into three stories; and the first story openings were arched doorways through the front and back walls. The second story had probably a window in the west wall and a door in the east wall, the latter opening into a gallery across the western end of the nave of the church, as in the old brick church at Smithfield. But the masonry is absent from the wall space between each opening and the doors below, and thus each pair of openings is merged in one, about twenty and eighteen feet high respectively. The third story was lighted by six loopholes, two in front and two on each side wall.[2]

September 19, 1676, this church was fired by a torch in the hands of Nathaniel Bacon, Jr.

The Fifth Church (Second Brick Church). This church was, like its immediate predecessor, of brick; and, as there is no trace of a new line of walls or tower foundations, there can be little doubt that it was a mere restoration of the fourth. The speed with which it was made ready for use goes to confirm the supposition; for as early as June 25, 1679, the vestry of Bruton church made its doors the model for the doors of the brick church building at Middle Plantation. It was then ordered[3] that "ye west door and chancell door (of Bruton church) be according to the dimensions of James Citty church doors, only to be one foot higher and 1/2 foot wider than they are."

In 1690, there assembled in the restored church the first regular convention of the clergy of Virginia, presided over by James Blair, commissary of the bishop of London, of whose diocese Virginia formed a part. This convention made itself memorable by digesting the scheme of a college, which they recommended to the governor and general assembly. This

[1] Yonge, *Site of Old Jamestowne*, 53.
[2] Hall, *Jamestown — History and Present Condition*, 24.
[3] *Church Review.*

was the last great connection of the Jamestown church with State affairs, and nine years later the seat of government was transferred to Middle Plantation, or Williamsburg.

The church building was, however, in active use in James City Parish for many years after this, and was regularly furnished with preachers. After seventy-five years or more, the difficulties of access to the Island and the dwindling population of the neighborhood suggested a change. In the time of Governor Dinwiddie (1751–1758) a "new brick church," [1] called the upper church of James City Parish, was erected on the Main farm, about three miles from Jamestown, near the road from Williamsburg to Barret's Ferry.

From this time preaching was discontinued at Jamestown, and the church, which doubtless demanded repair even before the desertion, fell rapidly into ruins; and before the end of the century the tower alone remained above ground.

The American Revolution produced a general awakening of interest in historic matters, and in 1803 William Wirt published his "British Spy;" and one of his best sketches has a sentimental account of a visit to the tower of Jamestown.

In 1804, John D. Burk printed the first volume of his "History of Virginia," in which the sufferings of the early settlers at Jamestown were graphically portrayed. This was followed in 1805 by a pictorial representation of the tower, by Frederick Bossler, which was published at Richmond, in a magazine alike pretentious in form and title, edited by Louis H. Girardin, formerly professor of modern languages, history and geography in William and Mary College, and later a teacher in a female seminary in Richmond. This magazine, entitled *Graphicæ Amœnitates*, with a half dozen other descriptive words, was a quarto, and its first number, which was also its last, contained, besides the Jamestown tower, five other colored plates by the same engraver.

Since that time the old tower has welcomed numerous sightseers, and witnessed many celebrations held in its shadow.

October 27, 1856, Jamestown was visited by Bishop William Meade, Rev. Dr. Silas Totten, of William and Mary, Mr. Richard Randolph (called the antiquarian), and Colonel

[1] *Va. Magazine*, V., 245.

Goodrich Durfey, a former proprietor of the place; and they made the first serious effort to take measurements, and discovered the foundations of the brick church to be fifty-six by twenty-eight feet; probably an outside measurement.

In 1901, excavations were made by Mr. John Tyler, Jr., under the auspices of the Association for the Preservation of Virginia Antiquities, and the inside measurement of the foundation walls was found to be fifty and six-tenths feet and twenty-two and seven-tenths feet respectively. Other valuable knowledge regarding the brick walls, acquired through the excavations, has been given in another place, but it remains to say that several graves and tombstones, as well as mortuary tablets, were discovered in the old foundations. In the chancel, lying with its head to the north, was an iron tablet, probably formerly a cenotaph, once embossed with inlaid brasses, now missing.

Over the foundations of the church has been lately erected, by the ladies of the A. P. V. A., a wooden shed, to protect the sacred relics thus exposed. The Colonial Dames of America have undertakened to erect next year (1907) a beautiful church on this hallowed spot.

Furniture and Service at Jamestown Church.

Some of the sacred vessels of Jamestown are still preserved, viz.: A silver chalice and paten, with an inscription on each; a silver plate, being part of a communion service; a silver alms-basin or plate; and lastly, a silver vase, or font for baptism. The first two pieces — the silver chalice and paten — are now in possession of Bruton church, in Williamsburg, and each bears the inscription, "*Mixe not holy things with profane*," and about the rim at the bottom, "*Ex dono Francisci Morrison, Armigeri. Anno Domi* 1661." (The gift of Francis Moryson, 1661.) Francis Moryson was at the time acting governor of the colony. The maker of this service, whose mark was " T. W.," was also the maker of a celebrated cup owned by the Blacksmiths' Company, London, 1655, and subsequently purchased at a sale for £378.

As to the third piece, the silver alms-basin, it is now at the Union Theological Seminary, in Alexandria. It has a Latin

JAMESTOWN CHURCH SERVICE.
Presented in 1661 by Col. Francis Moryson.

inscription which shows that it was given in 1694 " for the use of the Jamestown Church," by Sir Edmund Andros, knight, governor of the colony.

Finally, the fourth article, which is now in the possession of the Monumental church in Richmond, the vase for baptism, was presented to the Jamestown church in 1733 by Martha Jaquelin, widow of Edward Jaquelin, and their son Edward.

It may not be out of place to add, in this connection, that the stone font of the " Church on the Main " is preserved, with the other relics, in the old powder magazine in Williamsburg. This font was probably in use at Jamestown before worship was abandoned there, and was removed to the church on the Main at the time of its erection, in 1751–1758.[1]

The Churchyard.

A patent[2] to John Howard, in 1694, shows that the enclosure about the churchyard was of " rails;" and we are told by Bishop Meade[3] that John Ambler and William Lee erected the present brick wall after the American Revolution from the brick of the church, then deserted and falling to ruins. The same patent discloses the fact that the railing furthest from the water ran " north 87 degrees westerly," or nearly east and west; and thus it is probable that the two other sides were nearly north and south. The area of the present enclosure is about one-sixth of an acre, which is known to have been much less than the original extent. Bishop Meade, who received his information from nearly first sources, states that the original churchyard covered an area of about half an acre, in which he is doubtless right. The patent of John Howard appears to give the length of the railing on the north side as 3 $\frac{23}{100}$ chains (two rods or 33 feet to a chain), which would make that side about 130 feet long. With this breadth a tract included between the road and the river could not have exceeded half an acre.

The yard must have been a burying place from the earliest days. The finding of a human skeleton crossed by a wall of

[1] The font in Bruton church, sometimes said to be the font in which Pocahontas was baptized, was brought from England for the use of Bruton church in 1691. *Va. Calendar of State Papers*, I., 35.
[2] *Va. Land Register*, VIII., 320.
[3] Meade, *Old Churches*, etc., I., 112.

the church near its southeast corner shows that there was a burial ground at its site before the brick churches were built, and possibly even before the building of the timber church, 1617–1619, which covered almost all the ground occupied by its successors. It is hardly presumable that the hundreds who died during the periods of the first and second wooden churches could have been buried in the limited enclosure of the stockade.[1] At one time there must have been a great many tombstones in the churchyard, for comparatively recently monuments of massive make, like those of John Ambler and William Lee, have disappeared.

Among the objects which attracted attention in 1807, during the jubilee of that year, was a young sycamore tree, whose trunk had become fastened between the tombstones of Dr. James Blair and his wife, Sarah Blair, and tended incessantly to propel them from their centers.[2] This sycamore, now grown into a large tree, shattered both tombstones and carried some six feet from the ground a fragment of the monument of Mrs. Blair, imbedded partially in its trunk. The writer has often seen the fragment thus suspended above the ground, but when, in 1895, the tombstones were temporarily removed for the purpose of cleaning the yard, this piece of marble was unfortunately released from the embrace of the tree, which has since proceeded to close the cavity. Here, then, is authentic evidence of one tree, at least, upwards of a hundred years old in Virginia.

At the east end of the Island, in a clump of trees, is the private burial ground of the Travis family, in which some tombstones may still be seen.

Tombstones in the Yard of the Church.

Fragment of Lady Frances Berkeley's tombstone. It will be remembered that generally she called herself Lady Berkeley, even after she was Mrs. Ludwell.

yeth the Bod
LADY FRANC
KLEY

[1] Yonge, *Site of Old Jamestown*, 48.
[2] *Proceedings of the Jubilee at Jamestown*, 1807.

9

Fragment of the tombstone of Philip Ludwell, second of the name; the inscription partially supplied from the *Richmond Dispatch* for May 15, 1857.

> Here lies interred the body of PHILIP LUDWELL who died the 11th of January 1726 in the 54th year of his age, sometime auditor of his Majesty's revenue and twenty-five years member of the Council.

Tombstone of Mary Knight.

> Here lyeth the body of
> Mary the wife of John
> Knight who departed
> this life Febr 11th 1732–3 in
> the 59th Year of her age
> Waiting for a joyful resurrection.

Tombstone of Ursula Beverley, now missing. Description from *Richmond Dispatch* for May 15, 1857.

> Here lyeth inter'd the body of URSULA BEVERLEY, late wife of Robert Beverley, and daughter of ye very Honorable Wm. Byrd, who departed this Life the 11th day of October 1698, being much lamented by all that knew her, aged 16 years 11 months and 2 dayes.

Tombstone of Elizabeth Edwards, now missing. Inscription partially supplied from *Richmond Dispatch* for May 15, 1857. Parts in brackets added by the author.

> Here lies interred the body of [Elizabeth Edwards,] wife of William Edwards of [James] Citty, Gent1 and daughter of [Benjamin Harrison] of ye [county of Surry, who was born the] sixth day of January —, [and died] the 14th. day of — — [aged] seventeen years and — — dayes.

---

1 William Edwards and Elizabeth his wife are parties to a deed, among the Ambler MSS., for lands at Jamestown, dated 1709.

Tombstone of John Ambler, Esq., now missing. Supplied from *Richmond Critic*, January 20, 1889.

JOHN AMBLER, ESQUIRE, BARRISTER AT LAW
Representative in the Assembly for
Jamestown and Collector of the District
of York River in this Province.
He was born the 31st of December 1735,
and died at Barbadoes 27th of May, 1766.
In the relative and social duties — as a son, and a brother
and a friend — few equalled him, and none excelled him.
He was early distinguished by his love of letters, which he
improved at Cambridge and the Temple, and well knew how
to adorn a manly sense with all the elegance of language.
To an extensive knowledge of men and things he joined
the noblest sentiments of liberty, and in his own example
held up to the world the most striking picture of the
amiableness of religion.

Tombstone of Hon. William Lee (now missing), of " Greenspring who died June 27, 1795 Aged fifty-eight Years."

Tombstone of James Blair, D. D.

Very little of Commissary Blair's tombstone remains, but by comparing the fragments with the version given in Meade, *Old Churches*, etc., Dr. L. B. Wharton made the restoration as follows :

H. S. E. [Hic sepultus est]
Vir Reverendus et Honorabilis
JACOBUS BLAIR, A. M.
In Scotia natus,
In Academia Edinburgensi nutritus
Primo Angliam deinde Virginiam
venit :
In qua parte terrarum
Annos LVIII Evangelii Preconis,
LIV Commissarii,
Gulielmi et Mariae Praesidis,
e Britanni[a] Principum
Conciliarii,
Concilii Presidis,
Coloniae Prefecti,
munera sustinuit ;
ornavit
eum oris venusti Decus ;
[Accepit orn]ate, hilari, sine Luxu, hospitali[modo ;]
munificent —
issimo egenis [dedit] largo
omnibus ; comi [animo]
superavit.
Collegio bene diversam

fundaverat,
moriens Bibliothecam suam
ad alendum Theologiae studiosum
[et] juventutem pauperiorem instituendam
Testamento legavit.
[ante] Cal. Maii in die [XIV decessit],
MDCCXLIII
aetat: LXXXVIII.
[exim]iam desideratissimi
senis Laudem
suis nepotibus commendabunt
[o]pera marmore perenniora

Translation.

Here lies buried
The Reverend and Honorable
James Blair A.M.
Born in Scotland,
Educated in the University of Edinburgh,
He came
First to England, then to Virginia;
In which part of the world
He filled the offices
For 58 years of Preacher of the Gospel,
For 54 of Commissary,
Of President of William and Mary,
Of a Councillor
to the British Governors,
Of President of the Council,
Of Governor of the Colony.
The comeliness of a handsome face
adorned him.
He entertained elegantly, in a cheerful, hospitable manner, without luxury;
most munificently
he bestowed charity upon all needy persons;
in affability
he excelled.
For the College a well varied Library
he had founded.
Dying his own Library
by will he bequeathed
for the purpose of informing students in Theology
and instructing the poorer youth.
He departed this life the XIV day before the Calends of May [April 18th].
MDCCXLIII.
At the age of LXXXVIII.
Works more lasting than marble
will commend to his nephews
The surpassing praise of a well beloved old man.

Tombstone of Mrs. Sarah Blair.

Mrs. Blair's epitaph was published in the *Petersburg Constellation* for September 17, 1835, which gave the account of a visit to Jamestown, copied from the *Norfolk Beacon*. Only a few fragments of the tombstone remains.

Memoriae Sacrum.
Here lyes in the hope of a Blessed Resurrection
ye Body of Mrs. SARAH BLAIR, wife of
Mr. James Blair, Commissary of Virginia,
Sometime Minister of this Parish.
She was daughter of
Col. Benjamin and Mrs Hannah Harrison of
Surry. Born Aug. ye 14th 1670. Married
June ye 2d 1687.
died May ye 5, 1713 exceeding beloved and
lamented.

[Then follows a long Latin inscription partly concealed by the tree which clasps it.]

Tombstone of Rev. John Clough.

Here Lyeth [the]
Body of [the Rev.]
JOHN CLOUGH [late Minister]
of this Place Who [departed]
This Life [February 15th, 168¾]
And Waiteth [in hopes of]
A joyful Res[urrection]

Tombstone of William Sherwood.

[H]ere Lyeth WILLIAM SHERWOO[D]
That was Born in the parish
of White Chappell near
London. A Great sinner
Waiting for a joyfull
Resurrection

Tombstone of Hannah Ludwell.

Under this Stone lies interred
The Body of
Mrs. HANNAH LUDWELL
Relict of
The Hon. Philip Ludwell, Esq.,
By whom She has left
One SON and Two DAUGHTERS.
After a most Exemplary Life
Spent in chearful Innocence
And The continual Exercise of
Piety Charity and Hospitality
She Patiently Submitted to
Death on the 4th Day of April 1731 in the 52d
Year of Her Age.

Tombstones in the Burial Ground of the Travis Family.
In the eastern portion of the Island.

Tombstone of Edward Travis.

Here lyeth the Body of EDWARD TRAVIS
who departed this life the 12th day of
November in the year of our Lord 1700.

Tombstone of John Champion.

[Skull and cross bones.]

Here lyeth in the hope of A glorious Resurrection
the body of JOHN CHAMPION who was borne
the 10th day of November in the yeare of our
Lord 1660 and departed this life the 16th
day of December in the year of our Lord
1700
And likewise JOHN CHAMPION the son of John
Champion who was borne the 11th day of Decr
in the yeare of our Lord 1695 and departed
this life the 11th day of September in the yeare
of our Lord 1700.

Tombstone of Susanna Travis.

SUSANNA TRAVIS wife of
Edward Champion Travis and
Daughter of John Hutchings
of the Borough of Norfolk Mercht
And Amy his Wife who Departed
this life October the 28th : 1761 in the
33rd Year of her Age much Lamented
by all her Acquaintance
And leaving Issue three Sons and
one Daughter.

Nigh this Place are also Interred
The Following Children of the said
Edward Travis and Susannah his wife
ELIZABETH who was born August
24th 1748 and Died September 22d 1749
AMY who was born October 9th 1752
and Died October 2nd 1755
JOHN who was born December 9th 1755
and Died November 25th 1759.

Ministers.

Rev. Robert Hunt, first minister of Jamestown church, was
probably the Rev. Robert Hunt, A. M., who was appointed to

the vicarage of Reculver, Kent, January 18, 1594, and resigned in 1602.[1] On the recommendation of Dr. Richard Bancroft, archbishop of Canterbury, the post at Jamestown was offered to Richard Hakluyt, the friend of Gilbert and Raleigh, at a salary of 500£, but Hakluyt sent Hunt in his place.[2] All parties unite in praise of him, as he was not infrequently the means of reconciling the warring factions at Jamestown, and was tireless in waiting on the sick and administering religious consolation to the dying. He is thought to have performed the marriage ceremony for John Laydon, a carpenter, and Anne Burras, the maid of Mrs. Forrest — which was the first English marriage in America. He certainly died before October, 1609.

Rev. Richard Buck came to Virginia with Sir Thomas Gates, and is said to have been a graduate of Oxford University. While in the Bermudas, he baptized John Rolfe's infant daughter, Bermuda, by his first wife, but the child soon died. He reached Jamestown with Gates, May 23, 1610, and, on landing, held services in the church, and made " a zealous and sorrowful prayer " over the spectacle of death and starvation in the fort. On the arrival of Lord Delaware, he divided with the minister whom the latter brought over the duties of the church at Jamestown, " the two preachers taking their turns weekly." He united in marriage John Rolfe and Pocahontas, about April 5, 1614, and July 30, 1619, acted as the chaplain of the first general assembly that ever met in Virginia, being mentioned as " a verie good preacher." His opening words were that it would please God " to guard and sanctifie all our proceedings to his owne glory and the good of this Plantation."[3]

He purchased on December 18, 1620, from William Fairfax, " yeoman and ancient planter, who had remained eight years in the country, and Margery his wife, an old planter also that came into the country married to said Fairfax," twelve acres of land, a mile from Jamestown, in the eastern part of the Island, on which were " a dwelling house and another little house."[4]

[1] Brown, *Genesis of the United States*, II., 929.
[2] Smith, *Works* (Arber's ed.), II., 958.
[3] Brown, *Genesis of the United States*, II., 835.
[4] *Va. Land Register*, I., 650.

He patented also 750 acres and had a glebe of 100 acres.[1] The glebe land is still known as such, and is situated at Archer's Hope, across from the east end of the Island.

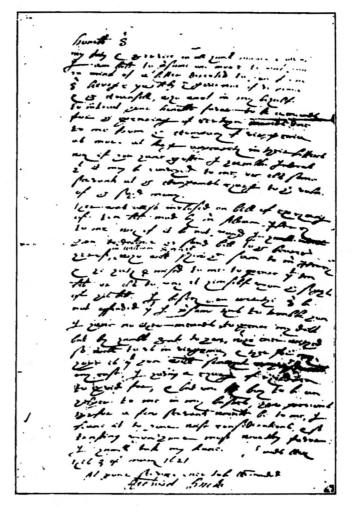

LETTER OF REV. RICHARD BUCK.

He had four children[2] (probably five) (1) Marah, who appears to have been the second wife of Richard Adkins;

1 Hotten, *Emigrants to America*, 270.
2 Neill, *Virginia Vetusta*, 164.

(2) Gershon, who in 1636 left[1] " 500 acres upon a creek between the Glebe land, and adjoining the land of the orphants and heires of Mr. Richard Buck," to his brother—(3) Peleg; (4) Benoni, "the first idiot born in Virginia;" (5) probably Elizabeth, who married Sergeant Thomas Crump,[2] and appears to have been in 1655 the solitary representative of Mr. Buck in Virginia. His widow married secondly, John Burrows, and thirdly, John Brumfield.

Poole and Glover. Sir Thomas Dale mentions that Mr. Poole preached on the afternoon of his arrival at Jamestown, which was Sunday, May 19, 1611, and in the second expedition of Sir Thomas Gates, which arrived in August, came Glover, " an approved preacher in Bedford and Huntingdonshire, a graduate of Cambridge, reverenced and respected," one who was in easy circumstances and advanced in years. He lived but a short time after his arrival.

Rev. Hawte Wyatt came to Virginia with his brother, Governor Francis Wyatt, in October, 1621, and was minister of Jamestown till about 1626, when they returned to England on the death of their father, George Wyatt, Esq. He was of the illustrious Wyatts of Boxley, Kent county, England, and was grandson of Sir Thomas Wyatt, the younger, beheaded for stirring up rebellion against " Bloody " Queen Mary. Another of his ancestors, Sir Henry Wyatt, received from Henry VII. the highest honors — was privy councillor, etc. His picture was taken with a cat at his side, because, when confined by Richard III. in a cold and narrow tower, where he had neither food nor fire, a cat brought him regularly every day a pigeon for his dinner, and kept the warmth in his body by permitting him to fondle and caress her.

Rev. Hawte Wyatt, after leaving Virginia, was inducted rector of Boxley, in Kent, October 3, 1632, and died there July 31, 1638. He was twice married, and two of his sons, Edward and George, settled at Middle Plantation, in Virginia. The Wyatt monumental tablet in the church at Boxley states that " Hawte Wyatt left issue living in Virginia."[3]

[1] *Va. Land Register*, I., 532.
[2] Hening, *Statutes at Large*, I., 405.
[3] *William and Mary Coll. Quart.*, III., 35–38.

Rev. Francis Bolton[1] also came with Governor Wyatt in 1621, and was minister first at Elizabeth City, and in 1623 at the plantation on the Eastern Shore of the Chesapeake Bay. After Wyatt's departure to England he was minister at Jamestown, where he was witness in February, 1630, to the will of Thomas Warnett, a leading merchant.

Rev. Thomas Hampton[2] was the next minister, so far as the writer knows, being probably the Thomas Hampton entered among the Oxford matriculates, as son of William of Reigate Surry, *sacerd.* He matriculated at New College 11th March, 1625, aged sixteen, and received the degree of B. A. from Corpus Christi College, January 30, 1627; was probably brother of Rev. William Hampton, who, at the age of seventy-seven, died in 1677, while rector of Bletchingly, in Surry.[3] Rev. Thomas Hampton came to Virginia before 1637, in which year he secured several grants for land in the Upper County of New Norfolk (afterwards Nansemond county). In 1640, he received from the general court an order for 100 acres in addition to the 100 acres of glebe belonging to the rectory of James City Parish. November 4, 1639, he received a grant, pursuant to an act for building James City, dated February 20, 1637, for land on a ridge between two swamps behind the church, running in length east and west eighty-two poles, and in breadth northerly and southerly thirty-six paces (five feet to every pace). Another patent, June 12, 1644, gave him eight acres on a ridge behind the church, extending from the easternmost bounds of his former lot, westerly 112 paces, and running the same breadth northerly to Back River.

About 1646, Mr. Hampton moved to York County, where he was rector of Hampton Parish. An order of York County does not present him in a very enviable light.

Whereas it appears to the court that " Mr. Thomas Hampton clerk obteyned the guardianship of the orphans of John Powell late of yis county dec and hath possesst himselfe with yere estates & hath also removed one of ye sd orphants with most of ye sd estate out of yis county and left behind ye other orphan by name Wm Powell without necessary pvon, to say even starke naked whereupon ye court upon ye petn of ye sd Wm Powell doth order yat Thomas Harwood shall have into his keeping Wm Powell orphan," &c. York Court, Nov. 26, 1646.

[1] Neill, *Virginia Vetusta*, 174.
[2] Neill, *Virginia Carolorum*, 70.
[3] Foster, *Oxford Matriculates.*

This order, however, must be taken with some grains of allowance, as the people of that day, even the justices, were good haters, and never spared any person they disliked. There was no such thing as moderation in expression.

Mr. Hampton's tombstone was formerly to be seen at King's Creek, York County, according to which he died January 5. 1647 (really 1648, as the year then did not begin till March 25).

Rev. Thomas Harrison is said by Calamy in his *Nonconformists' Memorial* to have come to Virginia with Sir William Berkeley in 1642 and officiated as chaplain at Jamestown. Probably the only foundation for all this is that he sometimes preached at Jamestown on special occasions. The records of Lower Norfolk County show[1] that, instead of coming with Berkeley, he qualified as minister of Elizabeth River Parish May 25, 1640, being then in his 25th year, at a salary of 100 pds. sterling. When, on the invitation of the Puritans of Nansemond County, the ministers John Knowles, William Thompson and Thomas James, came from New England to Virginia, Harrison used his influence to have them silenced and banished from the colony. Soon after occurred the Indian massacre of April 17, 1644, and the Puritans heralded this as a judgment of God upon the country for its rejection of the godly ministers. Harrison became a changed man, and turned Puritan himself.

He declined to read the book of common prayer, or administer the sacrament of baptism according to the prescribed canons; and the court of Lower Norfolk County ordered him to be summoned before the governor. But Berkeley did not proceed to extremities at once, and gave Harrison and his followers ample time for repentance. Three years passed, and at length Harrison and his elder William Durand were directed peremptorily to leave the colony. William Durand emigrated to Maryland with more than 1,000 settlers from Virginia, while Harrison visited Boston where he married Dorothy Symonds, a cousin of Governor Winthrop. He then sailed to England, and in 1649 obtained an order from the council of State directed to Governor Berkeley to permit his return to Virginia. Harrison, however, did not return to America, but became chief chaplain to Henry Cromwell, lord lieutenant of Ire-

[1] *Lower Norfolk County Antiquary.* No. i, part 3.

land, and in Christ Church Cathedral he preached a sermon on the death of his father, Oliver Cromwell.

Rev. Philip Mallory appears in the Virginia records as early as 1656, but was probably in Virginia much earlier. He was a son of Dr. Thomas Mallory, dean of Chester, matriculated at Corpus Christi College, May 28, 1634, aged seventeen; was B. A. from St. Mary's Hall, 1637; M. A., 1640; and vicar of Norton, Durham, in 1641. His brother, Rev. Thomas Mallory, was ejected by the Parliamentary party from his living during the civil war, but was reinstated canon of Chester in 1662 by King Charles II. Rev. Philip Mallory married Catharine, daughter of Robert Batte, vice-master of Oxford University, and removed with his wife's relatives, the Battes, and settled in Virginia.

He was a man of high character and exemplary piety, and stood at the head of the church in Virginia. In 1656, he was authorized by the general assembly, in connection with Mr. Roger Green, to examine into the competency of all ministers in the colony. He officiated at the two assemblies at Jamestown March, 1658 and 1659, and had charge of the religious services when Charles II. was, with great rejoicing, proclaimed at York, Virginia, October 20, 1660. In March, 1661, the legislature testified[1] that "Mr. Philip Mallory, had been eminently faithful in the ministry, and very diligent in endeavoring the advancement of those means that might conduce to the advancement of religion in this country," and appointed him " to undertake the soliciting of our church affairs in England." He reached London, but died soon after and his will was proved July 27, 1661.[2] In 1660, his nephew, Roger Mallory, obtained from York court a certificate for a grant of land " for the use of Mr. Philip Mallory." Roger Mallory settled in King and Queen County, and had a son William, who was ancestor of the distinguished family of his name, resident in Elizabeth City County, Virginia.

The Battes, who have been numerously represented in Virginia, were of Okewell, County York, England. (See *Genealogist* for October, 1898, pages 86-88.) John Batte, brother

---

[1] Hening, *Statutes at Large*, II., 34.
[2] *Va. Magazine*, XII., 4.

of Mrs. Mallory, married her husband's sister, Martha Mallory, and was a royalist. He was fined £364, and is said to have been a captain at the battle of Adwalton. The pedigree says that two of his sons, Thomas and Henry, came to Virginia. (See *Genealogist.*) In April, 1668, "Thomas Batte and Henry Batte, sonnes of Mr. John Batte decd." obtained a patent for 5,878 acres, 2 roods and 8 rods on Appomattox River for 118 "head-rights," or emigrants; and among the names represented were John Batte, Sr., John Batte, Jr., William Batte, Thomas Batte, Henry Batte, Philip Mallory, Nathaniel Mallory, Sr., Nathaniel Mallory, Jr., William Mallory, Thomas Mallory, Elizabeth Mallory, and Roger Mallory. So it seems from this that John Batte, the cavalier, and all his sons, John, William, Thomas and Henry, came to Virginia, as well as a whole host of Mallorys. Mrs. Mallory had also two uncles in Virginia, William and Henry Batte.

Rev. Roger Green was another minister in the colony who sometimes officiated at Jamestown. He was at Jamestown in 1656, and in 1661 published in England a pamphlet entitled *Virginia's Cure or an Advisive concerning Virginia, Discovering the true ground of that Church's unhappiness.* In 1653, he was a minister of Nansemond County, and on his petition the general assembly granted 10,000 acres of land to the first 100 persons, who should settle on the Roanoke and Chowan Rivers. He was still alive in 1671, when the general assembly ordered the vestry of the parish of James City to pay to Mr. Green 1,200 pounds of tobacco for the accommodation of their minister, Mr. Samuel Jones.[1]

Rev. Morgan Godwin entered Oxford in 1661, and received, March 16, 1665, the degree of A. B., and soon after came to Virginia, where he took charge of Marston Parish in York County. His father, Rev. Morgan Godwin, was archdeacon of Shropshire, his grandfather, bishop of Hereford, and his great-grandfather, Thomas Godwin, bishop of Bath and Wells. He resided for a short time at Jamestown, and, after visiting the West Indies, returned to England, where, in 1680, he published a dissertation against slavery, called *The Negroes' and Indians' Advocate.* Five years later he preached a sermon at

[1] Neill, *Virginia Carolorum,* 233, 234, 290, 420.

Westminster Abbey against the evils of the slave-trade, thus preceding Wilberforce and Clarkson more than a century.[1]

Rev. Justinian Aylmer was born in 1635, and was probably the Justinian Aylmer who matriculated at Trinity College, Oxford, July 23, 1656, and became B. A. October 24, 1657, and erroneously stated, as I believe, by Foster to have been rector of Ipswich in 1699. The pedigrees of Aylmer and Hone, and the connection of those families in Virginia, render it reasonably certain that he was a grandson of Theophilus Aylmer, archdeacon of the diocese of London. In 1661, he was minister of Hampton Parish, York County, and there are some depositions about a quarrel which he had with the Quakers of York County. He appears to have been a little later minister of Jamestown, but died not long after, and his widow, Frances Armistead, married Lt.-Col. Anthony Elliott of Elizabeth City County, who died in 1666, and, thereupon, she married Captain Christopher Wormeley.[2] The following order[3] throws some light upon the church at Jamestown in November, 1671 :

Whereas at last court Capt. Christopher Wormeley as marrying the relict of Mr. Aylmer decd late minister of James Citty obteyned Judgm^t ag^t Major Hone and Mr May as members of the vestry for sixteene pounds thirteen shillings foure pence due to the said Aylmer as officiating in his said ffunction. And whereas the said Hone and May sued Mr. Walter Chiles and Capt. ffra Kirkeman the prsent churchwardens, It is now ordered that the said Maj^r Hone & Mr. May be repaid the said sum of sixteene pounds thirteen shillings foure pence by the said parish according to agreem^t made wth the said Mr Aylmer, according to an order of the said vestry, with costs als exec.

Rev. Samuel Jones was minister after Aylmer's death, but hardly anything else is known of him.[4]

Rev. James Wadding filled the place of minister at Jamestown in 1672. He married Susannah, the widow of Mr. Walter Chiles, son of Walter Chiles, Esq., of the council.[5] Mr. Wadding moved to Gloucester County, where he was minister of Petsworth Parish at the time of Bacon's Rebellion. He was a loyalist and refused to take the oath of allegiance exacted by

[1] Neill, *Virginia Carolorum*, 345.
[2] *Va. Magazine*, V., 429; VII., 284; *William and Mary Quart. Mag.*, VI., 31, 32; XI., 30-33.
[3] *General Court Records*, 1665-1676.
[4] Neill, *Virginia Carolorum*, 420.
[5] *Ambler MSS.*, in Library of Congress.

Bacon, and encouraged others to refuse. Thereupon, Bacon "committed him to the Gard, telling off him that it was his place to preach in the church, not in the camp. In the first, he might say what he pleased, but in the last, he (Wadding) was to say no more than what should please him (Bacon) : unless he could fight to better purpose than he could preach." Not long after this, Bacon was taken very sick, and Wadding was the minister who attended him in his last illness at Major Pate's house on Poropotank Creek in Gloucester County.[1]

Rev. John Clough was minister of Jamestown during Bacon's Rebellion. He was an active supporter of Sir William Berkeley; being captured by Bacon, was condemned to death. but pardoned. He was minister of Southwark Parish in Surry in 1680, but appears to have returned to Jamestown Parish. His tombstone is still in the churchyard at Jamestown, according to which he died February 15, 1684.[2]

In 1680, *Rowland Jones*[3] appears as minister for Jamestown, as well as for Bruton and Martin's Hundred parishes. He was the son of Rowland Jones, vicar of Wendover, in Buckinghamshire; was born in 1640 at Swinbrook, in County Oxford, England; was an alumnus of Merton College, Oxford University; was minister of the church of Middle Plantation (Williamsburg), and died there April 23, 1688, "after fourteen years of service." His tombstone which is in the churchyard at Williamsburg, describes him as *" pastor primus et dilectissimus."* Among his descendants in Virginia was Martha Dandridge, wife of General George Washington.

Rev. John Clayton was minister at Jamestown from 1684 to 1686. He was probably a graduate of Oxford University, as there are several John Claytons among the Oxford matriculates who might be taken for this man. In May, 1688, he was rector of Crofton at Wakefield, in Yorkshire. He was a member of the Royal Society, and was a great admirer of Hon. Robert Boyle, the philosopher and naturalist, to whom he wrote[4] from Jamestown, June 23, 1684, describing a remarkable instance of animal electricity and the fly called the "fire-fly." He wrote

[1] An. Cotton, *Bacon's Proceedings.* (Force, *Tracts,* I., No. xi, 28.)
[2] His name has been often rendered from the tombstone *Gough,* but Clough is right.
[3] *William and Mary Coll. Quart. Mag.,* V., 192–197.
[4] Boyle, *Works,* V., 646.

after his return to England several letters about Virginia, which were published in the *Transactions* of the Royal Society. He was very fond of scientific studies, and his reflections on Virginia might have been more valuable but for his loss on the way thither of his scientific apparatus — "books, chymicall instruments, glasses, and microscopes." As it is, we are under great obligations to him for his description of Jamestown Island, and of the soil, animals, and inhabitants of Virginia. In 1680, Thomas Clayton was a resident of Jamestown, and, in 1705, arrived in Virginia John Clayton, son of Sir John Clayton. He became attorney-general, judge of the Admiralty,

and died, aged seventy-two, in 1737. He was father of John Clayton, a celebrated botanist, who wrote "*Flora Virginica,*" and had a botanical garden at Windsor, his home, in Gloucester County, Va. Whether Thomas Clayton or John Clayton, the attorney general, was related to Rev. John Clayton is not known.

Rev. James Blair, D. D.,[1] became minister of Jamestown in 1694. He was born in 1655, received in 1673 the

REV. JAMES BLAIR, D.D.

degree of master of arts of the University of Edinburgh, and came to Virginia in 1685. He was, at first, minister of the churches in Henrico, and lived at Varina, on James River, where, inspired by his residence near the site of the old college formerly proposed by the London Company, he early conceived the notion of reviving that great undertaking. In 1689, he was appointed commissary of the bishop of London, and by virtue of his office presided in 1690 over the convention of the clergy at Jamestown, where he obtained the endorsement of his project of a college, and immediately brought the matter before the governor and the general assembly. Both endorsed him,

1 Sprague, *American Pulpit,* V., 7.

and in 1692 he was sent by the general assembly to England as their agent to solicit a charter and money for the enterprise. Having proved successful, he determined, in 1694, to accept a call to Jamestown, so as to be nearer to the institution of which he had been appointed president. He was also made a member of the council, and thus his influence was felt in church, college and state. On Sunday, April 25, 1703, Rev. George Keith entered the following in his journal: "I preached at Jamestown on John I. 3, at the request of Reverend Mr. Blair, minister there, and commissary, who very kindly and hospitably entertained us at his house."

Dr. Blair remained minister of Jamestown till 1710, when he accepted the office of rector of Bruton Church and removed to Williamsburg that he might be still closer to the college which had been destroyed by a fire and was then being rebuilt. Under him the first full professorships of mathematics and natural science in the United States were established at the college. Dr. Blair acted as chief executive in the absence of Sir William Gooch in the Carthagena expedition, from June, 1740, to July, 1741. He was ever found battling for morality and the right, though he was often dictatorial and not always charitable in his opinion of others. He married Sarah Harrison, daughter of Col. Benjamin Harrison, and while he left no children, his brother, Dr. Archibald Blair, is numerously represented in Virginia and in the South.

Rev. John Warden, a Scotch clergyman, served six months as minister at Jamestown, after his arrival in Virginia in 1712. He afterwards served at Weyanoke and Martin Brandon parishes, and in 1717 became minister at Lawne's Creek, Isle of Wight County, but in 1725 being accused by the vestry to the council for "notorious immoralities," he promised to depart the colony.[1]

Rev. Peter Fontaine was a son of Rev. James Fontaine, a French Huguenot, descendant of the noble family of the Fontaines in Maine, France. Like Warden he preached a short time at Jamestown after his arrival in Virginia in 1716. At the end of six months he left for Westover Parish in Charles City County, where he was the friend of the eminent William Byrd

[1] Council Journal.

of Westover. In 1728–29, he was the chaplain to the Virginia commission appointed to lay out the boundary line between Virginia and North Carolina, the history of which was so entertainingly written by Colonel Byrd. He died in July, 1757, and he has many descendants in the male and female lines.[1]

Rev. Hugh Jones came to Virginia from England in 1716, upon the recommendation of the bishop of London, and was appointed to the chair of mathematics in the college of Wiliam and Mary. While resident in Williamsburg he preached at Jamestown, and served also as chaplain of the general assembly and lecturer in Bruton Church. He left the province for England in 1722, and in 1724 brought out in London his valuable book on "The Present State of Virginia," written in a sprightly and suggestive style. Returning to America in the latter year he resumed his parochial work in St. Stephen's Parish, King and Queen County, Virginia, but in 1726 he went to Maryland where he served in several parishes, viz.: William and Mary Parish, in Charles County, North Sassafras Parish and St. Stephen's Parish in Cecil County. He remained minister in Maryland for many years, and persuaded the people to build brick churches instead of cheap wooden structures. At length he died September 8, 1760, and was succeeded by his nephew, Rev. William Barroll. In his will he expresses the desire to be buried with his feet to the westward, contrary to the usual mode of burial. "He wished," he said, "to be facing his people as they arose from their graves. He was not ashamed of them." [2]

Rev. William Le Neve[3] arrived in Virginia from England on St. Matthew's Day, 1722. He took charge of the church at Jamestown October 5, 1722, where he preached two Sundays in three. Every third Sunday he preached at Mulberry Island church, and in the afternoon he officiated as lecturer at Williamsburg. He received from Jamestown sixty pounds sterling; from Mulberry Island thirty pounds sterling, and from Williamsburg twenty pounds sterling — in all about 110 pounds sterling — the equivalent of about $2,500 at the present time.

[1] Maury, *A Huguenot Family in America*, 332–355.
[2] Sprague, *American Pulpit*, V., 9–13; *William and Mary Coll. Quart.*, X., 202.
[3] Perry, *Papers relating to the Church in Virginia*, 264–266.

His congregation at James City Church consisted of about 130 persons, that at Mulberry Island of about 200, and at the lecture at Williamsburg he generally had above 100 persons in attendance. He let the glebe by the year, and James City Parish gave him about seven pounds sterling per annum for furnishing his own house and keeping it in repair. He stated that his parish of James City was about twenty miles long and twelve miles broad, and there were in it seventy-eight families. The church was decently and orderly provided with church service. How long Mr. Le Neve served is not known, but he

COLLEGE OF WILLIAM AND MARY.
As it appeared during the presidency of Dr. James Blair.

was living at the James City Glebe in 1737, when he published an advertisement in the *Gazette* for a manager.

Rev. William Preston represented James City Parish in the convention of the clergy in 1755.[1] He was son of Rev. William Preston, of Brougham, Westmoreland County, England, and was professor of moral philosophy in William and Mary College. He was a master of arts of Queen's College, Oxford University, and a great scholar. In 1757, he resigned his chair at the college because of the complaint of the college authorities that " contrary to all rule of seats of learning he had married[1] and kept his wife, children and servants in College, which occasioned much confusion and disturbance." Neither was he

---

[1] Perry, *Papers relating to the Church in Virginia*, 412, etc.; *William and Mary Coll. Quart.*, III., 139, 140.

as abstemious from liquors as his calling required. After his return to England he was rector of Ormside. He died in 1778, aged fifty-nine. His son, William Stephenson Preston, became rector of Warcop, in County Westmoreland, England, and this position was held by his great-grandson, Rev. Charles Mayes Preston, in 1894. Rev. William Preston was probably the last minister who officiated at Jamestown, for the church on the Main, about three miles from Jamestown, was built about this time, and became the regular church of James City Parish, in James City County.

According to Bishop Meade, *Rev. Mr. Berkeley* was minister of James City Parish in 1758, but I know nothing of him.

Rev. John Hyde Saunders[1] was the son of John Hyde Saunders, of Cumberland County, and was in 1763 student of William and Mary College. In 1772, he was minister of James City Parish, and in 1773 was elected minister of St. James Southam, in Cumberland County, where he continued for many years. He was a great patriot during the Revolution, and in 1775 was a member of the county committee.

Rev. William Bland[2] was rector of James City Parish in 1774. He was a member of a family long distinguished in Virginia, ever since the arrival of the emigrant, Theodorick Bland, of Westover, in Charles City County. Mr. Bland married Elizabeth, daughter of President William Yates, of William and Mary College, and she was buried at the upper church, in James City Parish, which was afterwards generally known as the "church on the Main," or "Main church." Mr. Bland was a warm supporter of the Revolution, which brought him into notice. He afterwards served as minister in Norfolk, about 1791. From him is descended General Roger A. Pryor, formerly of Virginia, now of New York.

Rev. James Madison,[3] D. D., preached at the "Main church," during most of his ministry. He was a cousin of James Madison, the eminent president of the United States, and, like his distinguished relative, was a man of consummate ability. As first bishop of the Episcopal Church of Virginia,

---

[1] *William and Mary Coll. Quart.*, IV., 43.
[2] Meade, *Old Churches*, etc., 113, *note*.
[3] Sprague, *American Pulpit*, V., 318–324.

president of the college of William and Mary, and professor in it of natural philosophy and mathematics, and afterwards of political economy and international law, he was necessarily a man of influence. He was an ardent patriot of the American Revolution, and the story is told of him that in his sermons and prayers he would never speak of heaven as a kingdom, but as that "great republic, where there was no distinction of class, and where all men were free and equal." He was born August 27, 1749, was educated at the college, and in Europe, died March 6, 1812, and lies buried in the college chapel.

Some years before Mr. Madison's death, the congregation at the Main had almost dwindled away, and for this there were two reasons. Population had withdrawn from the rivers, and the old plantations situated thereon had fallen into the hands of a few rich proprietors. Then most of the people had abandoned the Episcopal faith, and become

RT. REV. JAMES MADISON, D. D.

members of the Baptist and Methodist denominations. The little remnant of Episcopalians soon ceased to meet at all. The church on the Island had long before fallen into ruins and gradually the Main church fell into ruins also. Now scarcely is there enough brick left to tell the site of the building, which often echoed the voice of one of the best and purest of men — James Madison, the honored president of William and Mary College.

VIII.

BLOCK HOUSES.

In early American history the block house was universally used as a means of defense against the Indians. It was a structure made of heavy logs, having its sides loop-holed for musketry.

The first block house at Jamestown was erected in the Spring of 1609. It was built at the beginning of the neck connecting the Island with the mainland, and was kept by a garrison, who prevented all ingress or egress, without the president's order.[1]

When Sir Thomas Gates arrived in May, 1610, during the horrors of the " Starving Time," he found the Indians " as fast killing without the fort as the famine and pestilence within. Only the block house (somewhat regarded) was the safetie of the remainder that lived; which yet could not have preserved them now many dayes longer from the watching, subtile and offended Indians who (it is most certaine) knew all this their weakness, and forbare too timely to assault the forte, or hazard themselves in a fruitless warr on such whome they were assured in short time would of themselves perish, and being provoked, their desperate condition myght draw forth to a valiaunt defense; yet they were so ready and prepared, that such whome they found of our men stragled single beyond the bounds, at any time, of the block house, they would fiercely chardge (for all their pieces) as they did 2 of our people not many dayes Gates was come in, and 2 likewise they killed after his arrival 4 or 5 dayes."

When Sir Thomas Dale arrived, on the 19th of May, 1611, besides other works undertaken by him was a second block house, " on the north side of our Back River, to prevent the Indians from killing our cattle." The description here should be taken to mean " on the Back River, on the north side of the Island."

[1] Smith, *Works* (Arber's ed.), I., 154.

[150]

A block house on the northern side of the Back River would have been too exposed and remote. Nobody was living in that quarter then. It was completed by Gates, who arrived in August, 1611.

So Ralph Hamor, writing in 1615, spoke of two block houses within the island, "to observe and watch least the Indians, at any time, should swim over the Back River and come into the Island."

A patent to Thomas Sully, of the *Neck of Land,* yeoman, August 14, 1624, described his lot of six acres as "butting

A BLOCK HOUSE.

Eastward upon a peece of ground called the blocke howse feild cleared in the time of the governm^t of Sir Thomas Gates, Westward extending towards the path leading to the new blocke howse *lately built,* northward and upon a great marsh of the Back River, and Southward unto the markes there appointed, close to the highway by the swampe."

This third block house was erected probably in consequence of the Indian massacre of 1622, and as it was west of the old and separated from it by a lot of six acres, it stood doubtless further out on the neck. A grant[1] to Richard Sanders in 1643.

[1] *Va. Land Register,* II., 12.

shows that this later structure was standing twenty years afterwards; for the land is stated as "Neare the block house, bounded west upon the River, East upon the marsh, North upon the block house land, and South upon the Land of Edward Challes." This block house was decayed in 1656, when a grant[1] for fifteen acres, sixty-nine poles was made to John Bauldwin, of which five acres and sixty-nine poles were said to be located "at the *old* block house, beginning at the head of a swamp issuing into Back River." Bauldwin's tract was sold to William Sherwood, and a more accurate survey showed it to contain twenty-eight and one-half acres, as stated in another place.

In 1694, a patent[2] to Sherwood for 308 acres, embracing Bauldwin's tract, described the land as "situate in James Citty and James Citty Island, beginning on James River at the head of a branch of Pitch and Tar swamp next above the State House," and proceeding by devious courses to Back River, and up the same to "Sandy Bay to a Persimmon tree under *Block house hill,* thence under the said Hill west six chaines to James River, and down it to the head of the first mentioned branch."

Block house hill, as proved by Sherwood's plat of 1680, preserved among the Ambler MSS., stood on the first ridge about 900 feet from the north end of the present sea wall; and therefore a wide interval of water intervened between it and the present shore of the Island.

[1] *Va. Land Register,* IV., 88.
[2] Ibid., VIII., 384.

IX.

The Second Supply reached Jamestown in October, 1608, and brought eight Dutchmen and Poles to teach the colonists how to make glass, tar, pitch and soap ashes.[1] Soon after a house for the manufacture of glass was erected,[2] under the supervision of President John Smith, in the woods on the other side of the isthmus or connecting neck, " neare a mile from Jamestown;" and when Newport returned to England in December, 1608, he carried with him as a portion of his cargo the specimens of glass which had been thus produced.[3] In the spring of 1609 the manufacture of glass was continued by the colonists with success.[4]

Near the glass house, in February, 1609, Captain Smith had a hand-to-hand fight with Wowinchopunck, chief of the Paspaheghs. He had gone to the glass house to apprehend one of the Dutchmen, who, sent to Powhatan to build a house, had employed much of his time in training the Indians to fire-arms. Returning from the glass house alone, Smith encountered the Indian chief by the way, who, seeing that Smith had only his sword, tried to shoot him, but Smith prevented the attempt by grappling with him at once. The Indian dragged Smith into the water to drown him, but the president got a firm hold on his throat and drew his sword to cut off the Indian's head; but Wowinchopunck begged so piteously that Smith relented, and took him prisoner to Jamestown, whence he shortly after escaped. After that Wowinchopunck continued his devilish practices, and, with his warriors, would lie in wait near the glass house and kill such of the whites as ventured too far. He was one of the " mightiest and strongest salvages " that Powhatan had. At length, February 9, 1610, during the " Starving Time," President George Percy sent forth Ensigns Powell and Waller to surprise Wowinchopunck

[1] Smith, *Works* (Arber's ed.), 122, 434.
[2] Ibid., 467.
[3] Ibid., 441.
[4] Ibid., 150, 471.

[153]

and bring him, if possible, alive to town;" but finding that they could not do this, Ensign Powell rushed upon him, and " thrust him through with an arming sword." The savages, " with a mighty quickness and speed of foot," recovered the werowance's body and carried it off with a horrible yelling and howling. But Lieutenant Puttock, of the block house, followed hard upon them, and closing with one of the " cronockoes," or chief men, threw him down, and with his dagger sent him to accompany his master out of the world.[1]

In 1612, Strachey mentions that " the country wants not salsodiack to make glasse of, and of which we have made some stoore in a goodly howse sett up for the same purpose, with all offices and furnases thereto belonging, a litle without the Island where Jamestown stands." [2]

After this time, nothing more is heard of the glass house till 1621, when some private adventurers, with consent of the London Company, contracted with Captain William Norton to go over to Virginia and set up a glass furnace. Norton took four Italians and two servants with him, restored the glass works, and made all manner of glass, especially beads, for trade with the Indians.[3]

In 1622, the Indian massacre caused an interruption of the work, as everybody had to make tobacco to provide necessities of life.

In 1623, Norton died, and George Sandys (treasurer of the colony and brother of Sir Edwin Sandys), who had been appointed to oversee the glass works, in case of Norton's death, took charge, but he met with great difficulty in the work. On one occasion he sent his shallop as far as the Falls for sand, but the glassmen could not find any that would suit; he had then sent it to Cape Henry where he obtained better material, but the quality was still so unsatisfactory that Sandys wrote to John Ferrar to send him two or three hogsheads from England.[4]

The Italians had no heart in the work, and in order to get an excuse to return to England, Vincenzio, the foreman, broke the furnace with his crowbar; and Sandys was so disgusted

[1] Strachey, *Travaile into Virginia Britannica*, 59.
[2] Ibid., 71.
[3] Neill, *London Company*, 231.
[4] Bruce, *Economic History of Virginia*, II., 440.

that he used some strong prose in referring to the glass workers, "a more damn'd crew hell never vomited." [1]

Sandys, doubtless, was more expert in writing verses and raising silk worms in Captain Peirce's house in Jamestown, than in managing a glass factory.

In February, 1625, there were still five of these glass workers at the glass house near James-town.[2]

The glass house fell into disuse, and about twelve years later Sir John Harvey granted[3] the

GEORGE SANDYS.

twenty-four acres on which it formerly stood to Anthony Cole-man, whose heir, Edward Knight, conveyed the land to John Senior. The latter assigned it to John Fitchett, who sold it to John Phipps, and he in turn assigned it to William Harris, and from Harris it came to Col. Francis Moryson, who patented it on June 1, 1654—paying a quit rent of six pence per year, to commence seven years after the patenting.

On this ground, where an old chimney stood, probably a relic of the glass factory, stirring scenes in 1676 were witnessed. On September 13th of that year, Bacon, having marched forty miles since daybreak, came at nightfall with his tired men into Paspahegh old fields, whence, advancing with a small body of cavalry on the sandy beach before the town, he fired his carbine in defiance to Governor Berkeley, and commanded his trumpeter to sound.

All the night was spent in cutting a trench and felling trees, and the sun rose on the 14th to find Bacon and his men behind a good breastwork, safe from the cannon of the ships and the town. The better to direct the movements of his troops, he stationed

[1] Neill, *Virginia Vetusta*, 121.
[2] Hotten, *Emigrants to America*, 235.
[3] *William and Mary Coll. Quart.*, XI., 88.

a constant sentry on the top of the brick chimney " to discover from thence how the men in town mounted and dismounted, posted and reposted, drew on and off, what number they were and how they moved."

On the 16th, Sir William's men made a sally with horse and foot, but Bacon's men received them so warmly that they retired in great disorder, leaving several of their men dead upon the neck.

Then Bacon managed to get some cannon, and in order to place them in position, he sent off and captured the wives of the leading councillors — Madam Elizabeth Bacon, wife of Colonel Nathaniel Bacon, Sr.; Madam Angelica Bray, wife of Colonel James Bray; Madam Elizabeth Page, wife of Colonel John Page; Madam Anna Ballard, wife of Colonel Thomas Ballard, and other ladies, and the next morning he presented them to the view of their friends and husbands in the town, their white aprons fluttering a truce from the top of his small bulwark. This ruse succeeded, and the guns having been placed in position, without a shot from town, the ladies were withdrawn, and the fire of the cannon directed upon the shipping and the works of Governor Berkeley across the neck.

The result was that, in a day or two, the governor, despairing of success, was compelled to take to his ships at night and leave the city to its fate, which the very next night was burned to the ground by Bacon — September 19, 1676.

The exposure and hardships to which Bacon was subjected in the " trenches " here are supposed to have given him the disease of which he died October 26,[1] 1676, at the house of Major Thomas Pate, in Gloucester County.

January 24, 1677, Sir William Berkeley held a court-martial at Greenspring, three miles distant, when Colonel James Crews, Captain William Cookson, and Captain John Digby (or Derby) were sentenced to death as rebels. These men, who, as particular friends of Bacon, had been in the fight at the glass house, were carried to the same place by order of Sir William Berkeley and hung. In 1703, the glass house land was owned

---

[1] This is the date given in the *British Calendar of State Papers*, Colonial, 1675–1676, p. 476, but the author of a *Narrative of the Indian and Colonial Wars* gives October 1, 1676.

by William Broadrib; and in 1709 his executors, Major George Marable, Benjamin Eggleston, and Broadrib's widow, Lydia, then wife of Christopher Smith, clerk of Jamestown church and master of the Indian School at William and Mary College, sold the same to William Brodnax.[1]

Among the relics of the past still picked up on the shores of Jamestown Island, and the Main, are beads and other trinkets of glass, probably the manufacture of this first American glass factory.

[1] *Ambler MSS.* in Library of Congress.

A VIEW OF THE RIVER FROM JAMESTOWN ISLAND.

X.

THE GOVERNOR'S HOUSE.

Captain John Ratcliffe had in the days of his presidency
(September 10, 1607, to July, 1608) started to build a house
for the governor near the fort, and Captain Smith (president
from September 10, 1608, to September 10, 1609) had " stayed
the work as needless;"[1] but in 1611–1614 Sir Thomas Gates,
who brought his daughters with him to Virginia, erected " at
the charges and by the servants of the company," a governor's
house of framed timbers at Jamestown.[2] There was a garden
attached, in which Gates planted the seeds of the English
apple and pear with the view of grafting them upon the
native crab.[3]

This house was enlarged by Sir Samuel Argall in 1617, and
was confirmed to the governor's use, in 1618, by instructions
from the London Company to Sir George Yeardley.[4] It
probably stood outside of the stockade on the fourth ridge
where the " New Towne " was afterwards laid out. Sir George
Yeardley's wife was a widow, Temperance West, and she
and her children, Elizabeth, Argall and Francis were living at
Jamestown in 1625. Yeardley's successor, Sir Francis Wyatt,
who was governor from 1621 to 1626, doubtless lived in the
governor's house built by Gates, which would identify its
location with that of the ruins of the Jaquelin-Ambler House.
Yeardley then a member of his council lived on the second
ridge north of Wyatt, and to his west was a park. Wyatt's wife
was Margaret Sandys, niece of Sir Edwin Sandys, and " Good
Newes from Virginia "[5] has some quaint verses in her honor.

[1] Smith, *Works* (Arber's ed.), 121.
[2] *A Breife Declaration* in State Senate Doc. (extra), 1874, 80.
[3] Hamor, *True Discourse*, 23.
[4] *Va. Magazine*, II., 158.
[5] Neill, *Virginia Vetusta*, 147–153.

But last of all that Lady faire
 that woman worth renowne
That left her Countrey and her friends
 to grace brave James his Towne.

The wife unto our Governor
 did safely here arrive
With many gallants following her
 Whom God preserve alive

What man would stay when Ladies gay
 both lives and fortunes leaves
To taste what we have truly fowne —
 truth never man deceaves.

In 1626, Wyatt returned to England with his family and Yeardley was then governor till November, 1627, when he died and was succeeded, first, by Francis West, and then by John Pott. In 1630, Sir John Harvey became governor, and we are told that his private residence was a kind of public guest house, not only for strangers but for members of the council and their retinues, who sometimes stayed with him a month at a time. To meet the public expectations he was under the necessity of applying his domestic servants to the

COL. PHILIP LUDWELL.

public use and to kill even some of his own draft oxen to supply his table. When Wyatt succeeded him as governor in 1639, he purchased the new brick house of Richard Kempe, and probably resided in it till the incoming of Sir William Berkeley, who appears to have made the same building his residence till he sold it to Walter Chiles in 1649.[1]

After that time Berkeley probably lived in a brick house adjoining the state house, which upon his retirement, in 1652, from the government to his country house at Greenspring, he sold in 1655 to Richard Bennett.[2]

---

[1] *Ambler MSS.* in Library of Congress.
[2] Hening, *Statutes at Large*, I., 407.

Greenspring is situated upon Powhatan Swamp in James City County and takes its name from "a very green spring that is upon the land," which was reported[1] by Rev. John Clayton as "so very cold that 'tis dangerous drinking thereof in summer time." This spring is still one of the attractions of the place. Greenspring estate was granted to Sir William

LUCY HIGGINSON.
First wife of Col. Philip Ludwell.

Berkeley by the quarter court in Virginia, June 4, 1643, and comprised at first 984 acres, but it was subsequently increased to 1,090 acres.[2] Near it on Powhatan Swamp was a tree called Powhatan's Tree, being probably the oak tree on which at Opechancanough's request was hung the brass having upon it the words of the peace concluded at the marriage of Pocahontas in 1614.

Berkeley's brick house was two stories and a half high, and had six rooms and a large hall ten feet wide, and the dimensions of its present

ruins are: length forty-eight feet, width forty-three feet six inches. There were also two wings, which may have been added at a later day — one of which is still standing — length twenty-six feet two inches, breadth sixteen feet six inches. Greenspring was plundered by Nathaniel Bacon and his followers in 1676, and after Berkeley's death, in 1677, his widow, Frances Culpeper, married Col. Philip Ludwell, of Rich Neck in the same county (brother of Thomas Ludwell, the secretary of state), and thus the place descended in the

[1] Force, *Tracts*, III., No. xii, 13.
[2] *Va. Magazine*, V., 383.

Ludwell family, through three successive Philip Ludwells, till it came to Hon. William Lee, who married Hannah Philippa, the eldest daughter of the last Philip. During the occupancy

of the Ludwells, the lawn at Greenspring was beautifully terraced, and there were hothouses in which southern plants were grown. Thus Hon. John Blair, in his diary under date of March 18, 1751, speaks of "gathering oranges" there during a visit.[1]

Col. Herbert Jeffreys, who succeeded Berkeley in 1677, had his residence at Middle Plantation — Jamestown being in ruins, as the result of Bacon's Rebellion; and Sir Henry Chicheley, governor in 1679, resided[2] at Rosegill, on the Rappahannock, having married Agatha Eltonhead, the widow of the former proprietor, Col. Ralph Wormeley.

Lord Thomas Culpeper, a cousin of Lady Frances Berkeley, became governor in 1680, and had his residence,[3] while in the colony, at Greenspring, which he rented for £150 sterling.

Culpeper's successor, Lord Howard, of Effingham, who was governor from 1684 to 1688, lived[4] like Chicheley, during most of his time, at Rosegill, then the residence of Col. Ralph Wormeley, Jr.

Nathaniel Bacon, Sen., who, as president of the Council, was acting governor from the

departure of Lord Howard to the arrival of Francis Nicholson, lived during the time on York River, at the left side of King's Creek, first settled by Capt. John Utie in 1630.

[1] *William and Mary Coll. Quart.*, VII., 137.
[2] Ibid., VI.. 152.
[3] *Culpeper's Report.*
[4] *William and Mary Coll. Quart.*, VI., 153.

II

Col. Francis Nicholson and Sir Edmund Andros lived at
Jamestown, but when, in 1699, the capital was transferred to
Williamsburg, Nicholson, then serving his second term as gov-
ernor, had his residence at Mr. John Young's ordinary[1] in
Williamsburg.

Nathaniett Bacon D

In 1705, a large brick house for the governor, called the
palace, was erected at Williamsburg. It had a handsome
cupola, which was lighted up at night on public occasions, a
large green lawn in front, and extensive grounds adorned with
ponds, gardens and terraces.

The palace was burned during the Revolution, while it was
occupied as a hospital for the American army; and, long

ffa. Nicholson

after, the site became the property of William and Mary
College. After the collapse of Bacon's Rebellion, Richard
Lawrence, Thomas Whaley and John Forth, Bacon's
friends, fled to the woods in snow ankle deep, and were never
heard of again. But Thomas Whaley left in York County a
son, James Whaley, who married Mary Page, daughter of
Matthew Page, of Jamestown, and niece of Colonel John
Page. This couple had an only son Mattey (Matthew), who
died while a child, and so " to eternalize Mattey's name forever," Mrs. Whaley established, in 1706, near Williamsburg,

Mary Whaley

a free school for boys.
Mrs. Whaley died in Eng-
land, in 1742, leaving most
of her estate to this school.
To get the money the
church wardens of Bruton Parish, who had charge of the
school, sued the executor in England. But soon after the suit
was instituted, the Revolution broke out and the school suspended; and the fund in England was lost sight of. Nearly
a hundred years later, in 1867, some money belonging to this

---

[1] Perry, *Papers Relating to the Church in Virginia,* 170.

charity was handed over by the English courts to the authorities of William and Mary College, who, undertaking to administer the trust, erected the brick building now standing where the palace once stood, and established in it a school called " the Mattey Whaley Observation and Practice School of William and Mary College."[1]

In the churchyard of Bedfont Parish, England, is the tombstone of Mary Whaley, and in the churchyard of Bruton Parish, Virginia, lies buried her husband, James Whaley. The upright marble slab, which forms the eastern end of James Whaley's box tomb, has upon it engraved these words:

> MATTHEW WHALEY lyes Interred here
> Within this Tomb upon his FATHER dear.
> Who Departed
> This Life the 26th of
> September, 1705. Aged
> Nine years. only child
> of JAMES WHALEY
> and MARY his wife.

[1] *William and Mary Coll. Quart.*, IV., 3-15.

XI.

THE STATE HOUSE.

The first general assembly of Virginia, which met July 30, 1619, held its meetings in the new timber church erected not long before at the present brick tower. It consisted of the governor, six councillors, and twenty burgesses representing ten plantations. The burgesses of Martin's Brandon were refused a seat because of the independence asserted by the proprietor, Captain John Martin. The speaker of the assembly was John Pory, a master of arts of the university of Cambridge, and at that time colonial secretary of state. As is the custom in the house of commons to-day, the members wore their hats, and insisted on their privileges. Many important acts were passed, and the earliest assembly in the oldest of the original States, at its first session, took measures for the education of the Indians and for the erection of a university and college.[1]

In imitation of a Scotch parliament, the governor, council, and burgesses in the first assembly sat as one body, but it is probable, however, that this practice prevailed only during the existence of the company, and that, when the assembly came together in 1628 after the dissolution of the charter, the burgesses in imitation of the house of commons sat apart. We have none of the early journals of the general assembly after 1619 and previous to 1652, but in Hening's *Statutes at Large* one of the acts passed[2] in the year 1647 has a reference to the "members of both houses," showing that the council and burgesses sat apart at that time, and probably had been doing so ever since the reorganization in 1628. From 1652 on, there is plenty of evidence of the bicameral nature of the general assembly. Thus in the orders published by Hening for the sessions during the commonwealth (1652–1660) the burgesses clearly act as an organized

[1] *Journal of the Assembly of* 1619, in State Senate Doc. (extra), 1874.
[2] Hening, *Statutes at Large*, I., 341.

body independent of governor and council,[1] are called a house,[2] and have their own clerk[3] and rules of government.[4] The same condition of things is revealed by the journal after the Restoration,[5] and we have the authority of Rev. Roger Green,[6] who had been to Jamestown and wrote in 1662 as follows: "Whatever is of public concernment in Virginia is determined by their Grand Assemblies, which are usually held once a year and consist of Governor and Council, which make the upper house, and the Burgesses which represent the People, and make the lower house, and are chosen out of every county by the People, after the manner that Burgesses are chosen for Parliament in *England* * * *. Whatsoever passes into an act of Assembly must be agreed'd upon by the major part of the Burgesses * * *." And in 1676, T. M.'s narrative shows that the council and burgesses had different rooms in the state house.[7]

With this evidence it seems impossible to reconcile Beverley's statement[8] that "the council and burgesses were joined till 1680, when Lord Culpeper, taking advantage of some disputes among them, procured the council to sit apart from the assembly." And yet probably Beverley's words must not be taken too literally as there was some commingling of the two houses previous to 1680 or, at least, previous to 1676, which did not exist after that time. A resolution[9] of the burgesses in 1658 that "all propositions and laws "—" shall be first discussed among the Burgesses only " * * * in private * * * and not in presence of the Governor and Council," indicates that previous to 1658 the governor and councillors sat sometimes as advisers with the burgesses. After 1658, it was the practice for two councillors to sit, in

---

[1] See Hening, *Statutes at Large*, I., 371, 372, 373, etc.
[2] Ibid., I., 507, 509, 511.
[3] Ibid., I., 377.
[4] Ibid., I., 507.
[5] Ibid., II., 204, 206.
[6] *Virginia's Cure* (Force, *Tracts*, III., No. xv).
[7] Force, *Tracts*, I., No. viii.
[8] Beverley, *Virginia*, 187. In another place in his history, page 37, the language might be interpreted to mean that the council and burgesses never joined their houses again after the first meeting.
[9] Hening, *Statutes at Large*, I., 497.

an advisory capacity, with the committees of the house, but this practice was discontinued about 1680, so that Beverley may have had this in mind when he wrote.

It is almost certain that more than one session of the assembly was held in the old church, but how many we may never know. During Harvey's administration the council, and probably the burgesses, held their sessions at his residence, which was described as "a general harbor for all comers."

It was the scene of an interesting incident in Harvey's time, when the colony was excited over the disruption of Virginia's territory by the charter of Maryland to Lord Baltimore. Harvey, who was very unpopular as a friend of Lord Baltimore, suppressed a petition addressed by the people to the king on the subject of the tobacco trade and justified an attack by Lord Baltimore's men upon a pinnace of Claiborne engaged in the fur trade from Kent Island. At York on April 5, 1635, a meeting of protest was held at the house of William Warren, near the present Yorktown, where the chief speakers were Captain Nicholas Martian, an ancestor of Washington, Captain Francis Pott, and William English, the sheriff of Charles River County (York). Harvey was enraged at the proceeding and caused the leaders to be arrested and threatened them with the gallows. Then he called a council at his house at Jamestown, and demanded the execution of martial law upon the prisoners; and, when the council declined to give the order, he paced up and down the council room in great anger. After a while, he took his seat, and with a frowning countenance demanded an immediate answer to this question: "What do you think they deserve that have gone about to persuade the people from obedience to his Majesty's substitute?"

George Menifie, of Littletown, to whom the question was first directed, adroitly evaded it by saying, "I am but a young lawyer, and dare not upon the sudden deliver my opinion." The governor required this answer to be set down in writing; and when William Farrar of Henrico, another member, complained of the unreasonableness of the question, Harvey, in his majesty's name, forbade him to speak until his turn. Captain Mathews, of Denbigh, not deterred by this, commenced with a

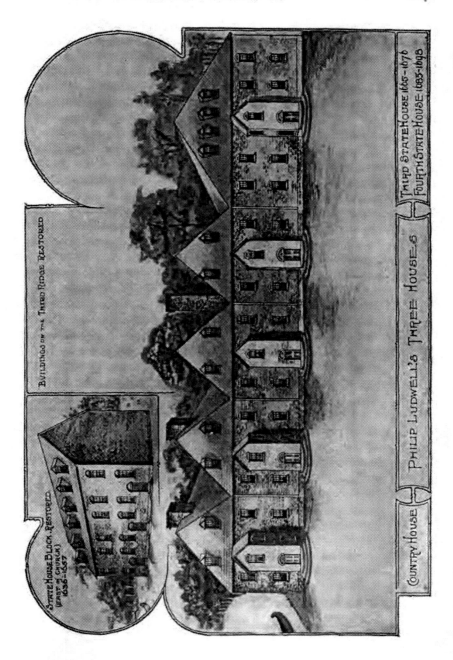

STATE HOUSE BLOCK, RESTORED.
(FIRST & FOURTH)
1656-1657

BUILDINGS ON THE THIRD RIDGE RESTORED

COUNTRY HOUSE

PHILIP LUDWELL'S THREE HOUSE

THIRD STATE HOUSE 1665-1676
FOURTH STATE HOUSE 1685-1698

remark similar to Farrar's, and was interrupted by a like command. But after this, the rest of the council began to speak, and refused to be so questioned. The next day there was another meeting, and Harvey sternly demanded the reason of the country's opposition to him. When Menifie informed him, Harvey rose in a great rage, and said to Menifie, "And do you say so?" He replied "Yes." In a fury Harvey clapped Menifie on the shoulder and said, "I arrest you on suspicion of high treason to his Majesty." Captain John Utie, who was nearest, returned the blow, and said in a loud voice, "And we the like to you, sir." And, thereupon, the councillors crowded around Harvey; and Captain Mathews, throwing his arms about him, forced him into a chair, telling him to be quiet as no harm was intended to him. In the meantime, Dr. John Pott, who stood at the door, waved his hand, and fifty armed musketeers, previously concealed, appeared. In May, an assembly was convened, which ratified the work of the council, and confirmed as governor Captain John West, brother of the late Lord Delaware; and Harvey was soon after put aboard a ship and sent off to England in the custody of Francis Pott and Thomas Harwood. The deposition of Sir John Harvey was the first vindication on the American continent of the constitutional right of a people to order their own government.

In 1637, Harvey had returned, and in 1639 he wrote that a levy had been laid by the general assembly for building a state house, and an act, passed in January, 1640, provided for a further levy of two pounds of tobacco. George Menifie was sent to England for mechanics, and about this time the country house in "New Towne" was erected for their entertainment. But it is not believed that a state house was actually built.

In the vicissitudes of party, Wyatt succeeded Harvey in November, 1639, and Wyatt's council ordered all the late governor's property to be sold to pay his debts. And, accordingly, Harvey on April 7, 1641, conveyed[1] to the colonial government for 15,700 pounds of tobacco "all that capital, messuage or tenement now used for a courthouse, late in the tenure of Sir John Harvey situate and being with-

---

[1] Robinson's *Abstracts of Council Proceedings.*

in James Citty Island in Virginia, with the old house, and granary, garden, and orchard, as also one plot of ground lying and being on the west side of said capital and messuage, as the same is now enclosed." This property is believed to have been the two houses and orchard which were presented[1] by the general assembly, in 1642, to the new governor, Sir William Berkeley. The latter built a third brickhouse adjoining the two, and the three formed a block, of which the middle, the "old courthouse," was what is referred to in the records as "the state house." Probably Sir William Berkeley lived in the last of the buildings; and when he removed to Greenspring after the change in government, he sold[2] it for 27,500 pounds of tobacco to Richard Bennett, Esq., describing it as "the westermost of those three brick houses which I then built."

Several grants of land show that this first state house was in the "New Towne" east of the churchyard. There is first a grant[3] of an acre, 23 rods long, to John White, dated August 28, 1644, placing the churchyard on the west, the land appertaining to the state house on the east, and the land of Rev. Thomas Hampton towards the north. There is the lease[4] of one acre in 1643 to Captain Robert Hutchinson, "Anciently belonging to Mr. Samuel Mole, bounded South upon the River, North towards Passbyhaes, West upon the land of John Osborne and towards the State House." "Passbyhaes," referred to here, was a general direction, as any of the country outside of the Island was in the Indian district "Passbyhaes."

The state house must have ceased to be used for government purposes sometime previous to June, 1656, since in December of that year Thomas Woodhouse, an ordinary keeper, was allowed[5] by the assembly 2,500 pounds of tobacco "for the quarter courts (general court) setting at his house two courts and for the committee's accommodation." The two previous quarter courts sat in June and September, 1656.

Abstracts of three deeds of Sir William Berkeley, dated

[1] Hening, *Statutes at Large*, I., 267.
[2] Ibid., I.. 407.
[3] *Va. Land Register*, II., 10.
[4] Ibid., I., 944.
[5] Hening, *Statutes at Large*, I., 425.

April 3, 1670, once on record in the general court, affirm that the state house was destroyed by fire, and that it was the middle building of three, each forty feet by twenty, all of which were generally referred to as the "State House." By the terms of the deeds mentioned, Sir William conveyed "the ruins" of all three buildings to Henry Randolph, of Henrico, and the westernmost, which sold for twenty-five pounds sterling, was described as "the remains, foundations and brick work of a certain house or messuage that was burned, forty feet long by twenty feet broad, being the westermost part of the ruined fabric or building adjoining the old State House, which said ruined messuage was formerly in the occupation of Richard Bennett, Esq.," including half an acre adjacent.[1]

SIR THOMAS LUNSFORD, KNIGHT.

There is a grant[2] to Thomas Ludwell and Thomas Stegge, dated January 1, 1667, for an half acre in James City, lying on the river side, and adjoining to the westermost of those three houses, "all of which joyntly were formerly called by the name of the State House," beginning "close to the wall where the said westermost house joynes to the middle house, thence running southwesterly 34 degrees 67 feet to high-water mark, thence northwesterly 56 degrees up the river side 120 feet, thence northeasterly 34 degrees 181 feet and halfe, thence southeasterly 56 degrees 120 feet, thence southwesterly again 34 degrees through the said old State House, and the partition wall dividing the said westermost house and middle house, 114 feet and halfe to the place where it first began." It appears then that the three buildings

---

1 Va. Magazine, VIII., 408.
2 Va. Land Register, VI., 223.

which the state house was the middle constituted a block which was distant 67 feet from high-water and had a frontage 20 feet and a depth of 20 feet. They stood in a lot extending along the river 280 feet and running back 181 feet. Henry Randolph did not long retain the buildings; for April 1671, he sold the westernmost fabric to Thomas Ludwell and Thomas Stegge, the middle building to Nathaniel Bacon, Sr., executor of Miles Cary, deceased, and the eastern building said to have been formerly in the occupation of Thomas Liley) to Colonel Thomas Swann. Then by his will proved May 15, 1671, Thomas Stegge left to Thomas Ludwell his interest in a house bought jointly with Ludwell of Henry Randolph.[1] Subsequently Ludwell got a patent for half an acre of land adjoining this tenement, and on March 17, 1672, reconveyed the tenement with the land so adjoining to Sir William Berkeley, who originally owned it, for 150 pounds sterling.[2]

As for several years after December, 1656, there is no further payment made by order of the assembly to ordinary keepers, the general assembly probably hired a building for governmental purposes. It therefore constituted the second " state house," and stood like the first on the fourth ridge; for in October, 1656, John Bauldwin patented[3] ten acres on the river at the western shore of the Island, which is described as " South upon the slash which lyeth between the State House " and Richard James' land. James' land was bounded by a southern line from " Frigett Landing," and east of this line Pitch and Tarr Swamp became the southern boundary of the fourth ridge. The second state house appears to have perished by fire before October, 1660, as during the assembly held that month an act was passed for allowing Thomas Hunt, an ordinary keeper, 3,500 pounds of tobacco for the use of his house for the assembly, and Thomas Woodhouse 4,000 pounds for the use of his house for governor and council. Indeed, in October, 1666, reference is made in an act to " two severall fires," which had destroyed some of the records in the secretary's office.

[1] New England Hist. and Gen. Mag., XXXIX., 161.
[2] Va. Magazine. VIII., 409.
[3] Va. Land Register, IV., 88.

In October, 1660, Sir William Berkeley was asked by the general assembly to contract for a new state house, and subsequently in March, 1661, a general subscription was started in order to avoid a tax levy. The governor, councillors, and burgesses headed the list; and an order was passed that the several county courts and vestrys take subscriptions from the other inhabitants.[1] Probably no great sum was raised, and the assembly continued to hold their meetings at the ordinaries for several years. September 16, 1663, the question was submitted in the house of burgesses: "Since the charge the country is yearly at for houses for the quarter courts and assemblies to sit in would in two or three years defray the purchase of a State House; whether it were not more profitable to purchase for that purpose then continue forever at the expense, accompanied with the dishonour, of all our laws being made, and our judgments given, in ale houses." The next day, Col. William Barber, Col. Gerard Fowke, Lieutenant Colonel Kendall, Mr. Warren, Mr. Rawleigh Traverse and Mr. Thomas Lucas were appointed a committee to confer with the governor about the matter.[2]

The assembly had in December, 1662, passed an act to build a town of thirty-two brick houses at Jamestown, and April 1o,

1665, Thomas Ludwell, the secretary of state, wrote[3] to Lord Arlington that they "had already built enough to accommodate the affairs of the country," by which it is supposed that the state house had been erected. The new state house, instead of standing like the other two on the river shore east of the church, stood on the third ridge above it, and its dimensions were seventy-four feet by twenty feet within the walls. It was two stories high, had probably garrets and dormer windows, and its roof was covered with tiles. The space in the first story was divided into two rooms, and the eastern division, which was about forty-three feet long, was used by the council

---

[1] Hening, *Statutes at Large*, II., 38.
[2] Ibid., II., 204, 205.
[3] *British State Papers*, Colonial, 1661-1668, p. 290.

in discharge of its triple duty as the general court, advisory body to the governor, and upper house of legislation. The western room, about thirty-one feet long, was probably used as a waiting room for those having business at court.[1] On the north of the building was a wing, and on the south a porch connected with it by a hall in which ran the stair-case to the upper story containing the apartments of the house of burgesses, and the office of Thomas Ludwell, secretary of state.[2]

Joining on to the state house was Philip Ludwell, Jr.'s block of three houses in length 3¾ chains or 123¾ feet, and westerly attached by a common wall was a "Country House," which must not be confounded with the country house in "New Towne." These four united buildings were each about forty feet square within the walls, and were divided longitudinally by a middle wall, in the nature of a prolongation of the northern wall of the state house, which suggests that these houses were enlarged to just twice their original size, being first forty by twenty feet, according to the specifications of the act of December, 1662, for rebuilding the town.[3] In February, 1903, the earth overlying was removed, and the brick foundations of this block of connected buildings, and of the state house, about two hundred and forty feet long, were disclosed.

·Here in June, 1676, occurred an interesting incident in the history of the colony. On the 5th of the month, the assembly convened in the state house to take measures against the savages, who had attacked the frontier settlers and committed many murders. Now, not long before, Nathaniel Bacon, one of the council, against the wishes of Governor Berkeley, went with an army and defeated the Occaneechees near the North Carolina line. So when he came to the assembly, as a delegate from Henrico County, Berkeley, in towering wrath, had him arrested by Major Theophilus Hone, high sheriff of James City County. Sympathy, however, with Bacon was widespread, and Berkeley, soon finding it to his interest, affected forgiveness, and offered to restore Bacon to his seat in the council on his making the proper apologies. Bacon was very unwilling to

[1] Yonge, *Site of Old Jamestowne*, 68.
[2] Ibid., 70.
[3] Ibid., 66.

humiliate himself, but was persuaded by his cousin Col. Nathaniel Bacon, Sen., to make the submission required of him, and this is how it was done, as told by " T. M." in his narrative of *Bacon's Rebellion*.[1]

The burgesses, having elected their speaker, marched in a body downstairs to the council chamber to hear the governor's address; and when they were all in the room, the governor, standing up before them, made this announcement: " If there be joy in the presence of the angels over one sinner that repenteth, there is joy now, for we have a penitent sinner come before us. Call Mr. Bacon." In response Mr. Bacon came forward, and resting " upon one knee at the bar, delivered a sheet of paper, confessing his crimes, and begging pardon of God, of the King and the Governor." After this there was a profound silence which was broken by Berkeley with the words thrice repeated: " God forgive you, I forgive you." Thereupon, Col. William Cole, of the council, and afterwards secretary of

state, asked " and all that were with him?" " Yea," said the governor, " and all that were with him." Apparently, in this way, the affair between Berkeley and Bacon was settled, and that evening, as T. M. passed the door of the council chamber, he saw Mr. Bacon in his " quondam seat," with the governor and council. But as it resulted, it was only a brief truce, and the quarrel soon broke out between the two men with greater virulence than ever.

Shortly afterwards, the house of burgesses appointed committee on Indian affairs, and the governor sent two members of the council to sit with them and give advice — The queen of Pamunkey, a relation of. Opechancanough was called before the committee, and she entered the chamber " with a comportment graceful to admiration," at-

[1] Force, *Tracts*, I., No. viii.

tended on her right by an English interpreter and on her left by her son, a young man of twenty years. She was clothed in a mantle of dressed deer skins, having the hair outward and cut in fringes six inches long, from her shoulders to her feet; and around her head she wore a "pleat of black and white wampumpeake," three inches broad. After she had taken her seat at the table, the chairman asked her how many men she could provide for the colony in the war which now threatened them. At first she declined to speak, and by a motion of the head passed the question to her son, who also remained silent. When the chairman reiterated his question, the queen, after further silence, broke out in vehement reproaches against the English for their injustice and ingratitude. Twenty years before, her husband, Totopotomoi, had been slain with many of his men while assisting the English in a battle with the Ricahecreans near a creek in Hanover County still bearing Totopotomoi's name, but she had never received the slightest compensation for her loss. "With a high shrill voice and vehement passion, she cried 'Totopotomoi Chipiack! Totopotomoi Chipiack!' Totopotomoi is dead, Totopotomoi is dead!"

When her harangue was over, the chairman of the committee, instead of showing sympathy, roughly pushed the question again: "How many Indians will you contribute?" The queen looked at him scornfully, and when he again demanded an answer she, in a "slow slighting voice," answered "*Six*"— although, at that very time, she had as many as 150 men in her towns in Pamunkey Neck. Further questioned, she said sullenly "Twelve," after which, as if disdaining to have any further treaty with the white men, she rose from her seat and abruptly quitted the room.

Several days later, the governor resolved to rearrest Bacon, and early in the morning sent soldiers to search Lawrence's house where Bacon staid. But Bacon received notice of Berkeley's intentions, and hastened from the town to his plantation at Curls Neck thirty miles up the river. Here his friends rallied about him, and presently finding himself with a sufficient force he set out for Jamestown a second time.

The governor, at first, was full of fight, but, finding his friends of a different mind, soon gave up the notion of defending the place. June 23, 1676, Bacon crossed to the Island unopposed, and following the " Old Great Roade " marched to the third ridge, where, after dispatching squads of troops to secure the fort, the ferry, and the neck by which he had crossed, he drew up the rest of his forces, " horse and foot," on the green " not a flight shot from the end of the State House." Shortly the drum beat for the assembly to meet, and Bacon sent into the state house to demand a commission against the Indians. Thereupon, Sir William Berkeley came out, and at first angrily refused, dramatically tearing open his breast and crying out: " Here, shoot me — fore God, fair mark." But Bacon only replied, " No, may it please your Honor, I come not, nor intend, to hurt a hair of your head, but I come for a commission against the heathen, who are daily spilling our brethren's blood; and a commission I will have before I go." Many more words passed, till Bacon, growing tired of the interview, turned to his soldiers, and swearing a mighty oath, called out: " Make ready, present ! " The soldiers promptly directed their pieces to the windows of the state house,

LUCIUS CARY, LORD FALKLAND.

crowded with burgesses and councillors.

One of these seeing the danger, shook a handkerchief out of the window and cried out to the soldiers: " For God's sake, hold your hands and forbear a little, and you shall have what you please." Upon which there was much hurrying and solicitation, and the governor was finally induced to give the commission demanded of him. Then, Bacon, who had now obtained all he desired, left town with his soldiers, and marched up to the Falls of the river, preparatory to going out a second time against the Indians.

As related on page 69, Bacon returned not long after and burned Jamestown, September 19, 1676; and this so greatly discouraged the general assembly that, after peace was restored, they had some thought of establishing the capital in some other place, but they soon set to work to re-establish Jamestown, and on December 4, 1685, Mr. Auditor Bacon[1] was ordered by the general assembly to pay "Col. Philip Ludwell £400 sterling out of ye money accruing from ye duty of three pence pr. gallon upon liquors for and in consequence of rebuilding ye State House, upon payment of which money Mr. Auditor is desired to take bond from Col. Ludwell for ye full compleating of ye House in such manner as shall be fully satisfactory to his Excellency, ye Council, and ye House of Burgesses, answerably good and equivalent to the condition of ye same."

The following extract from a message addressed to the house by the governor during the session of the assembly of 1685 shows that the third and fourth state house buildings occupied the same site and probably were of the same shape and proportions: "This day an addresse and some orders of yr House have been presented to me & ye Council by some of yr members, and doe much wonder, you should propose soe unreasonably, as to desire our concurrence, in ye memorial (removal?) of ye secretaries office, wch *ever since ye State House was first built, until burnt,* has been continued in ye place you allot for an office for ye Clerk, soe that Mr. Secretary justly claims it by prescription, and you yourselves have soe consented and alsoe desired, that it be enlarged as by ye agreement made ye last Gen'l Assembly with Col. Ludwell."

The new building then was the third state house restored, but, as indicated by the language of the order above cited, some changes were made in the assignment of the rooms. Contrary to the wishes of the governor, the house of burgesses appropriated to their clerk, Robert Beverley, the porch room adjoining their hall on the second story, deeming the proximity of the secretary of state "both inconvenient and incommodious to them whilst sitting: there being nothing spoken or proposed in ye House that was not equally to be heard there as

[1] Nathaniel Bacon, Sen.

well as in ye Assembly room itself, besides ye same gave continual opportunity to all sorts of persons to crowd before the Assembly room, under pretence of coming to ye Office." Lord Howard finally agreed to yield, if a room in the chamber adjoining the council room should be partitioned off and fitted up for the secretary of state with shelves, tables and benches, at the cost of the country (the colony).[1]

Robert Beverley, the clerk, who was at the bottom of this contention, was one of the most interesting men of his times. During Bacon's Rebellion he and Philip Ludwell, brother of Secretary Thomas Ludwell, had been Governor Berkeley's chief supporters, and when the war was over, they and other friends of Berkeley fell under the displeasure of the king's commissioners, Col. Herbert Jeffreys, Col. Francis Moryson, and Sir John Berry. In their zeal to get at the beginnings of Bacon's Rebellion upon which they were charged to report, the commissioners demanded the journals of the house of bur-

gesses, now composed of the friends of Sir William Berkeley; but Beverley, who had them in charge declined to hand them over. This was a most fortunate incident for the fame of Beverley, as it identified him with the dearest rights of the popular branch of the legislature. A few years later, in 1682, he became identified with another great principle, the personal liberty of the citizen; for being arrested by Governor Culpeper for participation in the conspiracy of the "Tobacco Plant Cutters," he underwent much persecution, and was denied the right of the *habeas corpus* writ, for which he applied. Still later he figured as the champion of the right of the assembly to lay taxes; for when Lord Howard, of Effingham, endeavored to induce the house of burgesses to authorize him and the council to exercise that power, Beverley was foremost in urging the burgesses to decline the request, which they did. As a consequence, he was deprived of his clerkship August 1, 1686,

[1] *McDonald Papers*, in State Library.

and the king, assuming the right of appointment, commis-
'sioned Captain Francis Page as his successor. Robert Beverley died about April, 1687, leaving a number of sons, among
whom was Robert Beverley, the historian.[1]

The site of the fourth state house at Jamestown Island, and
consequently of the third, is fixed by a patent[2] for land at the
west end granted in 1694 to William Sherwood, which
describes the head of a branch of Pitch and Tar Swamp, beginning at the west end of the Island, as "next above the State
House." This is further confirmed by recent excavations on
the third ridge, which have disclosed the extensive brick foundations already referred to, corresponding to the outward
manifestations described in 1837 by Mr. Richard Randolph,
who stated that there then existed on the ridge great quantities of bricks, plaster and other debris, prompting his conjecture that "they were the remains of the Governor's or
State House."[3]

October 31, 1698, flames once more attacked Jamestown, and
in this fire the state house and most probably all the other
buildings on the third ridge, except the powder magazine, were
destroyed. The consequences were fatal to the town, for no
attempt was made to rebuild, and in 1699 the seat of government was removed to Williamsburg. There at the east end
of a spacious avenue, facing the college at the west end, a
brick building, in the form of the letter H, too pretentious in
the eyes of Governor Nicholson to be called a state house, was
erected. It was the first capitol so-called in the United States.

It stood till 1746, when a fire broke out and destroyed it also.
A new capitol was erected soon after on the same walls, which
stood till 1832, when it was attacked by the same devouring
agent, and perished like its predecessor. In 1840, a portion of
the brick walls was used for the construction of a female

---

[1] *Va. Magazine,* II., 405–413; *William and Mary Coll. Quart.,* III., 149.
[2] *Va. Land Register,* VIII., 384.
[3] *Southern Literary Messenger,* III., 303. And in the *Ambler MSS.*
in the Library of Congress there is a deed in 1694 from William Sherwood to Francis Bullifant for two acres which are described as
"bounded west by James River, southerly by the slash or branch that
parts this land and the State House, easterly by the Greate Roade, and
northerly by the said slash that p[ar]ts this land and the block house
land."

academy, which was in use till the war of 1861–1865, when the school was discontinued, and after several years the building became the property of the Old Dominion Land Company, who pulled the academy down and removed the bricks.   In 1897 this company presented the site to the ladies of the Association for the Preservation of Virginia Antiquities, and they have laid bare the ancient foundations of the capitol and patriotically erected a monument on the spot where so much of the constructive work of the Revolution was performed.

THE LONE CYPRESS
300 feet from the western shore line of the   Island.

XII.

SOCIAL CONDITIONS.

Character of the emigrants. The emigrants sent over in the original ships and the " First " and " Second Supplies " were largely gentlemen of the fearless stamp of Drake and Hawkins, and many of them had endured all sorts of hardships on land and sea. Indeed, it is a truth generally conceded that in all affairs requiring courage, fatigue and endurance young men of birth and station are to be preferred. The emigrants were Christian Protestants, who were very exact in the performance of religious duties, and among the first things attended to was the service of God.

The misfortunes of the first two years are to be attributed not to the colonists, but to circumstances over which they had little control. These were the form of government, which produced discord and faction; the policy of the London Company, which, for a present return of profit, demanded the sacrifice of all measures necessary to the welfare of the colony; the place of settlement, which was without springs of fresh water, and was covered with huge trees, marshes and morasses; the scanty and ill conditioned provisions received at Jamestown; the absence of private property, the natural stimulus of labor; the severe and unceasing hardships and exposures experienced by the settlers; a climate singularly fatal to new comers; and the neighborhood of a numerous and ferocious body of Indians, who resented bitterly the intrusion of the whites upon their territory. Thus the conditions were in every respect the reverse of those of the Plymouth settlement on Cape Cod Bay; for there the Pilgrim Fathers had the control of their own government, the advantage of a dry and healthful situation, a sparkling stream of fresh water at their doors, open fields deserted by the Indians, whose nearest town was forty miles distant, a bay teeming with fish and a country abounding in animals whose skins brought a large profit in England. And

[181]

yet favored as they were, had they not been succored by Virginia ships, the settlers might have all perished of famine.[1]

As to the " Third Supply," who were afterwards stigmatized as a " lewd company " and " gallants packed thither by their friends to escape worse destinies at home," they appear from the broadsides issued by the company to have been chiefly artisans of all sorts. Probably Rev. William Croshaw stated[2] the case fairly in a sermon which he preached in 1610 that " those who were sent over at the company's expense were, for aught he could see, like those who were left behind, even of all sorts better and worse " and that " the gentlemen who went on their own account" were as good as the scoffers at home, and it may be " many degrees better." They had all the troubles of the early emigrants besides evils peculiarly their own, namely, imported pestilence and absolute want of victuals and leadership, so that it is no wonder that they nearly all died in less than nine months.

After the " Starving Time," for nine consecutive years, most of the emigrants who came were laboring men, but they did not endure as well as the gentlemen of the earlier times, and most of them died under the hardships of martial law as administered by the iron-handed Dale. Nor after the introduction of free institutions, in 1619, was the story of misfortune in any great degree changed. The emigration continued for many years to be that of laboring people, but climatic diseases slew them by hundreds; for we are told that the people on James River died like " cats and dogs " in the months of July and August,[3] and hardly one in five survived even the first year of his stay.[4]

When after 1642 the civil wars in England drove thousands of people to Virginia, two causes tended to reduce the death rate — the better material of the emigrants, being persons of genteel families, and the better health conditions in the colony itself, brought about by the opening of the forests. The mortality after this still fell chiefly upon the servants exposed to

[1] Bradford, *Plymouth Colony,* 150, 153.
[2] Brown, *Genesis of the United States,* I., 364.
[3] De Vries, *Voyages* (New York Hist. Soc. Coll., 2d series), 37.
[4] *William and Mary Coll. Quart.,* VII., 66, 114.

the malaria of the tobacco fields, and especially upon the criminal class who were most friendless and forlorn, and this continued until negroes took the place of white labor.

As the mortality among the white servants was so dreadful, Mr. Jefferson's estimate[1] of 4,000, as the number of convicts and their descendants in Virginia at the time of the Revolution, appears not far fetched. The influence of this class, forming as they did a small percentage of the servants, never amounted to anything as the law of Virginia forbade any convict from ever holding any position of honor or trust in the colony.

About the close of the seventeenth century negro labor was substituted for white labor, and thus the bulk of the white emigration of the eighteenth century was composed of free citizens, the greater part being thrifty and intelligent Scotch-Irish people driven by persecution to Virginia. This emigration was very large as shown by the census — the total white population in 1700 being about 70,000, whereas in 1776 it was about 296,852. In the nineteenth century a very small percentage of the immense European emigration to the United States came southward; so the South missed the flood of paupers and criminals, against whom in the end the Federal Congress found itself compelled to pass stringent laws.

The white population of Virginia is thus the most strictly homogeneous American population on the continent.

The following figures may be taken as approximately representing the population of the colony at different times from 1607 to 1776. The number of emigrants brought over to June 10, 1610, inclusive of Lord Delaware's company, was about 800. Between this time and December, 1618, 1,000 arrived, making a total of 1,800 persons, and of this number 1,200 died, leaving 600 survivors. Then in the interval between December, 1618, and November, 1619, 840 emigrants arrived, who made with the survivors 1,440 persons, of whom 540 died, leaving about 900 survivors. There were sent to Virginia between November, 1619, and February, 1625, 4,749 emigrants, who with the 900 of November, 1619, made a total of 5,649, of whom only 1,095 were living in Virginia February 20, 1625; showing a total mortality

---

[1] *Writings of Jefferson* (Randolph), I., 406.

in about eighteen years of 6,294 persons out of 7,389 imported.[1] After this time the violent fluctuations of the early years ceased, and there was a slow but steady increase. In 1629, the population of Virginia was about 3,000;[2] in 1634, 5,000;[3] in 1649, 15,000 (of whom 500 were negroes);[4] in 1654, 21,600;[5] in 1665, 40,000 (of whom 2,000 were negroes);[6] in 1681, 70,000 or 80,000;[7] in 1715, 95,000 (of whom 23,000 were negroes);[8] in 1755, 295,672 (of whom 120,156 were negroes);[9] and in 1776, 567,614 (of whom 270,762 were negroes).[10]

Houses. In Jamestown the first houses were log cabins, but in 1614 framed houses were built two stories and a half high, which being of sappy timber soon decayed. Afterwards, about 1619, seasoned timber was used, and about 1630 the first brick houses were erected,[11] after which the houses in Jamestown were chiefly of brick, two stories high, with dormer windows.

Outside of Jamestown where rural conditions prevailed, the buildings pursued the same general development, but wooden structures always remained in the majority. About the middle of the seventeenth century the typical country house was a framed building one story and a half high, with brick chimneys at either end,[12] but as shown by the inventories, there were framed buildings in each county two stories high with garrets besides. The country brick houses were generally one and a half story like the Cocke residence at Malvern Hill, but there were also, as in the case of the wooden houses, some brick houses two and a half stories high, of which " Bacon's Castle " in Surry, " Ringfield " in York County, built about 1680, and the Burwell house in Gloucester, built in 1694, have survived to the present day. We are told by Beverley that the

[1] Brown, *First Republic*, 285, 329, 612.
[2] *Calendar of State Papers*, Colonial, 1574–1660, p. 89.
[3] Ibid.
[4] *A Perfect Description of Virginia* (Force, *Tracts*, II., No. viii).
[5] Jefferson, *Notes on Virginia*, 151.
[6] *Winder Papers*, I., 187.
[7] *Culpeper's Report.*
[8] Chalmers, *American Colonies*, II., 7.
[9] *Dinwiddie Papers*, II., 345.
[10] Jefferson, *Notes on Virginia*, 151.
[11] The house of Sir John Harvey, afterwards called the state house, was certainly of brick.
[12] Hammond, *Leah and Rachel* (Force, *Tracts*, III., No. xiv, 18).

Virginians of the seventeenth century did not like "towering fabrics," because of the high winds which often prevailed.[1] Thus the "great gust" of August, 1667, blew down 15,000 houses in Maryland and Virginia, though from notices in the county books the victims were chiefly tobacco barns and other outhouses. After the forests were cleared away, these violent storms became less frequent.

During the eighteenth century the great influx of wealth arising from the employment of negro labor resulted in greatly improved architecture. The generality of the country houses remained the typical house of one story and a half, but they were much larger than their predecessors of the seventeenth century, and the woodwork was much superior, being handsomely planed and polished. Many of the rooms were panelled to the ceiling, and the banisters leading upstairs were made of the best lumber and finely carved. Many specimens of these houses still survive.

The brick houses, which were now become numerous, were as a rule large square buildings two stories and a half high, situated on the waterways at intervals of about two or three miles; and some of them like Westover and Shirley had large brick wings in the form of a court.

In 1781, a French traveller, who visited Virginia, wrote as follows: "As we advance towards the South, we observe a sensible difference in the manners and customs of the people. We no longer find, as in Connecticut, houses situated along the road at small distances, just large enough to contain a single family, and the humblest furniture, nothing more than is barely necessary; here are spacious habitations consisting of different buildings, at some distance from each other, surrounded with plantations that extend beyond the reach of the eye, cultivated not by hands of freemen, but by those unhappy blacks whom European avarice and injustice has taken from their native regions of Africa to cultivate possessions not their own, on a foreign soil. The furniture here is constructed out of the most costly kind of wood and the most valuable marble, enriched by the elegant device of the

[1] Beverley, *Virginia*, 235.

artist's hand. Their riding machines are light and handsome and drawn by the fleetest coursers managed by slaves richly dressed."

Roads and Vehicles.[1] Until 1630 the settlements in Virginia were all upon the James River or Accomac shore, and communication between the settlers was chiefly by boat and sloop. In 1630, Chiskiack and York on the York River were planted, and in 1632 Middle Plantation was laid out. Settlements now began to spread into the interior, as shown by the grants of land, and at first, of course, the communication with the interior was by horse-paths, or bridle-paths, generally following some old Indian trail, which, as the settlements extended further inward and counties were formed, grew into roads. Thus the road that passes by William and Mary College up the Peninsula follows the Indian trail to Rockahock on the Pamunkey, which in the old records repeatedly comes up in the boundaries of patents. In 1632, the general assembly passed the first general law in regard to roads and ordered that "the Governor and Council, or commissioners for the courts, or parishioners of a parish, shall lay out highways, according as they might seem convenient." This order was entered, two years after the first settlement was established on the York. The parish churches, court-houses, ferries and ordinaries became the focal points for roads, and the existence of roads, if other proofs were wanting, would prove the existence of carts, for which they were necessary. Carts were used at Jamestown before 1624.

In 1658, the general assembly appointed surveyors of the roads, who were commanded to clear all the general ways from county to county and to church, and in 1662 the surveyors were required to keep the roads forty feet wide and to call out the citizens for that purpose.

Besides carts there were some carriages and coaches introduced during the last quarter of the seventeenth century.[2] Nevertheless, it may be said that in this century travelling by horseback was the usual way.

During the eighteenth century there were many coaches in.

[1] *William and Mary Coll. Quart.*, VIII., 37–43.
[2] Sir William Berkeley had a coach in 1677.

the colony, and Hugh Jones in 1722 declared that "most families of any note in Williamsburg had a coach, chariot, Berlin or chaise." In 1753, Francis Jerdone, a merchant of Yorktown, wrote [1] that "second hand goods were in no ways saleable in Virginia. Our gentry have such proud spirits that nothing will go down but equipments of the nicest and newest fashions. You'll hardly believe it when I tell you that there are sundry chariots now in this country which cost 200 guineas and one that cost 260."

As to the horses in use in the colony, Hugh Jones wrote in 1722: "Almost every ordinary person keeps a horse;" and in 1759 Burnaby declared: "The horses are fleet and beautiful, and the gentlemen of Virginia, who are exceedingly fond of horse-racing, have spared no expense or trouble to improve the breed of them by exporting great numbers from England." Brissot de Warville said in 1788: "The horses of Virginia are without contradiction the finest in the country, but they have doubled the prices of those in the Northern States."

Numerous laws have been passed on the subject of the roads during and since the colonial days, and there was never, in fact, any lack of roads in Virginia at any time, as they interlaced all parts of the country. The temptation has been to have too many roads, and the expense of maintaining them has proved too much for the scattered population of the country. Travelling in Virginia before the Revolution was very good nine months of the year, but in the winter months the roads, owing to the rains and ice, were generally bad. Of course, there were some roads that kept good all the year round, as for instance the roads from Yorktown to Williamsburg and Hampton, which a traveller in 1746 pronounced[2] better than most in England. Thus to quote a passage from this writer:

"The most considerable houses (in Yorktown) are of brick, some handsome ones of wood — all built in the modern taste, and the lesser sort of plaister. There are some very pretty garden spots in the town, and the avenues leading to Williams-

[1] *William and Mary Coll. Quart.*, XI., 238.
[2] *Itinerant's Observations in America* (London Magazine, 1746).

burg, Norfolk, etc., are prodigously agreeable. The roads are, as I said before, some of the best I ever saw, and infinitely superior to most in England. The country surrounding is thickly overspread with plantations, and the planters live in a manner equal to men of the best fortune, some of them being possessed of 500 or 1,000 a year sterling."

Table Diet. The mode of living was distinctively higher than in the Northern colonies. We are told of excellent gardens in Virginia at a very early date, and Jamestown Island was famous for its figs and Littletown for its peaches. In 1656, Hammond wrote:[1] " The country is full of gallant orchards," and besides fruits of many kinds, " the gallant root of potatoes is common, and so are all sorts of roots, herbes and Garden Stuff." " Beef, veal, milk, butter, cheese," and " other made dishes," pork, bacon and pigs, oysters and fish were plentiful. Poor people could not fare badly under such conditions, and though their diet was chiefly pork, corn bread and vegetables, this seemed to be quite as good as the fare in other colonies. In New England, as late as 1725, the popular dinner of the lower classes consisted of salt meat stewed with cabbage and other vegetables served on wooden trenchers.[2] The condition of things in Virginia during the last quarter of the eighteenth century is thus described by Beverley.[3] " Hogs swarm like vermin upon the earth, and are often accounted such, insomuch that when an inventory is taken by the executors the hogs are left out and not listed in the appraisement." " The Virginians have," said he, " plenty and variety of provisions for their table." They had abundance of beef, pork, turkeys, capons, ducks, oysters and venison. Their bread was either of wheat or corn. The soil of New England was too cold for melons and other fruit, but the Virginians had " all the culinary plants that grow in England, and in greater perfection than in England," besides " several roots, herbs, vine fruits and sallard flowers peculiar

---

[1] Hammond, *Leah and Rachael* (Force, *Tracts*, III., No. xix).
[2] Weeden, *Economic and Social History of New England*, 541.
[3] Beverley wrote his book in 1703, and it was published in 1705; and, therefore, his description of things may be taken to represent Virginia in the last quarter of the century.

to themselves." "The gentry pretend to have their victuals dressed and served up as nicely as if they were in London."

Education.[1] The benefit of schools was early recognized by the settlers, and one of the subjects discussed in the first assembly in 1619 was the establishment of a university at Henrico. Friends of the colony also raised funds for a free school to be established at Charles City, and lands were appropriated for the purpose and servants sent over; but an Indian massacre in 1622 destroyed both university and school. Nevertheless, the colony was not left without an educational system. Now as early as 1619 it was the custom of the richer classes to send their children to England for education, and afterwards the vestries of the different churches had the supervision of all poor children, and saw that they were taught reading and writing. The county courts had an annual " orphan's court," which looked after the vestries, and there are numerous orders in the vestry books and county court records having in view the education of children.

In 1635, the first free school was established, that of Benjamin Syms, located on a branch of the old Pocoson or Back River in Elizabeth county. In 1659, Thomas Eaton established a free school close to that of Benjamin Syms; and a fund amounting to $10,000, representing these two ancient charities, is used to carry on the Syms-Eaton Academy in Hampton. In 1655, Captain John Moon of Isle of Wight County left a legacy for the education of " poor fatherless children;" in 1659, Captain William Whittington left 2,000 pounds of tobacco for a free school in Northampton County; in 1668, Capt. Henry King of Isle of Wight County gave 100 acres of land for the maintenance of a free school; in 1675, Henry Peasley of Gloucester County gave 600 acres together with ten cows and a breeding mare; in 1691, Hugh Campbell, for the support of persons to teach school, gave 200 acres in each of three counties, Norfolk, Isle of Wight and Nansemond; and in 1700, William Horton endowed a free school in Westmoreland County.

Beverley, who wrote in 1703. says: "There are large tracts of land, houses and other things granted to free schools

[1] *William and Mary Coll. Quart.,* V., 219–223; VI., 1–7, 71–86, 171–186; VII., 1–9, 65–77.

for the education of children in many parts of the country, and some of these are so large that of themselves they are a handsome maintenance to a master; but the additional allowance which gentlemen give with their sons render them a comfortable subsistence. These schools have been founded by the legacies of well inclined gentlemen, and the management of them hath commonly been left to the direction of the county court or the vestry of their respective parishes."

After this time we learn of many such schools in the county records, the most interesting being Mrs. Mary Whaley's free school in York County established in 1706, Samuel Sanford's in Accomac established in 1710, and William Broadrib's in James City County, established about the same time. Whenever such schools were wanting, the citizens clubbed together and organized private schools, of which there were sometimes as many as four in a parish. In 1693, the college of William and Mary was established, and most of the leading Virginians were educated there. In the eighteenth century, there were many tutors employed by wealthy landowners, and many young planters attended the English universities. Jefferson wrote to Joseph C. Cabell in 1820 that "the mass of education in Virginia before the Revolution placed her among the foremost of her sister States." This is borne out by an examination of records published and unpublished.

The inventories preserved in the county books in Virginia show that nearly every independent settler from the very earliest times had a few books; and the marriage bonds prove that a large proportion of the population during the eighteenth century could read and write, a result doubtless due to the argus-eyed churchwardens, who reported to the court parents neglectful of their children.

There were several reasons why Virginia, despite its scattered population, was able to preserve so good an educational appearance in an age when the masses everywhere had limited opportunities. The great Puritan emigration to New England from 1628 to 1642 brought with it many Englishmen of the stamp of Winthrop and Bradford whose writings compare favorably with the best productions of their contemporaries in England. But after 1642 the emigration stopped, and New

England concentered became exceedingly narrow and isolated, so that native born New Englanders had little of the literary graces of their emigrant ancestors. The Theocracy that grew up cut society entirely off from the finer fields of poetry and art, and after Bradford and Winthrop there is no work of real literary excellence in New England down to the Revolution, except the history of Thomas Hutchinson. In Virginia, on the other hand, contact with the better opportunities of the mother country was continually kept up. All ministers were obtained from England, and, though their morals were not always of the best, they were necessarily university graduates. Then the emigration of teachers and men of cultivation from England was not for one generation, as in Massachusetts, but for many generations.

Particularly noticeable was the great cavalier emigration in 1649, and after that there was a constant succession of emigrants of wealth and leisure. The libraries of Virginia were superior to those of any other colony in numbers and literary value; and the native literary output, if not as abundant, was not inferior to that of Massachusetts. Parallel with Bradford and Winthrop as writers were John Smith, Ralph Hamor, John Rolfe, William Strachey, and George Sandys. Then to be noticed are the accounts of William Bullock, Henry Norwood, John Hammond, and the numerous documents and letters written during the eighteenth century by men like Yeardley, Wyatt, Ludwell, Moryson and other officials upon the affairs of the colony. At the dawn of the eighteenth century appeared the " History of Virginia," by Robert Beverley,[1] a writer described[2] by Professor Jameson, of the Carnegie Institution, as " the one American historian " of his time who was " not mentally annexed to Europe, but retained an original spirit." Later were the charming " Westover Manuscripts " of William Byrd, the " Present State of Virginia " by Rev. Hugh Jones, the " History of Virginia " by the accomplished William Stith, and the poems of Goronwy Owen, which, though written in the Welsh language, were composed in a frontier county of Virginia. Finally, we may quote what

[1] Son of Mayor Robert Beverley, of Bacon's Rebellion.
[2] Jameson, *Historical Writings in America*, 62.

a traveller, J. F. D. Smythe, wrote in 1773 in regard to colonial Virginia: "The first class are here more respectable and numerous than in any other province in America. These, in general, have had a liberal education, possess enlightened understandings and a thorough knowledge of the world that furnishes them with an ease and freedom of manners and conversation highly to their advantage in exterior, which no vicissitude of fortune or place can divest them of, they being actually, according to my ideas, the most agreeable and best companions, friends and neighbors that need be desired. The greater number of them keep their carriages, and have handsome services of plate; but they all, without exception, have studs, as well as sets of elegant and beautiful horses."

As there was no system of vestries and churchwardens in New England, some general education law like that of 1646 in Massachusetts proposing a system of common schools for the towns was a necessity. But this law, while it showed the good intentions of the lawgivers, was deficient in providing adequate machinery. Some of the larger towns levied taxes for the support of schools, but more generally the parents had to pay the teachers, and these were hard to get. So that oftentimes the order of the town meetings "to set up a school" this year was a mere formality.[1] Throughout the colonial period, in Massachusetts, teachers when obtained taught "but two or three months in the year," and "in most schools there was little progress beyond the elementary rudiments."[2] Few towns of Massachusetts escaped ·fines for neglecting their schools, and the records of town officers, and accounts preserved in private families, are "miserably illiterate."[3] As late as 1723 Harvard College Library contained no volumes from Addison or his fellows, nothing of Locke, Dryden, Smith or Tillotson. Shakespeare and Milton had been acquired recently.[4] That there was a large class of very ignorant people among the fishermen and small farmers of New England cannot be doubted, but that the fishermen were as degraded, as Mr. Adams said[5] in 1776; or that only

---

[1] Bliss, *Colonial Times on Buzzard's Bay,* 163.
[2] Weeden, *Economic and Social History of New England,* 283, 861.
[3] Bliss and Weeden.
[4] Weeden, 545.
[5] *Jefferson's Works* (Randolph's edition), I., 23.

one in ten of the men "could read writing, and still fewer could write," as the Baron Riedesel declared[1] in 1781, may well be doubted.

The people of Eastern Virginia came in part from South-western England, where the English slurred their "r's," which accounts for this phenomenon in some parts of Virginia. This element was found in early times, especially in the counties on the south of the James, and in Henrico county perhaps, which were practically colonies of the great south-western city of Bristol. Nevertheless, the bulk of the population, and especially the population on the north of the James, as far indeed as the great Potomac, were from *Middle Eastern* England, where the classic English language of Shakespeare prevailed.

It must be remembered that the great company of London merchants first controlled the colony, and the records of the old counties on the north of the James conclusively show that these London merchants were largely represented in that part of Virginia. The trade of the Peninsula counties and of the Gloucester, Rappahannock and Northern necks was, during the seventeenth century, almost entirely with the great English metropolis. In fact, the deeds and powers of attorney show that the population was largely from London and the environing counties — Middlesex, Essex, etc. There is perhaps, despite the universal neglect and injuries of war and fire, more evidence of refinement in Virginia preserved by means of tombstones, book-plates and records of libraries[2] than in any other of the colonies.

Moreover, there is plenty of evidence that the speech of the people of Virginia had from very early days comparatively little of the provincial or dialectic about it. A single witness suffices — the able professor of mathematics in the college of William and Mary in 1722 — Rev. Hugh Jones, A. M. In his " Present State of Virginia " he says that " the planters of Virginia, and even the native negroes, talk good English

---

[1] *Memoirs of the Revolution*, I., 226.

[2] Specimens of Virginia libraries have been published in *William and Mary Coll. Quart.* and the *Virginia Magazine.* John Eliot had the most comprehensive library in New England, between 1713 and 1745, but Eliot's library was largely exceeded by the libraries of William Byrd, Richard Lee, Charles Brown, William Dunlop and others in Virginia.

without idiom or tone, and discourse handsomely on most common subjects:" that they, in fact, looked down upon all Englishmen who did not come from London, affecting to be greatly amused at the jargon of persons from Bristol, the smaller cities in England, the rural districts, and from Scotland.

Criminal Code. Capital crimes were the common law offenses of rebellion, murder, arson, rape, crimes against nature, and house breaking, and in the first assembly selling fire arms to the Indians was made capital and afterwards horse stealing also. Persons were sent to prison, whipped and fined for religious opinions, but no one was ever put to death on that account. The same may be said of persons accused of witchcraft. The case of William Harding, of Northumberland County, who by order of the county court in 1656 was given ten stripes and banished from the county, was the worst case which has come under my notice.[1]

This comparative gentleness in an age when human passions were not held in subjection, as they are now by a more enlightened public opinion, finds curious expression in an act of the assembly passed the same year. A previous act had provided that criminal causes concerning life or member should be tried in the county court, " for the benefit and ease of the people." But in 1656 it was commanded[2] that the trial should take place in the quarter court, and the following was given as the reason: " We conceive it no ease nor benefitt to the people to have their lives taken away with too much ease. And though wee confesse the same to be done in England, yet wee know the disparity between them and vs to be so great that wee cannot with safety follow the example, for noe countrey (county) there but makes at least ten times the number of people here, and the juries there are more practised in criminall causes then (than), by the blessing of God, wee are here and have more to informe them in case they should err. And 'tis a maxim that *no deliberation can bee too much pondered that concernes the life of the meanest man."*

If two very respectable witnesses are to be believed, there

1 *William and Mary Coll. Quart.,* I., 127.
2 Hening, *Statutes at Large,* I., 397.

were very good reasons for a mild administration of the law in Virginia. John Hammond, the first of these in point of time, testified, in 1656, as follows:[1]

" I can confidently affirm, that since my being in England, which is not yet four moneths, I have been an eye witnesse of more deceits and villanies (and such as modesty forbids me to utter) than I either ever saw or heard mention made of in Virginia, in my one and twenty years aboad in those parts."

The other witness was Alexander Spotswood who in October, 1710, used this language to the bishop of London:[2]

" I shall conclude with doing justice to this Country as far as· my Discoverys have hitherto been able to reach, and declare sincerely to Yo'r Lord'p that I have observed here less swearing and Prophaneness, less Drunkenness, less uncharitable feuds and animositys, and less Knaverys and Villanys than in any part of the world where my Lot has been."

ALEXANDER SPOTSWOOD

Manufactures and Commerce. Many attempts to institute manufactures on a public scale were made in Virginia, but rural life was not favorable to their development. For private consumption, however, much cloth and other things were manufactured on the plantations, and about the time of the Revolution there was quite a number of iron factories, fulling mills, paper mills, and rope walks.

· Domestic commerce, in fact, was much more extensive than has been represented, for we are told that the rivers and creeks swarmed with small craft, all of which were made in Virginia. As early as 1690 ships of 300 tons were built,

[1] Hammond. *Leah and Rachel* (Force, *Tracts,* III., No. xiv).
[2] *Spotswood's Letters,* I., 27.

and afterward trade to the West Indies was conducted in small sloops of Virginia make.[1]   There are still many places on the rivers and creeks known as " Shipyards," and in 1693 Hon. Thomas Mathews presented to the county which bears his name (lying on Chesapeake Bay), a seal emblematic of " the mechanic inhabitants of the county of Mathews who have been in the habit of shipbuilding."[2]

Distinctions in Society.   The application of both official and conventional titles was a matter of careful observance in all the English colonies.   Only a small number of persons of the best condition had the designation of " Mr." or " Mrs." prefixed to their names, and this respect was always shown in Virginia to ministers, lawyers, justices of the peace, and vestrymen.   " Goodman " and " Goodwife " were the appropriate addresses of persons above the condition of servitude and below that of gentility.   In Virginia the term " Gentleman " was applied to men of large landed estates, and " Esquire " was strictly confined to members of the council and the sons of knights, of whom there were very few in the colony.   " Clerk " was a term descriptive not only of clerks of courts, but of ministers of the Gospel.

These remarks apply for the most part to the 17th century, for during the 18th century when negro slaves were substituted for white servants, race became a badge of aristocracy, and all free white men were addressed as " Mr;" and the poorer the white man the more he insisted on his independence and equality before the law.   Thus, in 1790, Marquis de Chastellux wrote that " a Virginian never resembles a European peasant," and, in 1842, Henry A. Wise explained[3] that " wherever black slavery existed, there was found at least (political) equality among the white population."

[1] Mair. *Bookkeeping Modernized*, 495.
[2] *Va. Magazine*, III., 313.
[3] *Congressional Globe*, 1841-1842, p. 173.

XIII.

POLITICAL CONDITIONS.

Divisions. The settlers of Virginia were mostly city people, and they naturally expected society to develop as in England; and, therefore, the political units were in the beginning settlements along James River called cities, boroughs, towns and hundreds. In 1619, these scattered settlements were gathered into four large corporations with a capital city in each.

I. The corporation of Elizabeth City (capital, Elizabeth City), extending from the bay up the river, on the south side, to about Chuckatuck Creek, and on the north side, to above Newport News.

II. The corporation of James City (capital, Jamestown), extending on the south side, from about Nansemond River to Upper Chippokes Creek, and on the north side, from Newport News to the Chickahominy River.

III. The corporation of Charles City (capital, Charles City, at the present City Point), extending, on the south side, from Upper Chippokes Creek to the beginning of the pale run by Dale, between the Appomattox and James rivers, so as to include Bermuda Hundred and Jones' Neck, and on the north side to Farrar's Island.

IV. The corporation of Henrico (capital, Henrico, on Farrar's Island), extending from Charles City corporation to the Falls.

Each corporation contained one or more boroughs, and each borough was represented by two burgesses in the general assembly, for the first time called in 1619.

This system of corporations did not continue long, because the wealth of water-courses and the cultivation of tobacco provoked separation and isolation, and society became very soon distinctly agricultural and rural. As a consequence, after fifteen years, borough representation was abandoned, and the whole colony was divided into eight counties or shires. All but two of these — Accomac on the Eastern Shore, over the bay, and Charles River County, subsequently York, on York River — were situated on James River, as follows:

I. Elizabeth City County, extending on both sides of Hampton Roads — on the south side to Chuckatuck Creek, and on the north side to Newport News, and including a small part thereof.

II. Warrascoyack County, subsequently, in 1637, Isle of Wight county, extending, on the south side, from Chuckatuck Creek to Lawne's Creek.

III. Warwick County, extending, on the north side, from Elizabeth City county to Skiffes (Keith's) Creek.

IV. James City County, extending on both sides of the river — on the south side from Lawne's Creek to Upper Chippokes Creek, and on the north side from Skiffes Creek to above Sandy Point.

V. Charles City County, extending on both sides of the river — on the south side from Upper Chippokes Creek to Appomattox River, and on the north side from Sandy Point to Turkey Island Creek.

VI. Henrico County, extending from Charles City County indefinitely westward.

In 1637, the part of Elizabeth City County lying on the south side of Hampton roads was made into New Norfolk County, which immediately after was divided into Lower Norfolk County and Upper Norfolk County (called in 1645–46 Nansemond county). In 1691, Lower Norfolk County was divided into Princess Anne and Norfolk counties.

In 1652, the south part of James City County was formed into Surry county. In 1702, the south part of Charles City County was formed into Prince George County. In 1720, the Chickahominy was made the boundary of James City and Charles City counties. In 1748, the southern part of Henrico was formed into Chesterfield County.

Government. The government under the first charter (1606) was that of a supreme council in England appointed by the king and a subordinate council in Virginia; and neither the London Company nor the settlers had any political authority. Under the second charter (1609) the government was centered in England in a treasurer and council, who selected a governor for Virginia having authority independent of the local council. The third charter (1612) vested the authority in England in the company, but the government in Virginia remained unchanged until 1619, when a popular assembly was called to share with the London Company in legislation.

In 1624, the London Company was abolished, and the government of the colony was vested in a governor and council, appointed by the king, and a general assembly composed of the governor and council and a house of burgesses elected by the people. The latter body gradually assumed the chief power, and for many years the governor and council acted a secondary part. The council, which was made up of the richest men in the colony, held three political relations: first they formed an advisory board, of which the governor was the executive; secondly, they formed a supreme court (styled originally the quarter court and afterwards the general court), of which the governor was chief justice; and thirdly, they acted as a senate, of which the governor was president; but they seldom originated legislation, and contented themselves for the most with revising the action of the house of burgesses. The governor's power was more in theory than in practice, for he seldom acted outside of the council meetings, where in all cases the majority controlled.

Suffrage.[1] Rural life, while it hindered co-operation, promoted a spirit of independence among the whites of all classes which counteracted the aristocratic form of government. Suffrage was looked upon not as a privilege, as in New England, but as a right, and down to 1670 every one above the condition of a servant voted for members of the house of burgesses. In that year suffrage was apparently limited to householders and freeholders, but as the law did not define the freehold, manhood suffrage remained practically the constitution of Virginia till 1736, when the first real restriction on the suffrage was made. Nevertheless, even after that time the proportion of voters in Virginia, as shown by Professor Jameson, was greater than in Massachusetts. To the influence of country life, which promoted the independence of the citizens, was added that of negro slavery, which made race and not wealth

[1] *William and Mary Coll. Quart.*, VI., 7-13; VII., 71-73; VIII., 81.

the great distinction in society.   In colonial Virginia there was, it is true, an aristocratic class who monopolized the offices, but their authority was a mere veneering on the social life, and went to pieces at the first shock of the Revolution.[1]

In New England, where there were annual elections, the government was in form more democratic than in Virginia, but in substance it was more aristocratic.[2]   There was a very limited suffrage in the different towns, and the peculiar forms of election made almost permanent the tenure of the office holders.   This was but natural, for it is the common experience of every one who has watched the proceedings of popular assemblies that the power is certain to be exercised by a few smart managers.   The ultimate consequences of society in Virginia and New England was seen after the Revolution, when for the first time the different communities had the opportunity of directing without foreign restraint the government of their country.   Virginia became the headquarters of the Democratic Republican party of popular ideas, and New England that of the Federalist party — the party of aristocratic ideas.

[1] Edmund Randolph, who was one of the F. F. Vs., referred to the influence of the aristocracy as "Little and feeble, and incapable of daring to assert any privilege clashing with the rights of the people at large."— Henry, *Patrick Henry,* I., 209.

[2] Weeden, in his *Social and Economic History of New England,* says that the New England institutions were "democratic in form but aristocratic in the substance of the administration."

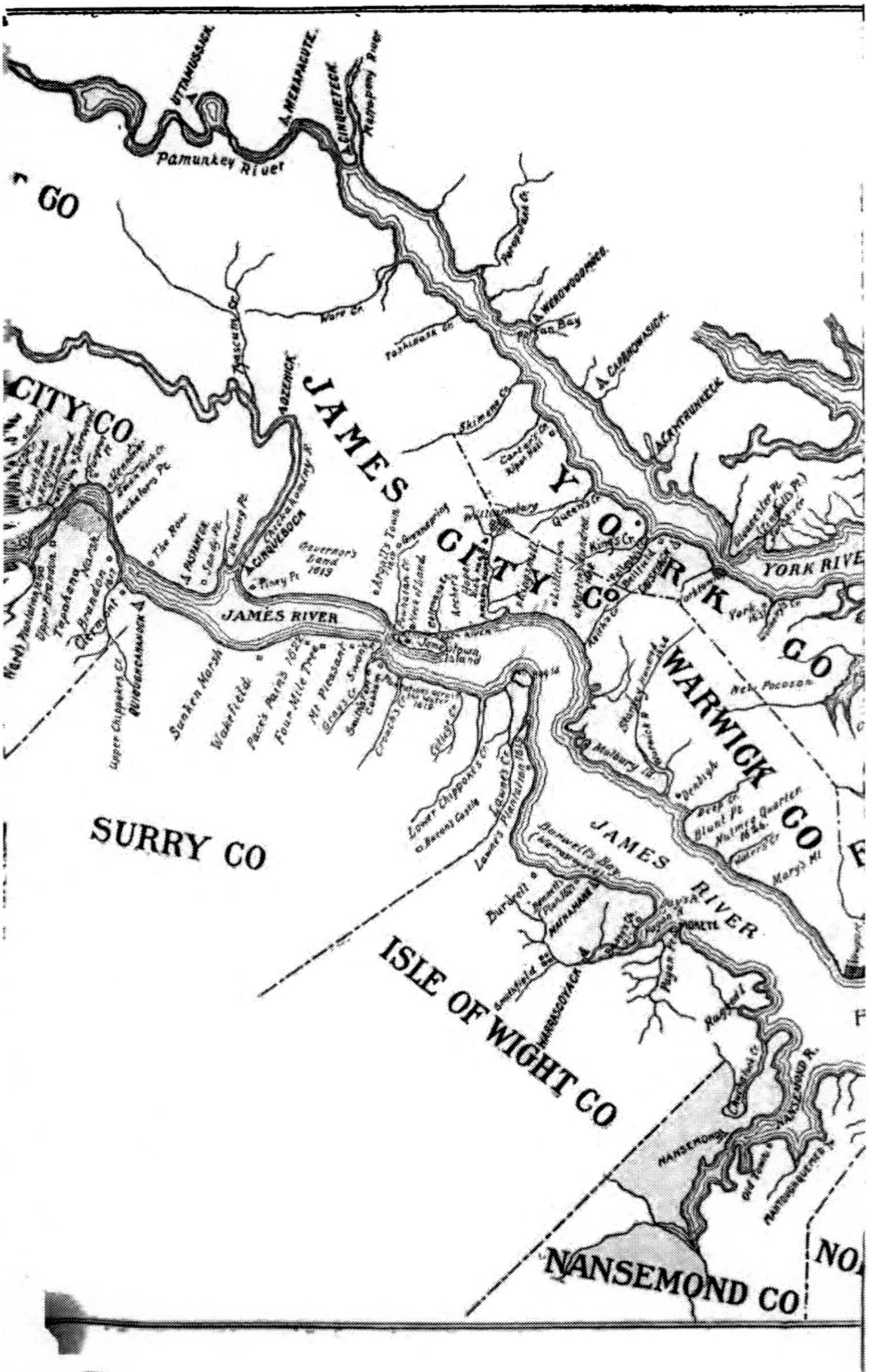

Pamunkey River
JAMES CITY CO
YORK CO
WARWICK CO
JAMES RIVER
YORK RIVER
SURRY CO
ISLE OF WIGHT CO
NANSEMOND CO
CITY CO
Jamestown Island
Governor's Land 1619

XIV.

(Named after King James I.)

Origin and History of Places Along James River.

The distance of Point Comfort to Richmond by the river is about 110 miles. The distance from Cape Henry to Richmond is about 127 miles.

South Side.

Cape Henry. Named in honor of Henry, Prince of Wales, son of James I. The cape opposite, separated by fifteen miles of water, is called Cape Charles, in honor of Prince Charles, another son, afterwards King Charles I. At Cape Henry, on April 26, 1607, the first settlers made their first landing. Three days later they set up a cross. In 1727, the establishment of a lighthouse was mooted in the general assembly of Virginia, but the first law in relation to it was not passed till 1752. Little or nothing was done under this law, and in 1772 the general assembly passed another act in conjunction with Maryland. In 1773, some rock and other material were brought to Cape Henry, but the American Revolution caused another delay. In 1789, Virginia ceded two acres at Cape Henry to the United States for a lighthouse, and not long after the structure, so many years in contemplation, was actually erected.

Chesapeake Bay. After passing the capes the visitor beholds the wide expanse of the bay of Chesapeake, which is an Indian name. The bay is 186 miles long, having an average width of twenty miles, and is a grand basin running parallel to the coast, which receives the waters of the James, York, Rappahannock, Potomac, Patuxent, Patapsco, Gunpowder, Susquehannah, Nanticoke, Choptank and several other rivers of Virginia and Maryland. Perhaps no bay in the world has such diversified scenery. The numerous rivers divide what is called Tide-water Virginia and Tide-water Maryland into long and narrow peninsulas, which are themselves furrowed by deep creeks, making numerous necks or minor peninsulas of land. Up these rivers and creeks the tide ebbs and flows for many miles.

Lynnhaven Bay. It appears on Smith's map as Morton's Bay, because here Matthew Morton and Captain Gabriel Archer were wounded by the Indians. Present name derived from the town of Lynn in England. It is at present famous for its oysters, said to be the finest in the world.

Hampton Roads. At Willoughby Point Chesapeake Bay connects with another bay called Hampton roads, into which discharge the waters of Elizabeth, Nansemond, James and Hampton rivers. This bay, which is one of the finest harbors in the world, receives its name from Henry Wriothesley, Earl of Southampton, treasurer of the London Company from 1620 to 1625, Hampton being a contraction for Southampton. Few men have a nobler memorial.

Willoughby Point. Named from Thomas Willoughby, a member of the Council from 1644 to 1650, who belonged to the family of Lord Willoughby, governor of Barbadoes.

Mason's Creek, which empties into Willoughby Bay, obtains its name from Captain Francis Mason, one of the leading settlers, who died about 1648.

Sewell's Point. From Henry Seawell, a burgess for Lower Norfolk county in 1639, now represented in Virginia by the descendants of his daughter Anne, who married Colonel Lemuel Mason. Sewell's Point is made by Elizabeth River and Tanner's Creek, which receives its name from Daniel Tanner, of Canterbury, England, who died on the creek in 1653, leaving a son John.

PRINCESS ELIZABETH.

Elizabeth River. Named for Princess Elizabeth, daughter of King James I., and afterward queen of Bohemia. Upon this river are situated the cities of Norfolk and Portsmouth. Norfolk was begun in 1680, when fifty acres for a town was condemned by the general assembly " on Nicholas Wise his land on the eastern branch of Elizabeth River at the entrance of the Branch." In 1705, it was given the name of Norfolk, and in 1736 granted a borough charter. During the Revolution it was burned, and its trade suffered very much by the results. It has a fine harbor and a population of 60,000.

Portsmouth is situated on the left bank of the Elizabeth River, immediately opposite to Norfolk, and was established in 1752 on the land of William Crawford; and is the seat of a U. S. naval hospital and navy yard. The Elizabeth River has three branches — Eastern, Southern and Western, and upon the Southern branch, twelve miles from Norfolk, occurred on December 9, 1775, the battle of Great Bridge, in which the Virginians under Col. William Woodford defeated the troops of Lord Dunmore, the royal governor.

Craney Island. This place, which, during the War of 1812, was fortified as a protection to Norfolk, received its name, at a very remote date, from an early resident of Norfolk county. Admiral Cockburn, with the British fleet, attacked it and was repulsed. In 1862, the Confederate iron-clad steamer Virginia, or Merrimac, was blown up in the waters nearby.

Nansemond River. From the Indians of that name, who had several towns upon it. Bennett's Creek, which derives its name from Governor Richard Bennett, who resided upon it, cuts off (Col. Thomas) Dew's point, where in 1680 the general assembly designated a town. The town did not materialize, and, in 1742, the general assembly established, about thirteen miles above "Old Town," the town of Suffolk, eighteen miles southwest of Norfolk. Suffolk is near the Dismal Swamp, which lies partly in Virginia and partly in North Carolina, and extends from north to south nearly thirty miles, and east and west about ten. In the interior is a beautiful lake called "Lake Drummond," which has been celebrated by Tom Moore, the poet of Ireland, in verses telling of the wanderings of a young man in search of his lady love:

> But oft from the Indian hunter's camp
> This lover and maid so true,
> Are seen at the hour of midnight damp,
> To cross the lake by a firefly lamp,
> And paddle their white canoe.[1]

[1] Howe, *Historical Collections of Virginia*, 403.

Chuckatuck Creek. About seven miles up the creek, on the road from Suffolk to Smithfield, is the village of Chuckatuck, an Indian name.

Naseway Shoals. From "Lt. Col. Tristam Norsworthy, of ye Ragged Islands in Virginia, Gent.," living in 1656. His name was originally pronounced "Nosory."

Pagan River. From "Pagan Point," probably so called because of the Indian village *Mokete,* on the south side ; originally Warrascoyack and afterwards New Town Haven River, and still later Pagan River. In 1680, a town was established on the left bank of the river about two miles from the mouth at "Pates field," not far from the site of the old Indian village of Warrascoyack. The spot is still known as "Old Town," and about four miles higher up the river is Smithfield, established in 1752 on the land of Arthur Smith. Within an hour's ride from Smithfield is an old church called St. Luke's, which, after having been deserted for a long time, has been lately rehabilitated and adorned with stained glass windows and memorial tablets. On the west side of Pagan River near its mouth was a tract of 300 acres patented by Captain Nathaniel Basse and others November 21, 1621. Here settlers were landed, but the low marshy country was very unhealthy to them, and many died. In 1622, the Indians killed twenty persons at *Basse's Choice.* Peter Knight patented it in 1640, and sold it to John Bland, who sold it to Thomas Taberer, who devised it in 1692 to his grandson, Joseph Copeland, of Isle of Wight county.

Day's Point. At the western point of Pagan River Bay, named from Captain James Day, formerly of London, who has left numerous descendants in Virginia.

Bennett's Plantation, or Warrascoyack. It was situated at the Rock Wharf on the present Burwell's Bay. Patented November 21, 1621, by Edward Bennett, a rich London merchant, in partnership with his brother, Robert Bennett, and nephew, Richard Bennett, governor of Virginia in 1652, and others. Edward Bennett's daughter, Silvestra, married Major Nicholas Hill, of Isle of Wight county. Another daughter, Mary, married Thomas Bland, whose daughter Mary married Captain James Day, of Day's Point. This early plantation became absorbed in the estate of Major Lewis Burwell.

Burwell's Bay. Named for Major Lewis Burwell (died 1710), who married Abigail Smith, niece of Colonel Nathaniel Bacon, Sr., and acquired, partly through his wife, a large estate in this quarter. Here Robert Burwell, his son, lived in a brick house two stories high, sixty feet long by twenty-six feet wide. Robert's only son, Nathaniel, was clerk of Isle of Wight from 1772 to 1787, and his daughter, Lucy, married Governor John Page, of Rosewell in Gloucester county, a patriot of the American Revolution.

Lawne's Plantation. In Isle of Wight county, patented by Captain Christopher Lawne and his associates. Captain Lawne arrived in Virginia April 17, 1619, and located his plantation near the mouth of Lawne's Creek (sometimes called " Lion's Creek "), which afterwards was made the dividing line between the counties of Surry and Isle of Wight. It was represented in the first general assembly by Captain Lawne and Ensign Washer.

Hog Island. It obtained its name as early as 1608 from being used by the colonists as a place for the safekeeping of hogs. Represented in the general assembly, 1624, by John Chew and John Utie, prominent colonists. John Bailey, who first settled at Berkeley Hundred in 1620, patented 600 acres here. He died before 1624, and his only daughter and heir, Mary Bailey, marrying Randall Holt, the island came into the Holt family, and continued their property for nearly 200 years. Of late years it was very much improved by Mr. E. E. Barney, and named " Homewood."

Lower Chippokes Creek. An Indian name. Enters James River on the west of Hog Island. Near by is an old brick house known as Bacon's Castle, erected about 1655 by Arthur Allen, ancestor of the late William Allen, of Clermont. It is probably *the oldest brick house* now standing in Virginia. During Bacon's Rebellion, it was fortified by Captain William Rookins, Robert Burgess, and other friends of Bacon.[1]

College Creek. On this creek there was a very old plantation known as the College plantation. How the name originated is not known, for it is not believed that any college was ever contemplated here. In August, 1667, " the great gust," or

---

[1] *William and Mary Coll. Quart.,* V., 189.

storm, which destroyed 15,000 houses in Maryland and Virginia, blew down at College Creek "three sixty-foot wall-plate tobacco houses," and one "fifty-foot rafted house." The two dwelling-houses, one "thirty foot" and the other "twenty foot" and a quarter "fifteen foot" withstood the fury of the storm. They had been erected by Anthony Stanford, merchant of London, and belonged at the time to Francis Newton, of Surry.[1]

Crouch's Creek. This creek, named for Lieutenant Richard Crouch, living in 1625, is situated nearly opposite to Jamestown Island, about five miles above Lower Chippokes Creek. In this quarter, in 1625, the poet George Sandys, then treasurer of the colony, had a settlement protected by a large stockade mounting one piece of ordnance. Among his other property were "a house framed for silkworms, a garden of an acre, and a vineyard of two acres." The total number of houses in this region in 1625 was eighteen dwellings, five stores, four tobacco houses, one stone house (the only one in the colony), and one silk house.[2]

Cobham. This place was established in 1772, at the mouth of Gray's Creek, but is now nearly deserted. It is a little west of "Scotland Wharf," the terminus of the Surry, Sussex and Southampton Railroad.

Gray's Creek. First called Rolfe's Creek, after Thomas Rolfe, son of Pocahontas, who had a plantation of 150 acres upon it "the gift of the Indian Kinge." In 1654, he sold the property to William Corker describing it as lying between "Smith's Fort old feild and the Divills woodyard swampe." "Smith's Fort" was two miles up the creek, on a bluff, and was probably the fort erected in 1608 to provide a refuge for the people at Jamestown in case of need.[3] In 1680, Smith's Fort was made by the general assembly the site of a town for Surry county. The creek gets its present name from Thomas Gray, who patented lands upon it in 1639, and is ancestor of numerous people in Virginia and other parts of the Union.

Swann's Point. From Colonel Thomas Swann, of the

[1] *William and Mary Coll. Quart.*, V., 190.
[2] Brown, *First Republic*, 623.
[3] *William and Mary Coll. Quart.*, V., 190.

council of Sir William Berkeley (1676), son of William Swann, an early settler. His son, Samuel, speaker of the North Carolina assembly, married Sarah, daughter of Colonel William Drummond, hanged for supporting Nathaniel Bacon, Jr., in 1676. Colonel Swann's tombstone with his coat-of-arms upon it was still to be seen a few years ago in a neighboring field. Here, in 1677, the commissioners sent over by the king to enquire into the causes of Bacon's Rebellion held court. This commission consisted of Colonel Herbert Jeffreys, Sir John Berry and Colonel Francis Moryson.

Four Mile Tree. This name preserves the memory of a tree on the south side of James River, which marked, in 1619, the western extremity on James River of the corporation of James City as defined by Governor Argall.[1] Here, in 1624, John Burrows patented 150 acres and called the place " Burrows' Hill." The place afterwards passed to one John Smith, whose executors sold the land, under the name of " Smith's Mount," to Col. Henry Browne, one of Sir William Berkeley's council, who in 1643 obtained a patent for 2,000 acres, including Pace's Pains. " Four Mile Tree plantation " remained in the Browne family for 200 years, and the handsome manor house is still standing. There is in the graveyard near the house the tombstone of Alice Jordan, daughter of John Miles of Branton, Herefordshire, and wife of Col. George Jordan, attorney general of Virginia in 1670. The tombstone states that Mrs. Jordan died January 7, 1650 (1651). There is only one older tombstone in Virginia — that of Col. William Perry at Westover, who formerly lived at Pace's Pains, and died in 1637. But the inscription on this tombstone is now entirely worn away.

Pace's Pains. Adjoining Burrows Hill was Pace's Pains, an estate of 600 acres planted by Richard Pace, Francis Chapman and Thomas Gates. In the massacre of 1622, Richard Pace saved Jamestown and many of the colonists. A converted Christian Indian, Chanco, who stayed with him, revealed the plot; and Pace, after securing his house, rowed off to Jamestown in the early morning and informed the governor. His widow, Isabella, married, secondly, Captain

[1] Brown, *First Republic*, 287.

William Perry, of the council. His son and heir was George Pace, who married Sarah, daughter of Captain Samuel Maycock, of the council, killed by the Indians in the massacre. George Pace moved to Captain Maycock's plantation, near Powell's Creek, in Prince George county, where his son Richard was living in 1659.

Wakefield. This was the residence of Nathaniel Harrison (1677–1727), and is distant about four miles from Upper Chippokes Creek.

Sunken Marsh. This is a very old name in the records, being found in the land books as early as 1642. In 1678, " Sunken Marsh Plantation " was one of the numerous plantations of the London merchant, John Bland, whose brother, Theodorick, was the founder of the prominent Virginia family of that name. It was situated opposite to Dancing Point on the other side of the river.

Clermont, and Upper Chippokes Creek. The Indian town of Quiyoughcohanock was near this creek, opposite to Paspahegh town on the other side. At a very early date Mr. Arthur Allen patented lands here on the east side of the creek, and his descendant Major William Allen, at the time of the war (1861–'65), owned 12,500 acres stretching along the river side. His brick residence " Clermont," pronounced " Claremont," is still standing, and gives its name to a town at the terminus of the James River Division of the Atlantic and Danville Railway.

Brandon. There are two Brandons in Virginia — Brandon on the Rappahannock, formerly the home of the Grymes family, and Brandon on the James, which last, as rich in soil as in memories, was patented in 1617 by Captain John Martin, one of the first council for Virginia, and the only man who protested against the abandonment of Jamestown in 1610, after the " Starving Time." In 1619, he sent to the first general assembly as burgesses from Brandon Mr. Thomas Davis and Mr. Robert Stacy, but that body would not allow them to sit, unless Martin would relinquish certain high privileges, which his patent conferred. Martin, then the only member of the original council living in Virginia, declined, and said: " I hold my patent for my service don, which noe

UPPER BRANDON (HARRISON)

LOWER BRANDON (HARRISON)

BACON'S CASTLE

CARTER'S GROVE (BURWELL)

newe or late comers can meritt or challenge." Martin's grant read: "He was to enjoye his landes in as large and ample manner to all intentes and purposes as any Lord of any Manours in England doth hold his grounde." He was afterwards fortunately induced to surrender this high authority.

Martin was son of Sir Richard Martin, and brother-in-law of Sir Julius Cæsar. His daughter, Dorcas, married Captain George Bargrave, son of Robert Bargrave, of Bridge in Kent. George Bargrave came to Virginia and was largely interested, with his brother, John Bargrave, in the trade of the colony. A Captain Robert Bargrave, as stated in a land grant in 1637, sold Martin's Brandon to Symon Sturgis, John Sadler and Richard Quiney, of London, merchants. In 1643, as stated in another grant, the general assembly confirmed to William Barker, John Sadler and Richard Quiney 4,550 acres known as "Martin's Brandon, between Chippokes Creek and Ward's Creek, due them by purchase from the heire of Captain John Martin, dece'd." So this Captain Robert Bargrave was doubtless a grandson of Captain John Martin. Brandon and Merchant's Hope, or Powell Brook, became the joint property of Richard Quiney and his brother-in-law, John Sadler.

The Quineys were from Stratford-on-Avon. Thomas Quiney married Judith, the daughter of William Shakespeare. Richard Quiney's wife, Ellen Sadler, daughter of John Sadler, was aunt of Anne Sadler, the wife of John Harvard, founder of Harvard College. Richard Quiney's moiety in Brandon, as well as in Powell Brook, descended to his son Thomas, who in his will left the same to his great-nephew Robert Richardson, and he in 1720 conveyed the same to Nathaniel Harrison, to whom the other moiety doubtless had not long before passed from the Sadlers.

The plantation has remained in the Harrison family ever since. It is divided into two estates — Lower and Upper Brandon. The house at Lower Brandon contains a collection of portraits of eminent persons, formerly the property of William Byrd, of Westover.

Ward's Creek. Captain John Ward came to Virginia in April, 1619, and was actively employed for several years with his ship in procuring fish and supplies for the colony. His patent seems to have called for 1,200 acres on the river side, and the land east of the creek which bears his name appears to have been included in a grant to Rice Hooe in May, 1638. Ward's plantation was represented in the first General Assembly by Captain John Ward and Lieutenant John Gibbs.

Flower dew Hundred. In 1618, Sir George Yeardley obtained a grant of 1,000 acres on the west side of a creek opposite to Weyanoke and called both creek and plantation " Flower dew Hundred." In 1619, the plantation was represented in the first general assembly by his nephew, Edward Rossingham and by John Jefferson, the ancestor of Thomas Jefferson. Sir George sold " Flower dew Hundred " before 1624 to Captain Abraham Peirsey, one of the leading merchants of Virginia. In that year there were on Peirsey's land (which included Windmill Point) twelve dwellings, three storehouses, four tobacco houses, and one windmill. Peirsey, who married Frances West, widow of Nathaniel West and daughter of Sir Thomas Hinton, died in 1627. After his death his widow married, thirdly, Col. Samuel Mathews, and his daughter Elizabeth married, first, Captain Richard Stephens and, second, Sir John Harvey, governor, and his daughter Mary married, first, Captain Thomas Hill and, secondly, Thomas Bushrod. Captain Richard Stephens' son, Captain Samuel Stephens, was the first husband of Lady Frances (Culpeper) Berkeley, wife of Sir William Berkeley. After Peirsey's purchase " Flower dew Hundred " was called " Peirsey's Hundred," but in 1635 Mrs. Elizabeth Stephens patented it as " Flower deue Hundred." Shortly afterwards, she sold it to William Barker, mariner.

At the close of the century, it was owned by Captain John Taylor, of Prince George county, who devised it to his daughters, Henrietta Maria and Sarah, who married respectively John and Francis Hardiman. They sold it to Joseph Poythress, and about the close of the century it became the property of John V. Willcox, whose descendants still own it.

Windmill Point. This in the early records is known as Tobacco Point, but it took its present name " Windmill Point " from a windmill established there, in 1621, by Sir George Yeardley, the first in the United States.

The Indians appear to have called the point Weyanoke Point.

Maycock's Plantation. This place is situated east of Powell's Creek, and was patented by Captain Samuel Maycock, who came to Virginia about 1618. He was made by Sir George Yeardley a member of his council, and continued as such under Sir Francis Wyatt till he was killed in the Indian massacre of 1622, when five others of the council perished. Among the killed at Captain Maycock's plantation of 200 acres adjoining Flower dew Hundred was Edward Lister, who came over in the *Mayflower* to Plymouth, Mass., and was a signer of the "Compact." After Captain Maycock's death, his daughter Sarah married George Pace of "Pace's Paines," whose father, Richard Pace, had saved Jamestown in 1622. There is a deed in the Charles City County records, by which "Richard Pace, of Powell's Creek, son and heir-apparent of George Pace, son and heire as the first issue by my mother Mrs. Sarah Macocke, wife unto my aforesaid father, both deced," confirms a sale of 800 or 900 acres "lying near unto Peirce's Hundred als Flower due Hundred" to Mr. Thomas Drew as per bill of his father, October 12, 1650. In 1723, John Hamlin sold "Maycock's," containing 250 acres, purchased of Roger Drayton in 1696, to Thomas Ravenscroft, of Wilmington Parish, James City County. In 1774, David Meade of Nansemond purchased 600 acres, including Maycock's. The land was poor except twelve acres about the house, but the situation was not inferior to any on the river. Meade was one of the earliest devotees of horticulture in the United States, and he arranged his twelve acres of fruitful ground in a way to produce the most charming and enchanting effect. "Forest and fruit trees are here arranged as if nature and art had conspired together to strike the eye most agreeably. Beautiful vistas which open many pleasing views of the river; the land thrown into many artificial hollows or gentle swellings, with the pleasing verdure of the turf, and the complete order with which the whole is preserved, altogether tend to form it one of the most delightful rural seats that is to be met with in the United States."[1]

---

[1] *Mass. Hist. Society Collections,* III., 90.

Powell's Creek. At the head of this creek on Flower dew Hundred Plantation was situated Weyanoke Indian Town. On the river was the plantation of Captain Nathaniel Powell, a valiant soldier, who came to Virginia among the first emigrants, and acted as governor on the departure of Samuel Argall in 1619. He married a daughter of Master William Tracy, but he and his wife and ten others were slain in the massacre March 22, 1622. His place of 600 acres lay on the west of Powell's Creek. Thomas Powell, of Powellton, Suffolk county, England, yeoman, his brother and heir, sold the estate to John Taylor, "citizen and girdler," of London, who in turn disposed of it to William Barker, mariner, Richard Quiney and John Sadler, merchants of London; and they in 1638 patented it (with 1,250 acres additional) as "Merchant's Hope, formerly known as Powle Brook." It finally passed to Nathaniel Harrison in 1720.

Near by there is still standing a very old brick church, known as Merchant's Hope Church. The courthouse of Prince George was first seated near the church on Chappell's Creek.

Chappell's Creek. Named for Thomas Chappell, who came to the colony in the ship of Captain William Barker in 1635. He has numerous representatives in the South.

Bicker's Creek. Named for William Bicker, or Bykar, killed in the massacre of 1622.

Chaplin's Choice. This place was first patented in 1619 by Captain Isaac Chaplin who represented it in the House of Burgesses. It lay east of Captain Woodlief's land, near Jordan's, and in 1686, Captain Nicholas Wyatt patented it anew, describing it as in area 361 acres, and as lying on James River between Parson's and Bicker's creeks. He states that it was for a long time in the possession of his late father, Captain Anthony Wyatt. By the burning of his father's house and that of the secretary at Jamestown, the original patent to Chaplin's had been lost.

Captain John Woodlief's Plantation. He was a member of the London Company, and came first to Virginia in 1609 from Prestwood in Buckinghamshire. When Berkeley, Thorpe, Tracey, Smith, and other Gloucestershire men, formed a company, he was empowered in 1619 to be governor of their new plantation at Berkeley Hundred. He afterwards settled on the south of the James, and left numerous descendants.

Jordan's Jorney, or Beggar's Bush. Captain Samuel Jordan, in 1619, patented at Jordan's Point on James River 450 acres, bounded by Captain Woodlief's land. At the time of the massacre in 1622, Captain Jordan gathered together his neighbors " at Beggar's Bush where he fortified and lived in despight of the enemy." He died the next year, when his widow Cecilly was courted by Captain William Farrar, after the minister Rev. Greville Pooley had received, as he alleged, a promise of marriage. The affair was brought before the council, who thought it of such ill consequence that they issued a proclamation prohibiting women in the future from contracting themselves in marriage to " two several men at the same time."

At Jordan's Jorney in 1676 the volunteers of Charles City County (Prince George County) had their encampment, previous to pressing Bacon into service to lead them against the Indians.

In 1677, the place had become the property of John Bland, of London, merchant; and nearly a hundred years later, was the residence of Richard Bland, " the antiquary," the first person to show in a formal pamphlet that America had no connection with England except the tie of the crown.

Bailey's Creek. From Temperance Bailey, who in 1626 had two hundred acres there.

City Point. This name is a contraction for Charles City Point, a public settlement begun by Sir Thomas Dale about Christmas, 1613. It was first known as Bermuda City, but the name was soon changed to. Charles City in honor of Prince Charles, afterwards King Charles I. In March, 1617, the three years' time of service of the incorporators of Bermuda City expired, and they being freed, " with humble thanks to God, fell cheerfully to their own particular labors."

Here it was, in 1621, that the company proposed to erect the East India School, which was to be a feeder to the college at Henrico.

The place is spoken of in the records of Prince George county in 1720 as " City Point," i. e., " Charles City Point." On April 24, 1781, the British force landed here under General Phillips and captured Petersburg.

In the war of 1861–65 it was an important military depot for the army of General Grant, who had his headquarters here. At City Point is the residence of the Eppes family, called " Appomattox," which has been in the Eppes family since it was first patented by Colonel Francis Eppes in 1635. President Lincoln was here on a visit to General Grant when Richmond was evacuated. It is connected with Petersburg by a railroad.

Appomattox River. Up the Appomattox is a number of fine old plantations: *Cawsons,* formerly a seat of the Blands, and the birthplace of John Randolph; *Conjurer's Neck,* the seat of the Kennon family; *Broadway,* named for Alexander Broadway, an early settler; and *Matoax,* a mile from Petersburg, which was the residence of John Randolph, father of John Randolph, of Roanoke. At the Falls of the Appomattox is *Petersburg,* founded in 1733 by Peter Jones, a descendant of Col. Abraham Wood, an early patentee for land in the neighborhood.

Bermuda Hundred. This place lies in Chesterfield county, near the mouth of the Appomattox, across from City Point. It was laid out by Sir Thomas Dale at the same time as Bermuda City, or Charles City. He named the place Bermuda Hundred " by reason of the strength of the situation," which likened it to those coral girt islands, the Bermudas. He annexed to it many miles of " champion and wood land in several hundreds, as Rochedale Hundred (afterwards known as the Neck of Land in Charles City, and now as Jones' Neck), the Upper and Nether Hundreds (Curls Neck and Bermuda), West's Sherley Hundred (Shirley)and Digges' Hundred."

In the first general assembly the plantations of Bermuda Hundred, Sherly Hundred and Charles City were represented by Samuel Sharpe and Samuel Jordan.

On May 2, 1781, the British forces under Generals Phillips and Arnold, returning from their attack on Petersburg, embarked at Bermuda Hundred.

For many years previous to the war, before the upper portion of the river was deepened, this was an important shipping point, and was the port of Richmond for large vessels.

In 1864, General Butler, with a force of thirty thousand men, was, in the language of General Grant, " bottled up " here by the Confederates, and just outside of this peninsula may still be seen many heavy outworks thrown up by him. Bermuda Hundred is now the terminus of the Farmville and Powhatan Railroad.

Neck of Land, or Rochedale Hundred. This place is now known as Jones' Neck, and was a part of Dale's settlement in 1613. It was first called Rochedale Hundred and afterwards " Neck of Land in Charles City " to distinguish it from " Neck of Land " in James City County. A creek on the western side still retains the name of Rochedale Creek.

On the west side of Jones' Neck is " Meadowville," the handsome estate of Mrs. Edward E. Barney, originally called " Woodson's," being the original seating place of Robert Woodson, the first emigrant ancestor of the Woodson family of Virginia.

Gatesville and Osborne's. In 1720, the name of Dale Parish was given very appropriately to that part of Henrico County on the south side of the river, the scene especially of Dale's labors.

The glebe of Dale Parish (one hundred acres) was opposite to the present Farrar's Island, and, in 1761, an act was passed authorizing the division of this land into lots for a town to be called *Gatesville* (in honor of Sir Thomas Gates, who was Sir Thomas Dale's superior officer). In April, 1781, the British forces captured and destroyed here about twenty-five vessels loaded with tobacco, flour, etc. On April 27, 1781, after a hot action with the British, the vessels of the small Virginia navy then in James River were captured and destroyed about four miles above Gatesville. After this, the little town of Gatesville, ceased to be mentioned, and the wharf near by is now known as Osborne's. For a number of years this was the shipping point for coal from the Clover Hill mines, in Chesterfield County.

Coxendale. This is the bend west of the bend called Farrar's Island across the river. When Sir Thomas Dale set to work in 1611 to build his city at Henrico, he ran a pale across this neck and secured it by several forts: Charity Fort, Elizabeth Fort and Fort Patience. He also built a retreat or guest house for sick people, called Mount Malado — which appears on Fry and Jefferson's map (1751) under the spelling of " Mt. Malawdy." In Coxendale Alexander Whitaker, son of the celebrated Dr. William Whitaker, a Puritan divine, had his parsonage.

Proctor's Creek. This creek gets its name from " Mistrisse (Alice) Proctor a proper ciuill modest gentlewoman," who, in 1622, defended her plantation here against the savages with great bravery. She afterwards refused to obey the order of the council to abandon her house, and would not retire till the officers had threatened to burn it down. She was the wife of John Proctor, an early settler.

Sheffield's Plantation. Three miles from Falling Creek. Thomas Sheffield, the first proprietor, was slain here by the Indians in 1622. About 1770, the place was the residence of Seth Ward and his family.

Drewry's Bluff. The Confederates had here strong fortifications during the war of 1861–1865, which were the means of inflicting a severse repulse, in 1862, upon the Federal fleet, including the iron clad Monitor.

Falling Creek. This creek was the *site of the first iron works in America.* In 1619, Sir Edwin Sandys informed the London Company of one Mr. King, who was to go with fifty persons to Virginia and set up iron works there, and the same year 150 expert workmen, chiefly from Warwickshire and Staffordshire, were sent over. The works cost the company four thousand pounds, the equivalent of one hundred thousand dollars in present money, and were first under the charge of Captain Bluett; but, he dying shortly after his arrival, the care of the iron industry was committed to John Berkeley, son of Sir John Berkeley, of the castle and manor of Beverston, in Gloucestershire, an eminent branch of the noble family of the Berkeleys of Berkeley Castle. The iron was made from bog ore found in the vicinity, and it was reported that " no better iron existed in the world." Unfortunately, in 1622, the works were broken up by the Indians, who killed

Berkeley, and all his employees, except a boy and a girl, who managed to hide in the bushes. Colonel Archibald Cary owned mills upon the creek at the time of the Revolution, which were destroyed by Tarleton; and a mill still exists near a picturesque little fall.

Ampthill. This was the estate of Colonel Archibald Cary, chairman of the committee of the Virginia Convention which drafted, in 1776, the Declaration of Rights and State Constitution — the first in America. The house, a fine square brick building, is still standing.

Warwick. The chimney standing on the right bank of the river near Ampthill marks the old site of the village of Warwick, established in the twenty-second year of the reign of George II. While the bar in the river above remained, it was a place of much importance. At the time of the Revolution there were here mills, warehouses, storehouses, rope-walks and a ship-building yard, which were all destroyed by the British in 1781. Chastellux, who was here in 1782, describes it, nevertheless, as a charming spot, "where a group of handsome houses form a sort of village, and there are several superb ones in the neighborhood, among others that of Colonel Cary, on the right bank of the river, and Mr. Randolph's on the opposite shore."

Goode's Creek. Named from John Goode, who was a supporter of Bacon in 1676. The name of his place is "Whitby," through which the creek runs.

NORTH SIDE.

The Falls, and Richmond. After the landing at Jamestown Island, May 14, 1607, President Wingfield, in accordance with instructions from the London Company, sent a body of men in a shallop to discover the part of the river above them. They left Jamestown May 21, 1607, under Captain Newport, and six days later arrived at an Indian town called Powhatan, consisting of some twelve houses pleasantly situated on a hill. Below it were three fertile islands, and it was separated from the river by a meadow of 200 acres, in which were planted Indian corn, tobacco, pumpkins, gourds and other vegetables. The town was distant three miles from the Falls, and the description of the place corresponds with either the present " Marin Hill," or " Tree Hill " plantation. It was the native country of Powhatan, but the chief here, in 1607, was Parahunt, a son of Powhatan, called Tanxpowhatan (Little Powhatan).

After the arrival of the Third Supply in August, 1609, Captain John Smith, in the absence of Sir Thomas Gates, the new governor, sent Captain Francis West with one hundred men to form a settlement at the Falls. West purchased a site from the Indians in a low place subject to overflow, now known as Rocketts, and called his settlement Fort West. After a time Captain John Smith came up the river, and finding West absent ordered the settlers to move to the hill on which the Indian town was situated, which he purchased from the Indians, and called " Nonsuch." After a while West returned, and not liking Smith's interference ordered the company back to their original settlement. But here they were attacked by the Indians, and the colonists returned to Jamestown.

After the second massacre, in 1644, a fort was built near this place. It was rebuilt in 1676, but was soon abandoned.

Finally Captain William Byrd became possessed of much of the land in this vicinity; and his son, Colonel William Byrd, had at the Falls several mills. In 1742, Richmond, having been surveyed by Col. William Mayo, was established as a town on land belonging to Colonel Byrd. A mile from Richmond is a place called Powhatan, long the home of the Mayos, who came from Barbadoes to Virginia.

Gillee's Creek. Named for Gilleygrow Marin, living in 1769.

Tree Hill. Formerly the residence of Colonel Miles Selden (died May 18, 1811), and for a long time celebrated for its race-track.

Chatsworth. This was formerly the seat of Colonel Peter Randolph (son of Colonel William Randolph, Jr.), member of the council and surveyor-general of the customs (died 1767). The last male of this immediate branch was Mr. William B. Randolph, who died since the war. This was the birthplace of Beverley Randolph, governor of Virginia; of Colonel Robert Randolph, of *Eastern View*, Fauquier County, Va., ancestor of the present Bishop Randolph, of Virginia; and of Mrs. Fitzhugh, of " Chatham," grandmother of Mrs. General Robert E. Lee.

Wilton. Colonel William Randolph, son of Colonel William Randolph, of Turkey Island, built the present brick mansion early in the eighteenth century. It stands nearly opposite to Falling Creek, on the opposite side of the river. The best known of his descendants who lived here was Innes Randolph, the poet, and Anne Randolph, who married Colonel Benjamin Harrison, of Brandon, a member of the first State executive council (1776). She was a noted belle of the period just prior to the Revolution, and was referred to as Nancy Wilton.

Chaffin's Bluff. Fortified by the Confederates in 1861–65. Next below is " Newstead," location of the Confederate signal station.

Farrar's Island, and Dutch Gap. In June, 1611, Sir Thomas Dale went up James River to search for a new site for the chief town, the London Company having become dissatisfied with Jamestown. The privy council had already named the proposed site, " Henrico," in honor of Henry, oldest son of King James I. In September, 1611, with permission from Sir Thomas Gates, who had in the meantime arrived as governor, Dale went up to Henrico, and began the settlement on the peninsula (now an island), known afterwards as Farrar's Island, after William Farrar, who patented it. He cut a ditch across the neck (Dale's Dutch Gap), such as he had learned to make while campaigning in Holland, and strongly faced it with palisades. There were in the town three streets of framed houses, and a church of timber. The foundations of the houses were of brick made on the spot by the brickmakers brought by Gates from England. For the town's security, there were five block houses upon the verge of the river. In the main, two miles from the town, they ran a pale from river to river two miles long and, on the other side of the river, they impaled the bend west of Henrico called Coxendale. Henrico was distant from Bermuda Hundred by water fourteen miles, but by land only five miles.

In the first general assembly Henrico and Coxendale, together with Arrohateck just above Henrico, was represented by John Dowse and John Polentine. But the place did not flourish, and it was reported as containing in 1619 only "two or three old houses, a poore ruinated church, with some few poor buildings."

At Henrico it was proposed in 1619 to build a college, and ten thousand acres of land were appropriated to the purpose. The first rector was to be the Rev. Patrick Copland, while George Thorpe was made superintendent of the buildings and plantation. The Indians, in 1622, put a stop to the project by almost wiping the place out of existence, and Virginia waited many years for a college. Finally, in 1693, Dr. James Blair, who was minister of this same parish from 1685 to 1694, inspired doubtless by the early memories of the place, consummated the original design, though the general assembly chose Williamsburg, many miles distant from Henrico, as the seat of the college.

In this locality the river makes great loops, and to avoid the Confederate battery at the extreme end of Farrar's Island, called Howlett's house battery, General Butler attempted, in 1864, to deepen Dale's old ditch or gap, so as to admit a passage from the rear to the river above. The work, however, owing to the Confederate sharp-shooters, was not completed at this time, but in 1871–72 the United States government deepened it to its present practicable condition, and thus reduced the distance to Richmond by seven miles.

Varina. A little more than a mile below the Dutch Gap Canal is *Varina*, so named, it is said, because of the superior character of the tobacco raised in the neighborhood, which resembled a high-price Spanish tobacco called *Varina*. This was long the county-seat of Henrico, and here, it is said, resided, after their marriage, John Rolfe and Pocahontas. At Varina was also the glebe of Henrico Parish, where resided James Blair, who founded William and Mary College, and William Stith, another of its presidents, who wrote the *History of Virginia*. Some forty years ago the sites of the glebe, court-house, jail and tavern were pointed out. Under the name of Aiken's Landing, Varina was well known during the war of 1861–65 as a place of exchange of prisoners.

Four Mile Creek. Opposite to the point of "The Neck of Land," or Jones' Neck. It receives its name from its distance — four miles — from Henrico (Farrar's Island).

Curls Neck. This place obtains its name from the surprising
" curls " which the river makes in this locality. To go six
miles from Farrar's Island to City Point, the river takes a
course of sixteen miles. Curls Neck was at first divided into
a number of small farms, which gradually became consolidated.
Chief among the inhabitants here in 1676 was the famous
Nathaniel Bacon, Jr. In 1698, William Randolph of Turkey
Island patented two certain tracts of land in the county of
Henrico — one tract called " Curles, formerly Longfield," the
other called the " Slashes," containing together twelve hundred
and thirty acres, " *late in the seizin and inheritance of Nathaniel
Bacon, Jun., Esq., dece'd, and found to escheat to his most
sacred Majesty by the attainder of the said Nathaniel Bacon,
Junr., of high treason.*" William Randolph purchased the land
for one· hundred and fifty pounds. " Longfield," originally
containing 400 acres, was first patented by Edward Gurgany
October 1, 1617, and was bequeathed, in 1619, by his widow,
Ann Gurgany, to Captain Thomas Harris, who patented it with
300 acres additional in July, 1637.

William Randolph, of Turkey Island, became the owner of a
large part of the Neck, and he left it to his son, Richard Randolph, grandfather of John Randolph of Roanoke. In later
years the estate, containing 3,000 acres, became one of the
numerous plantations of Major William Allen, of Clermont.
The present owner is Charles H. Senff, Esq.

Bremo, and Malvern Hill. Bremo was patented by Colonel
Richard Cocke in 1639, and continued the residence of the
Cockes for nearly 200 years. Near by, just back of Turkey
Island, is another estate of the Cockes, called " Malvern Hill,"
after some hills in England of that name, which divide the
counties of Hereford and Worcester. The old dwelling house
at Malvern Hill is still standing, and is described as " one of
the best specimens of colonial architecture." It was here that
one of the most sanguinary conflicts of the war took place in
1862 between the armies of General George B. McClellan and
General R. E. Lee.

Turkey Island. A short distance below Bremo is Turkey
Island Plantation. so called because the first explorers up the
river found in the neighborhood an island having many turkeys

upon it. But the description seems more applicable to the peninsula opposite, called Presque Isle, or Turkey Island Bend.

In 1676, Turkey Island was owned, in part at least, by Colonel James Crews, one of Bacon's most loyal friends, who was hanged at the glass house near Jamestown by Sir William Berkeley. In 1684, his heirs — Sarah Whittingham, wife of William Whittingham, of London, Gent., and daughter of his brother Edward Crews, and Matthew Crews, "citizen and haberdasher of London," son of his brother Francis

SIR JOHN RANDOLPH.

Crews — sold the land (600 acres) to William Randolph, "late of Warwickshire in England," a half-nephew of the poet Thomas Randolph and founder of the eminent Virginia family of Randolphs.

William Randolph married Mary Isham, daughter of Henry Isham, of Bermuda Hundred, and granddaughter of William Isham, of Northamptonshire, in England. He had issue, nine children: (1) William, of Turkey Island; (2) Thomas, of Tuckahoe, in Goochland

LADY SUSANNA RANDOLPH.

County; (3) Isham, of Dungeness, in Goochland; (4) Sir John, of Williamsburg, an eminent lawyer; (5) Colonel Richard, of Curls Neck; (6)

Elizabeth, who married Richard Bland, of Jordan's; (7) Mary, who married John Stith, and was mother of William Stith, president of William and Mary College; (8) Edward, a sea captain; (9) Henry, who died, unmarried, in England. William Randolph was the common ancestor of Thomas Jefferson, John Marshall, Robert E. Lee and Edmund Randolph. The old dwelling-house at Turkey Island was destroyed by the gunboats of General McClellan, when he took refuge here with his army after "the Seven Days' Battles." At one time during the late war the estate was owned in part by General George E. Pickett.

ROBERT CARTER.

Shirley. This place was first occupied in 1613, when Sir Thomas Dale established Bermuda Hundred. It was called originally West-and-Sherley-Hundred. It was originally the property of Thomas West, Lord Delaware, and his three brothers, Captain Francis West, Captain Nathaniel West, and Captain John West, who all resided in Virginia. Thomas West, Lord Delaware, married Cecilly, daughter of Sir Thomas Sherley. In 1664, 2,544 acres at Shirley Hundred were patented by Major Edward Hill, Sr., a man of great prominence in the colony. The land was inherited by his son Colonel Edward Hill, Jr., who left a son, Colonel Edward Hill, and two daughters, Hannah, who married Edward Chilton, the attorney-general, but died without issue, and Elizabeth, who married John Carter, secretary of state, and son of Robert (King) Carter. Colonel Edward Hill, third of the name, died in 1720 without children, and Shirley descended to his sister Elizabeth Carter, and has since remained in the Carter family. This was the birthplace of Anne Hill Carter, wife of "Light Horse" Harry Lee, and mother of General Robert E. Lee. The plantation is one of the finest in Virginia, and the buildings, which were erected about the beginning of the eighteenth century, are elegant examples of colonial architecture. Among the portraits at Shirley is an excellent one of Washington by Peale.

Cawsey's Care. Nathaniel Causey was an old soldier, who came in the First Supply in January, 1608, and patented 200 acres, called "Cawsey's Care," on Kimage's Creek December 10, 1620. John Causey sold this land in 1634 to Colonel Walter Aston, son of Walter Aston, of Longden, Stafford County, England. The latter patented, August 12, 1642, 1,040 acres on Kimage's Creek, of which Cawsey's Care was part. Colonel Aston left a son, Walter, who, in 1666, devised the estate to Mr. George Harris, of Westover, merchant. He died without issue, and Cawsey's Care fell to his brother, Thomas Harris, of London, merchant. This last sold the estate to Colonel Thomas Grendon, Jr., who by his will, proved December 3, 1684, devised the same to William Byrd, Jr., son of William Byrd, whereupon it became absorbed in the Byrd estate.[1] Sarah Grendon, the wife of Colonel Thomas Grendon, Jr., was one of the heroines of Bacon's Rebellion, being the only woman excepted from pardon in the act of "indemnitie and free pardon," passed in 1677.

Berkeley. On February 3, 1619, the London Company granted to Sir William Throckmorton, Sir George Yeardley, Richard Berkeley, George Thorpe and John Smith, of Nibley, a plantation in Virginia, which became known as Berkeley Hundred. On December 4, 1619, *The Margaret* arrived from Bristol at Jamestown, bringing thirty-five passengers, under the conduct of Captain John Woodlief. These were the first settlers of the "Town and Hundred of Berkeley," which was located between West-and-Sherley's Hundred and Westover. William Tracy, to whom Sir William Throckmorton assigned his interests, and George Thorpe came over in person and succeeded Captain Woodlief in the management of the settlement.[2] In 1621, Rev. Robert Pawlett, a kinsman of Lord Pawlett, was preacher at Berkeley Hundred. But in the massacre of 1622 nine persons were killed there, and the plantation was tempor-

---

[1] *William and Mary Coll. Quart.*, IV., 148.
[2] John Smith of Nibley, *Papers* in Bulletins of New York Public Library, 1899.

APPOMATTOX. (Epes)

MALVERN HILL. (Cocke)

SHIRLEY (Carter)

arily abandoned. In 1636, the plantation was patented anew by Captain William Tucker, Maurice Thompson, George Thompson, William Harris, Thomas Deacon and Cornelius Loyd, of London, merchants, and Jeremiah Blackburn, of London, mariner, who had purchased it from the " adventurers of the company of Berkeley Hundred." It was described as consisting of 8,000 acres, bounded east by the land (Westover) of Captain Thomas Pawlett (brother of Lord Pawlett), and on the west by King's Creek, and extending back into the woods. After some years their interests passed to John Bland, of London, merchant, whose only son, Giles, resided here till his execution in 1676 for complicity with Bacon. After this the estate went to Benjamin Harrison, the third of that name, who died April 10, 1710. It descended then to Col. Benjamin Harrison, speaker of the House of Burgesses, who died in 1744, and at the time of the Revolution was owned by his son, Benjamin Harrison, who was one of the signers of the Declaration of Independence, and father of William Henry Harrison, president of the United States, born at Berkeley, February 9, 1773.

Berkeley is better known to Northern soldiers and people as Harrison's Landing, headquarters of General McClellan after his retreat from Malvern Hill. At that time there were no less than 600 war vessels and transports anchored in the river near by, and the river shore for miles was covered with the camps of soldiers.

The handsome brick house of the Harrisons is still standing.

Westover. During the summer of 1619, Captain Francis West selected the site of Westover for the lands of Henry West, fourth Lord Delaware, son and heir of his brother, Thomas West, third Lord Delaware, governor of Virginia. The three brothers of Lord Delaware (who all acted as governors of Virginia), had separate plantations here — Captain Francis West, Captain John and Captain Nathaniel West. Only Captain John West is known to have left descendants in Virginia. His son, Colonel John West, of West Point, was the first child of English parents born on York River.

In 1622, six persons fell beneath the tomahawk at Westover. In February, 1633, the representative for Westover and Flower dew Hundred was Captain Thomas Pawlett, who, in January, 1637, patented 2,000 acres of the plantation called Westover.

Pawlett was brother of the first Lord Pawlett, and was born about 1578, and came to Virginia in 1618. He appeared in the first American assembly at Jamestown as a representative from " Argall's Gift."

Pawlett's grant describes the place as " 2,000 acres in Charles City County, bounding to the river south, northward to the main, eastward to the land of Captain Perry, west upon Berkeley Hundred land, extending by the river side from Herring Creek to a gut dividing Westover from Berkeley."

Captain Thomas Pawlett died in 1644, and his brother Lord John Pawlett, in 1666, sold Westover to Theodorick Bland, brother of John Bland, merchant, of London.

Theodorick Bland died in 1674, when the Westover tract went to his sons Theodorick and Richard Bland. In 1688, they conveyed 1,200 acres to William Byrd, Esq., son of John Byrd, goldsmith, of London, for three hundred pounds English money, and 10,000 pounds of tobacco.

WILLIAM BYRD, OF WESTOVER.
Fellow of the Royal Society.

Captain Byrd took part with Bacon during the civil war in 1676. He was living at that time near Richmond, and was Bacon's neighbor. At Westover, in 1690, he built a wooden residence, and died there in 1701.

He was succeeded by his son, Colonel William Byrd, who was by long odds the most accomplished man in America — statesman, scholar and fellow of the Royal Society. He built the present noble brick mansion at Westover, and gathered about him the finest library on the continent. He wrote several very entertaining tracts upon Virginia, which have no equal in colonial literature for grace of style and composition.

Buckland. This settlement adjoined Westover and contained the plantation of Captain George Menifie, of the council (who in 1635 took a prominent part in deposing Harvey), and of Captain William Perry (died August 6, 1637), who married Isabella, widow of Richard Pace, of Pace's Pains. Captain Henry Perry, son of Captain William Perry, married the daughter of Captain George Menifie, and became possessed of the whole of Buckland. Captain Perry left two daughters — Elizabeth, who married John Coggs, of Rainslipp, Middlesex County, England, and Mary, who married Thomas Mercer, a stationer of London.

In 1766, Buckland, containing 10,000 acres, was the property of Colonel William Cole.

This place, or a part of it, is now owned by the Willcox family, of Charles City County.

Swineyards. This place probably gets its name from Thomas Swinhow, whose wife and sons, together with four other persons, were slain in the massacre of 1622. The name of the place appears variously as "Swinhows," "Swiniares," "Swineherds," "Swineyards." It was owned in 1769 by Colonel William Cole, who also owned Buckland at that time.

Weyanoke. This place was called by the Indians "Tanks Weyanoke" (Little Weyanoke), to distinguish it from the territory from Appomattox River down to Powell's Creek on the south side of James River, which was called "Great Weyanoke." In 1617, Opechancanough presented to Yeardley a large tract of land at Weyanoke, and, in 1619, the London Company confirmed the gift. In their deed they described it as containing "twenty-two hundred acres, all that piece of marsh ground called Weyanoke, and also one other piece and parcell of land adjoining to the said marsh, called by the natives Kenwan, one parcel thereof abutteth upon a creek called Mapsock to the east, and the other parcell thereof towards a creek, there called Queen's Creek, on the west, and extendeth in breadth to landward from the head of said creek called Mapsock up to the head of said creek called Queen's Creek (which creek, called Queen's Creek, is opposite to the point there which is now called Tobacco Point, and abutteth south upon the river and north to the landward)."

About 1624, Sir George Yeardley sold Weyanoke and Flower dew Hundred, on the opposite side of James River, to Captain Abraham Peirsey. In 1665, Joseph Harwood located a grant in Weyanoke, and the place descended for many years in the Harwood family. Major Samuel Harwood was a distinguished member of the convention of 1776. The land descended, in part at least, to his descendants, the Douthats, who still reside there.[1]

Southampton Hundred. This land ran from " Tanks Weyanoke " to Chickahominy River, and contained about 80,000

COMMUNION CUP OF
SMITH'S HUNDRED.
(The oldest church plate
in America.)

acres. It was located in 1617 by a powerful association in England, of whom Sir Thomas Smith was the head. The hundred was at first known as " Smith's Hundred," but when Sir Edwin Sandys became treasurer of the London Company Smith sold his shares, and the name in 1619 was changed to Southampton Hundred, in honor of the Earl of Southampton, who was a member. The organization was a strong one, owning ships, etc., and had an interest in Hog Island as well. Sir George Yeardley was for many years captain or commander of the hundred.

It was represented in the first general assembly by Captain Thomas Graves and Mr. Walter Shelley.

Mrs. Mary Robinson gave £200 sterling and a silver gilt communion cup and other ornaments for " St. Mary's Church in Smith's Hundred in Virginia," which were brought to the colony in 1619. The cup is still preserved by the church at

---

[1] The descent seems to run thus: Joseph[1] Harwood, living in 1665, had issue Samuel,[2] who married Temperance Cocke, dau. of Capt. Thomas Cocke, Sr., of Henrico, and had issue: Samuel,[3] whose will was proved in Charles City Co., in 1745, by his widow Agnes. Samuel[3] and Agnes Harwood had issue: Samuel,[4] member of the State Convention, 1776, who married Margaret Woddrop, daughter of John Woddrop, of Nansemond, and had Anne,[5] who married Thomas Lewis. Agnes,[5] who married Fielding Lewis, son of Col. Warner Lewis, of "Warner Hall," in Gloucester County, and Eleanor Bowles, his wife; and Margaret[5] who married Robert Munford. Fielding Lewis' daughter, Eleanor, married Robert Douthat, Esquire.

Hampton, and bears the hall-mark 1617, with the inscription above mentioned. This plate is by long odds *the oldest church plate* in the United States. After the massacre of 1622 Southampton Hundred was abandoned, and in 1635 the associators in this company complained that they had spent upwards of £6,000 in planting settlements, and had nothing left but a stock of cattle in the hands of Captain John Utie. About 1637, the governor began to grant out the territory in parcels to new applicants; and Milton, Sherwood Forest, Sturgeon Point, Bachelor's Point, the Row, and Sandy Point — all lie in what was once Southampton Hundred.

Milton. This place, it is believed, was named after Richard Milton, who patented lands in Charles City County as early as 1636.

Sherwood Forest. This place reaches the river opposite to Brandon, and was the property in 1842 of Collier Minge, who sold the same to John Tyler, president of the United States. His residence still stands about two miles back from the river, and three miles further, near Charles City court house, is his birthplace, "Greenway," the former residence of his father, Governor John Tyler, Sr.

Sturgeon Point. This place appears to obtain its name from the sturgeons which were caught in great numbers in the river here.

Bachelor's Point. Here resided the family of William Hunt, a sympathizer with Bacon, and who died in 1676. His tombstone lies on the hill.

Sandy Point. This place is nearly opposite to Clermont, and is one of the most fertile tracts of land on the north side of the river. Here at the time of the arrival of the colonists was seated the Indian town of "Paspahegh." About 1700, it became the plantation of Colonel Philip Lightfoot, of the council of Virginia, grandson of Richard Lightfoot, rector of Stoke-Bruern, in Northamptonshire, England. It remained many years in the Lightfoot family. The house is said to have been built in the year 1717, and is called "Tedington," the name of a place near London.

Dancing Point. There is a waggish story that this point, which is at the mouth of the Chickahominy River, got its name

from a dancing match had here between the devil and Mr.
Lightfoot, who lived at Sandy Point, the stake being some
marsh land. Mr. Lightfoot outdanced the devil, and won the
land. But about 1637, many years before the Lightfoots settled at Sandy Point, this point was patented by John Dance,
and on Fry and Jefferson's map of Virginia the point is called
Dance's Point, which was readily corrupted into Dancing
Point.

Chickahominy River. This river is famed in the early his-
tcry as the seat of a numerous tribe of Indians who preserved
a *quasi-independence* of Powhatan. At the head of this river,
perhaps in New Kent county, John Smith was captured in
1607. During the war between the States, its extensive swamps
and morasses played an important part in determining military
results.

Governor's Land. In 1619, 3,000 acres were laid out as the
Governor's Land, extending from the Chickahominy to Jamestown, on the land " formerly conquered or purchased of the
Paspahegh Indians." It was tilled at first by employees of the
London Company for the support of the governor's office.
After the revocation of the charter in 1624, the land was leased
on terms of ninety-nine years to individuals, with a nominal
rent. This system was kept up till after the Revolution, when
the legislature, in May, 1784, vested " the lands near Jamestown, in the county of James City, and all the lots and houses
in Williamsburg, which are the property of the commonwealth,
and not yet granted " in the college of William and Mary.

Argall's Gift or Town. This place was located in 1617 about
a mile from Jamestown towards Chickahominy. Captain Argall contracted with some of the Martin's Hundred people to
cut down the wood on 300 acres for £600, and with Captain
William Powell to clear the ground and put up houses for £50.
In July, 1619, they were represented in the first house of burgesses by Captain Thomas Pawlett and Mr. Gurgany. But
inasmuch as this tract was embraced in the district of 3,000
acres appointed by the company for the Governor's Land, the
people petitioned the Assembly for relief from payment to
Captain Argall. Their petition was granted, and the place
appears to have been abandoned.

WEYANOKE (HARWOOD)

SHERWOOD (TYLER)

BERKELEY (HARRISON)

WESTOVER (BYRD)

Jamestown. Distant about sixty-eight miles from Richmond. Of this place I have already written at length.

Neck of Land. This was the country between Back River and Powhatan Creek, north of Jamestown Island. There were living here in 1624 sixteen persons, of whom Richard Kingsmill was the most prominent. It was represented in the general assembly in 1629 by Richard Brewster, and in 1632 by Lieutenant Thomas Crumpe, who, it is believed, married Elizabeth, daughter of Rev. Richard Buck.

Archer's Hope. The country between the mouth of Back River and Archer's Hope Creek was divided into three parts — the glebe land, Archer's Hope proper, and Fowler's Neck. In 1619, William Spence and John Fowler patented 500 acres called Archer's Hope, bounded on the west by the glebe land, and on the east by Fowler's Neck. Archer's Hope was assigned by Thomas and Sarah Brice to Roger Webster, and it was confirmed, in 1646, by grant to his three daughters, Lucy, Judith and Jane Webster. In the massacre of 1622 the Indians killed here, at Ensign William Spence's house, five persons, including William Fairfax, an ancient planter. The following order, entered by the general court of the colony, is preserved:

A Court at James Citty the 17th of September 1627 prsent Sir George Yeardley, knt., Governor, Dr. Pott, Capt. Smyth and Mr. Secretary: Divers examinacons being taken and had concerning the unquiett life wᶜʰ yᵉ people of Archers Hope lead through the scoldinges raleings and fallings out wᵗʰ Amy the wife of Christopher Hall and other abominable contencons happening between them to the dishonʳ of God and the breach of the Kings peace, the Court hath thereupon ordered that the said Amy shall be toughed round about the *Margarett and John* and ducked three times and further that Christopher Hall, John Upton, Robert Fitt and William Harrison and Amy the wife of the said Christopher Hall and Ann the wife of the said Robet Fitt shall be all bound unto their good behaviour and to appear at yᵉ Quarter Court after Christmas.

Midde Plantation. About 1632 Sir John Harvey ran a palisade six miles in length from Archer's Hope Creek to Queen's Creek, which empties in York River, and, about the center, on the ridge, he laid out a settlement called Middle Plantation. This became the seat of the college of William and Mary in 1693, and of the capital, after Jamestown was abandoned, in 1699. It is now called Williamsburg, and is distant seven miles from Jamestown. Its present population is about 2,500.

Kingsmill. This plantation gets its name from Richard

Kingsmill, who appears to have obtained a patent for 850 acres in a neck between Archer's Hope Creek and James River. A patent in 1637 to Humphrey Higginson for "Tuttey's Neck," in James City County, describes it as separated from Kingsmill Neck by a branch of Archer's Hope Creek. Elizabeth Kingsmill, daughter of Richard Kingsmill, married, first, Colonel William Tayloe, and, secondly, Colonel Nathaniel Bacon, Sr., of the council. The latter had no children, and left *Kingsmill* to his niece, Abigail Smith, who married Lewis Burwell. His son, Lewis Burwell, built an elegant brick mansion here, which was standing about 1800. It was described in 1780 as two stories high, four rooms to a floor, with two wings for offices; the ground in front of the house was terraced to the river, and there were on the place, besides, a large brick storehouse, stables, barns and coach house.

Littletown. This adjoined Kingsmill, and in March, 1633, was the residence of Captain George Menifie, of the council, one of the greatest merchants in Virginia. He had a garden of two acres on the river side, and it was full of roses of Provence, apple, pear and cherry trees, the various fruits of Holland, with different kinds of sweet smelling herbs, such as rosemary, sage, marjoram and thyme. He had growing around the house plenty of peach trees, which astonished his visitors very much, for they were not to be seen on the coast anywhere else. Here the governor sometimes held court. In 1661, Littletown was the residence of Col. Thomas Pettus, of the council. He married the widow of Richard Durant, and his widow, Elizabeth, married Captain John Grove, who died in 1671. Captain Thomas Pettus, Jr.'s, widow, Mourning, married James Bray, Jr., and thus the place passed to the Bray family till 1752, when, on the death of Colonel Thomas Bray, Littletown descended to his daughter, Elizabeth, who married Colonel Philip Johnson. Elizabeth Johnson, daughter of James Bray Johnson, son of Colonel Philip Johnson, married Chancellor Samuel Tyler, who died in 1812.

Utopia Bottoms. Adjoining Littletown are some deep ravines and bottoms, once owned by the poet George Sandys, called, in a patent granted to him, "Utopia," and still known as "Utopia Bottoms."

Wareham Ponds. These ponds constituted the east boundary of Harrop Parish, and the west bounds of Martin's Hundred. "Werrum's Run," a name given to a marshy branch near "Carter's Grove," is probably the place denoted by "Wareham Ponds."

Martin's Hundred. This was the plantation of the society of Martin's Hundred, organized by certain lords, knights and gentlemen in England. They got a grant in 1618 from the parent company — the London Company — for 80,000 acres, and settled a colony in the east end of James City county on the west side of Skiffes (Keith's) Creek. It was named in honor of Richard Martin, Esq., an attorney for the London

Company, and a leading member of the society. In October, 1618, the society sent the *gift* of *God* to Virginia with about 250 settlers for the plantation, and they arrived in Virginia about January or March, 1619.

On July 31, 1619, Martin's Hundred was represented in the first Virginia assembly by John Boys and John Jackson.

In the massacre of

RICHARD MARTIN.

March 22, 1622, this settlement suffered severely. Seventy-eight persons were slain, and Martin's Hundred was temporarily abandoned; but in February, 1624, two years later, twenty-four persons were living there.

In January, 1625, about thirty-one persons were resident there, of whom William Harwood was head. Martin's Hundred was represented in the Legislature, until counties were formed in 1634.

Till the Revolution, it constituted a distinct parish, and the foundations of the church may yet be seen on the roadside going into Blow's Neck. In Martin's Hundred, Robert Carter had a plantation on James River, called "Carter's Grove," which became the residence of his grandson, Carter Burwell, whose house, a handsome brick structure, is still standing. It is now the property of Dr. E. G. Booth.

Skiffes or Keith's Creek. This creek derives its name from Rev. George Keith, who was for a time a minister at Bermuda, but came to Virginia in 1617 in the ship *George.* He lived in the corporation of Elizabeth City in 1626, where he owned 100 acres of land. Mrs. Susan Keith, reported in 1624 among the dead at Jamestown, was probably his first wife. In 1634, he was "pastor of Kiskiacke," York County, at which time he obtained a grant of land on Chisman's Creek, due partly for the adventure of his wife (second wife), Martha, and for his son, John. In 1625, he was forty years old, and his son John eleven years old. George Keith may have been connected with the celebrated George Keith, who flourished at the close of the century and was at first an eminent Quaker, but, renouncing that faith, was equally as eminent as a minister of the established church, and as an author. His daughter, Anne, married George Walker, of Hampton, Va., whom Keith visited in 1704. She was still living in 1728, when the Quaker preacher, Rev. Samuel Bownas, visited Hampton. Her daughter, Margaret, married Thomas Wythe, a magistrate of Elizabeth City county. Their son was the celebrated George Wythe, distinguished equally as a statesman, a jurist, and a professor of law in William and Mary College. He was taught Greek by his mother, Margaret (Walker) Wythe, and became an accomplished scholar. He was the first professor of law in the United States.

Mulberry Island. Like Jamestown and Henrico, this, at the time the settlers came, was not an island, and is not an island now, although at high tide the water from the James and Warwick rivers join and may be seen in the road. It gains a place in our early history as being the point where, on June 8, 1610, Captain Edward Brewster, commanding the pinnace *Virginia,* met Sir Thomas Gates and the Jamestown colony on their way back to England, and gave the command from Lord Delaware for their return.

There was a grant here, before 1626, for 1,700 acres to John Rolfe, who married Captain William Peirce's daughter, Jane, and in January, 1625, the place was occupied by thirty of

Captain William Peirce's company. In 1635, Rev. Willis Heyley, "clarke and pastor of Mulberry Island," received a grant of 250 acres, and the consideration was stated to be two-fold, viz.: "his faithful pains in the Ministrie exemplified by a godly and quiet life, thereby seconding his doctrine, and next as a spur and encouragement for others of his calling to pursue so fair and bright an example." It seems that Robert Poole had 300 acres in 1627 on Warwick River, adjoining Stanley Hundred above, and that below him, at the mouth of the Warwick River, was Lieutenant Gilbert Peppet, with 250 acres of land.

The church of Mulberry Island was said to be west of Robert Poole's land.

By the side of the road going from Lee Hall into Mulberry Island is still pointed out the place where an old church once stood.

Stanley Hundred. In 1626, Sir George Yeardley, the governor, intimated his intention to the council to take up 1,000 acres, bounded northerly upon Blunt Point River (Warwick River) and southerly upon the main river, and easterly by a creek which separated him from the land of Robert Poole and Lieutenant Peppet. Governor Yeardley was buried at Jamestown, November 13, 1627, and on February 9, 1627-'28, Lady Yeardley acknowledged a sale of the land under the name of "Stanley Hundred" to Thomas Flint, who accordingly patented it September 20, 1628. It was described as adjoining the lands of John Rolfe, Esquire, and Captain William Peirce, in Mulberry Island. The place passed to John Brewer, who served as burgess for Warwick River and member of the council. He returned to England, where he was "citizen and grocer of London." Brewer's will was proved in London, May 13, 1636, and in it he bequeathed Stanley Hundred to his son, John, who settled in Isle of Wight county, and has descendants on the south side. The widow of John Brewer, Sr., married Thomas Butler, "clarke and pastor of Denbie."

Stanley is now the name of one of the magisterial districts of Warwick County, and includes Mulberry Island.

Denbigh. This was the plantation of Col. Samuel Mathews, who came to Virginia in 1622, and filled every office up to and including governor. A contemporary wrote in 1649 that he had a fine house, sowed much hemp and flax, and had it spun; kept weavers and a tannery, had forty negro slaves, whom he brought up to mechanical trades, and sowed large crops of wheat and barley. He also supplied vessels trading to Virginia with beef. He had plenty of cows, a fine dairy, and abundance of hogs and poultry, and is finally described as one who "kept a good house, lived bravely, and was a true lover of Virginia." He married Frances, daughter of Sir Thomas Hinton, and widow successively of Captain Nathaniel West, brother of Lord Delaware, and of Captain Abraham Peirsey, which last, at his death left "the best estate that ever was known in Virginia."

Denbigh, in 1678, was owned by John Mathews, "grandson of Samuel Mathews, Esquire," and was described as containing 2,944 acres lying on James River between Deep Creek and Warwick River. In 1630, Denbigh was represented in the house of burgesses by Thomas Ceeley, Christopher Stoakes and Thomas Key. In 1633, a public storehouse was established at Denbigh. Then, in 1680, a town was ordered by the ·assembly to be built there, "at the mouth of Deep Creek, on Mr. Mathews' land," and to be called Warwick Town. In 1691, this order was renewed, and it was stated that a brick courthouse and prison, together with several other houses, had been there built. The plantation of the Digges family, on Warwick River, was during the eighteenth century known as "Denbigh," and a district of the county still goes by that name.

Nutmeg Quarter. Below Blunt Point, in Warwick County, Sir Francis Wyatt had 500 acres of land planted in 1626. This was called "Nutmeg Quarter." It seems he increased this dividend; for in July, 1635, Joseph Stratton patented 500 acres, *part* of a dividend formerly belonging to Sir Francis Wyatt. It lay upon the river side, and had for bounds on the southeast a piece of land that "did once belong to Capt. John Smith," on the northwest land of John Laydon, whose marriage with Anne Burras was the first in the United States. Nutmeg Quarter was represented in the house of burgesses in October, 1629, by William Cole and William Bentley; in February, 1630, by Joseph Stratton; and in 1633, by Francis

Hough. After counties were formed, Nutmeg Quarter continued a separate parish till 1656, when on the petition of
Captain Thomas Pritchard, in behalf of the majority of the
inhabitants, it was united with Denbigh Parish.

Waters' Creek. The name of this creek is incorrectly given
in the Coast Survey as Watts' Creek, but it was named for
Captain Edward Waters, who, in 1624, got a patent for 100
acres on Waters' Creek, "two miles from Blunt Point."
Captain Waters had an eventful life. He was born in 1584,
and left England for Virginia in 1609, in the *Sea Venture,*
which bore Sir Thomas Gates. The ship was wrecked on the
Bermuda Islands, and Waters, with the rest, was compelled to
remain forty-two weeks till they built two cedar ships, the
Deliverance and the *Patience,* and by this means finally reached
their destination in Virginia.

Shortly afterwards, Waters returned with Sir George
Somers to the island for hogs, which abounded there in a wild
state. Sir George Somers died, and his nephew, Matthew
Somers, sailed with his body to England, leaving Waters and
two others to hold the island. During his absence, Waters
and his companions found a gigantic piece of ambergris
weighing 160 pounds, and worth £120,000 sterling (about
$3,000,000 in present money). The treasure was claimed by
the London Company, and Waters only received a small share
of its value.

He remained in Bermuda nine or ten years, during which
time he was a member of the council. In 1618 or 1619, he
moved to Virginia, and about 1620 married Grace O'Neil,
whose second husband was Colonel Obedience Robins, of
Northampton County. At the great massacre in 1622, himself
and wife were taken prisoners by the Nansemond Indians, but,
finding a small boat, they secretly escaped, and rowed over to
Kecoughtan. In 1625, he was living, aged forty, on Waters'
Creek, with his wife, aged twenty-one, and two children,
William and Margaret, both born in Virginia. He was a
captain, a burgess and a justice of Elizabeth City County, and
was still living in March, 1629. His descendants are numerous and highly respectable.

Mary's Mount. This place lay above Newport News. Upon
February 1, 1630, Daniel Gookin, Jr., conveyed to Thomas

Addison, late servant of Daniel, his father, 150 acres of land
above Newport News, at a place called " Mary's Mount." The
site of the plantation is still indicated by a point of land known
as " Merry Point." It is not improbable that this name is
derived from Morton's celebrated settlement of " Merry
Mount " in Massachusetts, as some of his men came to
Virginia.

Newport News. This place appears on Smith's map as
" Point Hope," but it seems to derive its present name from
Newcestown, near Bandon in County Cork, Ireland. Sir
William Newce was the founder of Newcestown, and in 1621
he came with Sir Francis Wyatt to Virginia, where he served
as marshal of the colony and member of the council. He was
preceded to Virginia by his brother Captain Thomas Newce,
who was by the London Company made superintendent of
the company's lands and tenants, and in 1620 settled at Elizabeth City.

The example of the Newces was followed by their friend
Daniel Gookin, Esquire, who, November 15, 1620, engaged
with the London Company to ship cattle to Virginia from
Ireland. Under date of January, 1622, the governor and
council thus noticed Gookin's arrival in Virginia. " There
arrived here, about the 22 of November, a shipp from Mr.
Gookin out of Ireland wholly upon his own adventure, without any relation at all to his contract with you in England,
which was so well furnished with all sortes of provisione, as
well as with cattle, as wee could wyshe all men would follow
their example. He hath also brought with him about fifty
men upon that adventure, besides some thirty passengers.
Wee have according to their *desire seated them at New Port's
News*, and they do conceive great hope, yff the Irish plantation prpr (prosper), yt (that) from Ireland great multitudes
of people will like to come hither."

Though hailing like the Newces from Newcestown in Ireland, Daniel Gookin, was nevertheless an Englishman, and
he named the port at which he landed New Port Newce in
honor of Newcestown and Sir William Newce. Gookin
obtained a patent of 2,500 acres, and the census of Virginia
in 1625 shows that Newport News was occupied solely by

16

"Daniel Gookin's muster." In March, 1622, with thirty-five men he successfully defended his settlement against all attacks of the Indians, and afterwards brought to England the first news of the massacre in Virginia.[1]

It is probable that he did not return but carried on his plantation in Virginia through his son Daniel Gookin, Jr., who was found in 1633 at Newport News by Peter DeVries, the Dutch ship captain, who narrates that at " Newport-snuw " there was a fine spring, from which all ships navigating the James obtained their water.

Daniel Gookin, Jr., was a Puritan in his sympathies, and left Virginia in May, 1644, for Massachusetts, where he became one of the most prominent men. His tombstone is at Cambridge with this inscription:

> Here lyeth Interred
> ye body of
> MAJOR GENERAL DANIEL GOOKIN
> Aged 75
> who departed this life
> ye 19th March 1686–7.

There is a grant dated April 20, 1685, to Hon. William Cole, Esq., secretary of the colony of Virginia, for land partly in Warwick County and partly in Elizabeth City County, " commonly called Newports News," containing, " according to the most ancient and lawful bounds thereof," 1,431 acres, " being all that can be found, upon an exact survey, of 2,500 acres *formerly granted to Daniel Gookin, Esquire,* except 250 acres formerly conveyed and made over to the said Gookin." And Daniel Gookin, Jr., and John Gookin conveyed the said land to John Chandler, who sold the same to Captain Benedict Stafford, from whom the said land was found to escheat by a jury April 3, 1684, and was then granted to Col. William Cole and Capt. Roger Jones, which last made over his interest to said Cole, the patentee in 1685. Susanna Cole, daughter of Col. William Cole, married Colonel Dudley Digges, of York county, son of Governor Edward Digges, and grandson of Sir Dudley Digges, master of the rolls to King Charles I. In 1787, Newport News was owned by William Digges, great-grandson of Dudley Digges.

---

[1] " Newport News, Origin of its Name," in *William and Mary Coll. Quart.,* IX., 233–237.

The waters off Newport News are made famous by two celebrated vessels both called *Virginia* — the pinnace *Virginia,* which in June, 1610, carried *the glad tidings* of the arrival of Lord Delaware at Point Comfort to the vessels coming down the river from Jamestown, and the Confederate iron-clad *Virginia, which on March 8, 1862, revolutionized naval warfare by defeating the powerful Federal fleet of wooden battle ships, splendidly equipped and gallantly manned.*

March 8, 1862, the *Virginia* with ten guns, supported by several small wooden steamboats, having eleven guns in all, engaged the Federal fleet armed with 204 guns, and powerfully aided by several lighter craft and by the batteries at Newport News. The engagement commenced at 3.30 P. M., and by 6 o'clock P. M., the *Virginia* had sunk the *Cumberland,* burned the *Congress,* disabled and driven the *Minnesota* ashore, and compelled the *St. Lawrence* and the *Roanoke,* to seek shelter under the guns of Fort Monroe. Two small steamers were also blown up, and two transport steamers were captured.[1] In the battle, however, Captain Franklin Buchanan was wounded, and the command of the *Virginia* devolved upon Lt. Catesby ap R Jones.

The next day the *Virginia* encountered the Monitor *Ericsson* — a vessel much more heavily armored, scarcely presenting any surface above water, and unlike her antagonist exceedingly nimble by reason of the lightness of her draught. It was the *first battle between iron clads ever fought,* and for four hours they battered one another with their guns without doing any particular damage, until at last a shell from the *Virginia* exploded in the turret of the *Monitor,* and blinded her gallant captain, John L. Worden. Thereupon, the *Monitor,* according to the official statement[2] of G. J. Van Brunt, captain of the *Minnesota,* steamed out of range of shot towards Old Point Comfort, and the *Virginia* having waited three quarters of an hour[3] for her antagonist to renew the fight (during which interval she fired eleven guns at the *Minnesota*), retired to Norfolk, as the tide was falling. Twice afterwards the *Virginia* returned to the Roads on April 11,

[1] *Official Records of the Union and Confederate Navies.* VII., 41.
[2] Ibid., VII., 12.
[3] Ibid., VII., 60.

1862, and May 8, 1862, but in each case the *Monitor*, though supported by the *Stevens Battery*, the *Naugatuck*, and other iron ships declined to risk a second encounter. The *Virginia* successfully protected the right wing of General Joseph E. Johnston's army by closing the entrances to the James and Elizabeth rivers; but when his left wing at Yorktown was turned and the Peninsula had to be evacuated, the Confederates blew her up May 11, 1862, near Craney Island, as her great draught of twenty-three feet prevented her from going up James River.[1] At the time of the combat between the *Virginia* and *Monitor* there were two or three houses on the shore at Newport News, but there has been a great change since. Its value as a strategic point was demonstrated during the war, and the wisdom of Daniel Gookin in selecting it as the site of his proposed town, has been vindicated by the phenomenal growth within a few years past of a city of 25,000 inhabitants.

In the great shipyard at Newport News was recently built an ironclad of the Federal Navy called also *The Virginia*, which is recognized as one of the finest battleships afloat on the waters anywhere.

Salford's Creek. This creek is on the east of Newport News, and receives its name from Robert Salford, who came to Virginia in 1611, and resided near its mouth with his wife Jane and son John. It is now known as Salter's Creek, but, in the Elizabeth City records, the name, as late as the 18th century, is written Salford's Creek. About 1639, Thomas Ceeley, a member of the house of burgesses, resided here, and in the 18th century the land was owned by Colonel Wilson Miles Cary, who lived in a handsome brick residence of two stories, with wings, commanding a splendid view of Hampton Roads. The plantation was called "Ceeleys" and contained some 2,000 acres. During the war (1861–65), the house was occupied by a settlement of negro squatters, and while in their occupation the residence was burned, and afterwards the walls were removed to furnish chimneys for the hovels of the negroes.[2]

[1] *Career of the Virginia*, by D. B. Phillips.   (Va. Hist. Soc. Coll. [new series], VI., 195.)
[2] *Va. Magazine*, IX., 104–109.

Kecoughtan.[1] Because the Kecoughtan Indians killed
Humphrey Blunt near Blunt Point, Sir Thomas Gates, on July
9, 1610, drove the werowance, Pochins, and his tribe away,
and built two small stockades near the mouth of James River
— Fort Henry and Fort Charles, named in honor of the sons
of James I. They were located on a rivulet which Lord
Delaware called Southampton (Hampton) River — in honor
of Henry Wriothesley, earl of Southampton, whose name was
also given to the splendid body of water into which the rivulet
entered — Southampton (Hampton) Roads. These forts
were abandoned the following fall, but were reoccupied by Sir
Thomas Dale in 1611.

Fort Henry was located where stands at present the
Soldier's Home on the Strawberry Bank, and a mile further
east was Fort Charles. Each of these forts in 1613 had
fifteen soldiers, but no ordnance; and in 1614 Captain George
Webb was the principal commander of both. In the latter
year, Hamor described them as "goodly seats and much corn
about them, abounding with the commodities of fish, fowle,
Deere and fruits, whereby the men lived there with halfe that
maintenáunce out of the Store which in other places is
allowed." In 1616, there were at Kecoughtan twenty men
governed by the same commander, Captain George Webb,
and of the number Mr. William Mease was minister and
eleven were farmers who maintained themselves. In 1619,
William Tucker was captain there, and he and William
Capps represented it in the general assembly, which was
convened that year in Jamestown. On the petition of the
inhabitants, who did not like the heathen Kecoughtan, the
name Elizabeth City, from Elizabeth, King James' daughter,
was given to one of the four great corporations in which all
the settlements were included.

About this time the land from the mouth of Hampton
River to the Bay was appropriated to public uses, and 3,000
acres were assigned to the London Company, 1,500 acres for
the common use and 100 acres for a glebe. The portion from
Hampton River to the end of Mill Creek was called "Strawberry Bank" and the portion between Mill Creek and the
Bay shore "Buck Roe."

[1] "Old Kecoughtan," in *William and Mary Coll. Quart.*, IX., 83-131.

In 1620, the company sent some Frenchmen to Buck Roe to teach the colonists how to plant mulberry trees and vines, raise silkworms, and make wine. They were selected by John Bonnell, silkworm raiser to the king at Oakland, from Languedock in France, and among them were Anthony Bonnell,[1] Elias La Guard,[2] James Bonnell, Peter Arundell and David Poole.

In 1621, Captain Thomas Newce came over as manager of the company's land, and received 600 acres in this region.

At this time the minister of Elizabeth City was James Stockton, son of William Stockton, parson of Barkeswell, County Warwick, England; and in May, 1621, he wrote a letter regarding the treacherous character of the Indians, and the futility of any attempt to convert them till "their Priests and Ancients" were put to death. He appears to have been the earliest exponent of the doctrine that "the only good Indian is a dead Indian." The next year occurred the massacre, and the warning of Mr. Stockton may have served the people at Elizabeth City to good purpose, for no one was killed there. After the first news Captain Newce called all his neighbors together at his house, which he defended with three cannon, and took measure not only for their relief, but built two houses and "a faire well of water mantled with brick" for the reception of emigrants daily expected from England; and, foreseeing the famine that must necessarily ensue, caused a large crop of corn to be planted around the fort. In all these works the captain acted the part of a sawyer, carpenter and laborer, but met with many difficulties. In the latter part of June Governor Wyatt, accompanied by his council and many other gentlemen, spent three or four days with him and ate up the crop of corn near the fort, before the ears were half grown. However, Captain Newce, sick and weak as he was, never tired of well doing; but when all was spent and the colonists had to live on crabs and oysters, distributed among them, as he saw occasion, a little milk and rice which he still had left, and behaved with such "tenderness

---

[1] He was probably ancestor of the Bonny (Anglocised from "Bonnell") family of Princess Ann and Norfolk Counties.
[2] He was probably ancestor of the Ellegood family.

and care " that he obtained the reputation of being the best commander in Virginia.[1]

September 9, 1622, his men were attacked at their labors by the Indians, which was their first assault since the massacre; and four men were slain. The captain, although extremely sick, sallied forth, but the Indians hid in the cornfields at night and escaped without any loss. About this time Samuel Collier, who had come, as a boy, to Virginia and was very useful as Indian interpreter, was accidentally killed by a sentinel; and in the general neglect of agriculture we are told that the vineyards at Buck Roe were greatly bruised by the deer. Captain Newce died the next year (1623) and he was preceded to the grave by his brother Sir William Newce, who had come a very short time before as high marshal to Virginia. In the revenge now taken on the savages no quarter was given, and Captain William Tucker, of Elizabeth City, was one of the commanders who led expeditions against them. In 1624 the population of Elizabeth City was 349; and in 1627 Rev. Mr. Stockton had the lease of 50 acres " within the Company's land at Elizabeth City," at the Indian House Thicket. It appears the irony of fate that an Indian school should now be seen near where once was an Indian thicket, and the prophetic Stockton announced his conviction of the original depravity of the Indian. As a result of the massacre, the Indians were driven far away from the settlements, and the colony in a few years again put on a prosperous appearance. In 1628, we are told that there was a great plenty of everything in the colony and " peaches in abundance at Elizabeth City." [2]

About 1630, Col. William Claiborne set up on the very site of the present town of Hampton a store house for trade with the Indians up Chesapeake Bay, and here he resided after being driven out of Kent Island by Lord Baltimore. He removed to West Point about 1661.

In 1632, the French vignerons at Buck Roe incurred the resentment of the general assembly by dropping into tobacco raising, and a law was passed inhibiting them from

[1] Smith, Works (Arber's ed.), 593, 595.
[2] Ibid. (Arber's ed.), 887.

so doing on penalty of forfeiting their leases and having to quit the colony.

In February, 1634, Leonard Calvert and his emigrants stopped here on their way to found the great state of Maryland at St. Mary's.

In 1635, Benjamin Syms left his famous legacy of land and cattle on Back River for the first free school in America, and in 1659 Dr. Thomas Eaton established another school near Syms'— two benefactions now represented by a fund of $10,000 and a fine brick building at Hampton having the name of the "Syms-Eaton Academy."

In 1637, after Fort Henry had been abandoned, the field of 110 acres on which it stood was granted to Captain Francis Hooke, Esq., of the Royal Navy, commander at Point Comfort, and one of the Council of State; and in 1648 the land fell to Major Richard Moryson, one of Captain Hooke's successors in command at Point Comfort.

The first church at Elizabeth City lay on the north side of the present trolley car line from Hampton to Phœbus, and its site is doubtless indicated by an old graveyard on the late Major Thomas Tabb's property. A grant to one Robert Partin in 1637 bounds his lease of forty acres as "south on the Fort Field and north towards the church." In this church during January of this year Sir John Harvey read his commission to be governor a second term, and in 1644 William Wilkinson, afterwards the second Protestant minister in Maryland, was its rector.

About 1667, a new church was built on the west of Hampton (at a place lately known as "Pembroke Farm"), and that year a burial took place in the "old church at Kecoughtan" and another at the "new church." In 1699, Walter Bailey was paid 400 lbs. of tobacco for "pulling down the old church and setting up benches in ye court house;" and in 1704 Rev. George Keith, a celebrated missionary of the Episcopal Church, visited his son-in-law, George Walker, on the Strawberry Bank, and "preached in the church at Kikotan," by which he must have meant the second church.

Elizabeth City had been the name adopted in 1619, but "Kecoughtan" adhered to the county around Southampton

River during the whole of the 17th century. The town of Hampton (contraction for Southampton) was not regularly established till 1680, and then it was laid out on land formerly attached to Col. William Claiborne's storehouse, and then belonging to Thomas Jarvis, a ship-captain, who married Elizabeth Bacon, daughter of Sir Edward Duke, and widow of Nathaniel Bacon, Jr.

In the waters near by occurred, on the 29th of April, 1700, the obstinate fight of the fifth-class English man-of-war *Shoreham* with a pirate ship, in which, however, the pirate was beaten. Among the casualties was the death of Peter Heyman, collector of the customs for the James River, and grandson of Sir Peter Heyman, of Summerfield, County Kent, England. He was shot down by the side of Sir Francis Nicholson, the governor, who was himself on board the *Shoreham* and participated in the affray.

BLACK BEARD, THE PIRATE.

Hither also came the gallant Captain Henry Maynard, after his victory, November 21, 1718, over the pirate Blackbeard, or Teach, in Pamlico Sound, North Carolina, swinging the pirate's head from his bowsprit and bearing captive the survivors of the pirate's crew, most of whom were hanged afterwards at Williamsburg. Blackbeard's head was set up at the mouth of Hampton River, and the point is still known as Black Beard Point.

On July 1, 1715, permission was granted by Alexander Spottswood, the governor, for the justices to remove from their old court-house and build a new one in Hampton town, and land was purchased from Captain William Boswell for the purpose.

When John Fontaine visited[1] Hampton in 1716, it was a place of 100 houses and had the greatest trade in Virginia. All the men-of-war lay before this arm of the river, and the inhabitants drove a great trade with New York and Pennsylvania, but " it has no church." Twelve years later, the church at Pembroke Farm had become ruinous, and, on June 17, 1727,[2] Mr. Jacob Walker and Mr. John Lowry were appointed by the court of Elizabeth City to lay off and value an acre and a half of ground on Queen's Street, joining upon Mr. Boswell's lots, for building the church thereon. The same day, Mr. Henry Cary, by order of the minister, church wardens and the court, was permitted to take wood, " at the rate of six pence per load to burn bricks for the church, from the School land." [3] But it seems that a portion of the people of the parish did not desire to remove from the old quarters, and they appealed the matter to the governor and council. They heard the complaint and decided[4] October 27, 1727, that " the new church should be built in Hampton Town as the most convenient place in the said parish." In 1760, Alexander Kennedy devised land to the poor of Elizabeth City county, and the sum of " 40 pds. sterling towards purchasing out of England a bell for the church of Elizabeth City Parish, provided the vestry and church wardens will undertake a belfry within twelve months after my decease."

Hampton was captured during the war of 1812 by the British under Admiral Cockburn, and subjected to pillage and outrage. During the war between the States, the inhabitants set fire to their own dwellings, rather than they should afford a shelter to the enemy. It has been called the " Gamecock Town," and has produced a number of prominent and distinguished men, of whom George Wythe, Commodore James Barron, and Commodore Lewis Warrington are perhaps the most distinguished.

---

[1] Maury, *Huguenot Family*, 293.
[2] *Elizabeth City Co. Records.*
[3] *Elizabeth City Co. Records.*
[4] *Council Journal*, 1727.

Little England. A place between Hampton and the mouth of Hampton River; anciently known as Capps' Point and agreeing with the description of some land patented in 1627 by a prominent settler named William Capps.

Point Comfort. This received its name at the first coming of the settlers because they found deep water here, permitting the passage of their ships into the water beyond. After Captain Smith's departure for England, in October, 1609, President George Percy sent Captain John Ratcliffe down to the mouth of the river to erect a fort as a precaution against an attack of the Spaniards, who claimed the continent. He chose the present site of Fort Monroe, and named the fort "Algernourne Fort," in honor of President Percy's ancestor, William Algernourne de Percy, who came to England with William the Conqueror.

After Ratcliffe, Captain James Davis had command for several years, and in 1614 the fort was described as a stockade " without stone or brick," containing 50 persons, men, women and boys, and protected by seven pieces of artillery; two of thirty-five " quintales," and the others thirty, twenty and eighteen — all of iron.

After Percy's departure for England, in April, 1612, the name Algernourne Fort was discontinued; and the place, for many years afterwards, was referred to as " Point Comfort Fort."

In 1632, the fort, having fallen into disuse, was rebuilt by Captain Samuel Mathews, afterwards governor, and furnished with a guard of eight men; and Captain Francis Pott, brother of Governor John Pott, of the ancient family of the Potts of Harrop, in Yorkshire, was made commander, and continued such till he was removed by Sir John Harvey in 1635.

In that year (1635) Francis Hooke, of the Royal Navy, " an old servant of King Charles," was put in command.

He died in 1637, and Captain Christopher Wormeley, who had been governor of Tortugas, was for a short time in charge.

Then, in 1639, succeeded Richard Moryson, son of Sir Richard Moryson, and brother-in-law of the noble cavalier, Lucius Cary, Lord Falkland, who married Letitia Moryson.

In 1641, he returned to England, and left his brother, Lieutenant Robert Moryson, in charge of the fort.

In 1649, Major Francis Moryson, another brother, who had served King Charles in the wars with the Parliament, came to Virginia with Colonel Henry Norwood, Colonel Mainwaring Hammond, and other cavaliers, and was appointed by Sir William Berkeley captain of the fort. After Major Moryson, his nephew, Colonel Charles Moryson, son of Richard Moryson, about 1664, succeeded to the command of the fort.

For the support of the captain, what were known as " castle duties " were established in 1632, consisting, at first, of " a barrel of powder and ten iron shot " required of every ship; and the captain kept a register of all arrivals.

By 1665, the fort was entirely out of repair, and the general assembly in obedience to orders from the king appointed Captain William Bassett to build a new fort, but the council substituted Col. Miles Cary and his son Thomas, as Bassett lived too remote.[1] Before the work was finished, however, the great storm of 1667 washed away the very foundations, and Col. Cary lost his life in fighting the Dutch, who made an attack the same year, and burnt the English shipping at the mouth of the river. Then the king sent new orders to restore the fort, but the assembly, who had very reluctantly obeyed in the first instance, now instead of doing what the king required, ordered five forts to be built at five other places, viz.: Nansemond, Jamestown, Tindall's Point, Corotoman and Yeocomoco. As an excuse for this action, they asserted in the preamble to their act the inefficiency of a fort at Point Comfort and the great difficulty of getting material to build a fort there. Of course, when the Dutch came in 1673, the fort was of little value in preventing their operations, and the shipping had the misfortunes of 1667 repeated upon them.

Not much is recorded of the fort for many years after this, but in 1722 we learn that George Walker, grandfather of George Wythe, was governor and storekeeper of the battery at Point Comfort.

In 1727, the resolve was taken by the assembly to build a durable fort at Point Comfort. When finished it was mounted

[1] Hening, *Statutes at Large*, II., 220; *Virginia Magazine*, V., 29.

by twenty-two guns, and about 1736 Governor Gooch reported[1] that: "no ship could pass it without running great risk." It was named Fort George, and was made of bricks, each nine inches long by four wide and three thick. The exterior wall was sixteen feet distant from the interior óne, and the former was twenty-seven inches thick and the latter sixteen inches. Then the two walls were connected by counter walls ten or twelve feet apart forming cribs, which were probably filled with sand.[2] The fort, however, in spite of its apparent durability did not remain effective very long, for it fell a victim, in 1749, to a great hurricane, which has been described as most terrific and disastrous. The officer in command was Captain James Barron, ancestor of a line of naval heroes distinguished in three wars. The barracks in which he stayed were a long row of wooden buildings with brick chimneys, running up through the centre of the roofs, and Captain Barron caused all his family, with the officers and soldiers of the garrison to muster on the second floor with all the weighty articles they could find; which, it was supposed, kept the houses firm on their foundation, and so preserved the lives of all concerned. The hurricane, however, entirely destroyed the fortification of Fort George, and Captain Barron removed with his family to the upper part of Mill Creek, not far off, where he resided during the remainder of his life.[3]

In 1756, Governor Dinwiddie, commenting on the fort, observed:[4] "It was built on a Sandy Bank; no care to drive the piles to make a Foundation; the Sea and wind beating against it has quite undermined it and dismantled all the Guns which now lie buried in the Sand." There is no evidence that the fort was ever restored, but as late as 1847 parts of its walls were seen and described.

The present Fort Monroe was commenced in 1819, and about 1830 the work of sinking rocks on the shoal opposite, called Rip Raps from the rippling of the water, was begun; and afterwards a fort was erected called Fort Calhoun, and subsequently Fort Wool.

[1] Va. Magazine, III., 119.
[2] Va. Historical Register, I., 22.
[3] Ibid., I., 24.
[4] Dinwiddie's Letters, II., 342.

Cape Charles. This is the extreme point of the Accomac Peninsula, and was named for Prince Charles by the first settlers. In 1614, Sir Thomas Dale established some men under Lieutenant Craddock at Smith's Island, near the cape, for the purpose of making salt out of sea-water. He called this colony " Dale's Gift," but it does not appear to have been a continuous settlement.

Cheriton (or Wissaponson?) Creek. The first permanent settler on the Eastern Shore of Virginia appears to have been Thomas Savage, who came as a boy to the colony in 1608, was given to Powhatan by Captain John Smith, resided for many years with the Indians, and learned their language. About 1619 he went to the Eastern Shore, and received from the "Laughing King" the neck of land between Cheriton Creek and King's Creek, known as Savage's Neck. In 1621, the Laughing King gave Sir George Yeardley all the land between Hungar's Creek and Cheriton Creek.

Old Plantation Creek receives its name from being the site of Capt. John Willcox's settlement which was made the same year (1621).

APPENDIX A.

SOME STATEMENTS.

See pages 26, 29, 116.

Mr. J. R. Bacon's statement June 2, 1900:

"My father, William E. Bacon, was employed by Colonel Goodrich Durfey as carpenter. I lived with him in the powder magazine on Jamestown Island, and, though but a small boy at the time, retain lively recollections of the appearance of the place. I remember that I used to sit on the roots of the cypress tree, now standing many yards in the water, and fish at high tide. At low tide its roots were dry. I remember that the boiler of the steamer *Curtisspeck*. blew up at the wharf while I lived there. The mail was carried to the Island over the causeway across the submerged neck. The pierhead of the wharf stood then about sixty feet from the shore. I was born in 1835, and was about ten years old when we removed."

Mr. J. R. Bacon's statement December 27, 1905:

"When I lived upon the Island the wharf where the steamboat stopped was above the church tower and its site is indicated by some old piles standing out in the water. Some years after our departure, Col. William Allen built the wharf below his residence.

While I did not again reside upon the Island, my father lived near by, and I was employed upon a schooner which plied upon the river. I was, therefore, a frequent visitor to the Island, and attribute the wearing away of the shore to the severe northwest and southeast winds that frequently attacked it."

Mr. John Gilliam's father was a carpenter employed by Colonel Durfey (who owned the Island from 1836 to 1846). The Gilliams lived in the brick magazine after the Bacons left it. Mr. Gilliam visited the Island with the author about eight years ago, and pointed out the cypress, now about three hundred feet distant, which in 1836-'46, stood on the shore about a hundred yards from the magazine. Mr. Gilliam died in 1899, aged about seventy years.

APPENDIX B.[1]

SIR WILLIAM BERKELEY'S DEED TO WALTER CHILES FOR KEMPE'S BRICK HOUSE.

This Indenture made the three & twentyth day of March Anno Domi. 1649 & in the second yeare of ye reign of o^r Lord Charles by ye grace of god King of England Scotland ffrance & Ireland defend^r of ye ffayth &c ye second of that name, Betweene the Honorable Sr Willm Berkeley Gou^r and Capt. gen!l of Virginia of ye one pt and Wal^r Chiles of James Citty in Virginia gent: of ye other pt. Witnesseth

---

[1] The papers printed in this appendix are copied from the *Ambler MSS.* in the Library of Congress except the grant to John Knowles. They all refer to Jamestown Island.

That ye sd Sr Wm Berkeley for and in Consideracon of ye some of
six & twenty thousand poundes of tobacco to him in hand payd by y^e
sd Wal^r Chiles before ye ensealing & deliuery Hereof, for wch hee
acknowledgeth himselfe fully satisfyed & from wch paym^t hee hath
fully discharged the sd Wal^r Chiles his heyres, execut^rs and Adm^rs
hath giuen granted Bargained & sold aliened assigned & sett ouer, &
doth by these p^rentes giue grant Bargain sell alien Assigne and sett
ouer, unto ye sd Wal^r Chiles his heyres and assigns for ever. All y^t
his messuage or mansion house, together wth All gardens orchards
yardes Backsides out houses buildings and hereditam^ts & appurtenances whatsoeuer to ye sayd messuage or mansion house belonging,
or in any wise Apperteyning scituate lyeing & Being in James Citty,
both in ye tenure and occupacon of Richd Kemp esq^r, and by him
Conveyed unto S^r ffrancis Wyatt k^t & purchased by y^e [sd] S^r Wm
Berkeley of Capt Wm Peirce attorney for ye sd S^r ffrancis Wyatt, all
wch writings remayne uppon records in ye Secretaryes office in James
Citty as relatn thereunto being had more at Large appeareth together
also wth one pcell or plott of ground granted to ye sd S^r ffrancis by ord^r
of court Conteyning three acres more or Lesse and being in James
Citty afforsayd adioyning to ye Land whereon the sayd messuage
standeth To haue and to hold ye sayd houseing laund and other the
p^r mises afforesayd wth his due shares of all mines and mineralls therein
Conteyened wth all rightes and priveledges thereunto belonging, unto
the sayd Wal^r Chiles his heyres & Asss for euer in as Large and ample
manner & forme to all Intents & purposes as ye sd p^rmises are or haue
beene formerly granted, unto them the sd Richd Kemp, S^r ffra: Wyatt,
or the sayd S^r Wm Berkeley, by vertue of any former deeds of grant
made unto them either by pattent, or Conveyance. To have and to
hold the afforesayd p^rmises and every pt and pcell thereof und^r the
tenures, rents, services, & Condiciones in ye sd deedes of grant menconed and expressed unto the sayd Wal^r Chiles his heyres and Asss
for euer. And the sayd Sr Wm Berkeley for himselfe his heyres
executors Adm^rs, doth Couenant and grant to & wth ye sd Wal^r Chiles
his heyres execut^res & Adm^rs y^t hee is at this p^rsent seized of an
undefeazible estate in ye p^rmises, in fee simple according to y^e
tenor and purport of ye fore menconed deeds of grant, and y^t
the p^rmises are free and Cleare and shall bee always made free
and Cleare by ye sd Sr Wm Berkeley [his] heyres execut^rs and Adm^rs,
from all former Bargaines, sales, [   ] dowres, Judgm^ts, execucons
or any other Incombrances whatsoeuer made donne or suffered by
ye sayd S^r Wm Berkeley, S^r ffra: Wyat: or Richd Kemp esq^r afforesayd, And the sayd S^r Wm Berkeley [by] these presents furth^r con-
enant & grant to an wth ye sd Wal^r Chiles his heyres & Asss. y^t hee
ye sayd S^r Wm Berkeley his h[eyres, execu^rs] Adm^rs shall and will at
all tymes heereafter warr^t & defend ye fore cited [   ] to ye sd Wal^r
[Chiles heyrs, assignes   ] exec^rs Adm^rs   [   ]
p sons what soe [uer   ] in witness whereof [ye sd S^r] Wm Berkeley hath heereunto putt his hand and seale the day and yeare aboue
written.

                                        WILLIAM BERKELEY.

Signed sealed and deliuered
in p^rsence of
                Al^r: Culpeper
                Ed^w: Hill
                Rich: Lee

DEED OF NATHANIEL BACON AND ELIZABETH HIS WIFE FOR THE ISLAND HOUSE.

To All to whom these presents shall Come Nathaniel Bacon esqr and Elizabeth his wife ye daughter & heyr of Richard Kingsmill decd sendeth greeting in our lord god Everlastinge Now know yee that wee ye s^d Nathaniell & Elizabeth Bacon for and in Consideracon of a certeine sume of mony and Tobaccoe in Cashe to bee paid by Nicholas Meriwether accordinge to an engagem^t vnder his hand bearinge date ye 30th of Aprill last past made vnto the s^d Nathaniell Bacon esqr, doe sell assigne & make ouer And by these presents haue sould assigned & made ouer vnto the said Nicholas Meriwether his heyrs & Assignes for Euer A deuident of Land belonginge to vs Scituate in James City Island Comonly called the Iland house Boundinge as Followeth Westwardly By or wth out an old Ditch cross ye old Feild nigh ye greate popler called mrs Harmers greate popler Northwardly by the Marsh or Back Creeke Eastwardly By Back Creeke and Kingsmills Creeke Southwardly by the Marsh or kingsmills Creeke and by a Branch of Pitch & Tarr Swampe, The said Land beinge formerly in ye possession of Richard kingsmill decd & is due vnto the sd Elizabeth Bacon as beinge ye daughter & heyr of the sd Richd Kingsmill To haue and to hold ye sd Land wth the, house Orchard & all other appurtenances thereto belonginge to him ye sd Nicholas Meriwether his heyrs & Assignes for Euer, And ye sd Nathaniell & Elizabeth Bacon for themselues theire heyrs Exrs & Admrs doe Couenant and grant to & wth ye sd Nicholas Meriwether his heyrs & Assigne [s] that ye sd nicholas meriwether his heyrs & assignes shall foreuer quietly & peseably haue hold occupy possess & enjoy ye aforesd Land wth all other ye premises wthout ye let trouble Molestacon or disturbance of ye sd Nathaniell & Elizabeth Bacon their heyrs Exrs Admrs or Assignes or either of them or any other pson or psons w^{ts}ouer In Witness whereof they haue put theire hands & seales this 26th day of Nouebr 1[6]56.

the Nathaniell Bacon
Marke E B *of* Elizabeth Bacon

Signed & Sealed in ye Presence
of   Rodger Parteridge
ye Marke of
John Bvrsh

JOHN KNOWLES'S GRANT.[1]

Grant to John Knowles of " 133 acres, 35 chains and nine decimal parts, part within and part without the liberties of James Citty, beginning at a corner stake by a Ditch near the house formerly belonging to John Phipps, thence along the said Ditch East South East one third Southerly 11 chains & 5 primes to a corner stake one chain short of an old corner persimmon tree, thence South West half westerly three chains to a corner stake, thence South East one fourth southerly, seven chains to a corner stake, thence North East half easterlv two chains Eight Primes to a corner persimmon upon the aforesaid Ditch, thence along the same South East half southerly one chain and 46 Decimal parts to the corner of said Ditch, &, thence South West ¾ southerly one chain 38 decimal parts to a corner stake, thence along a Ditch

[1] *Va. Land Register*, V., 63.

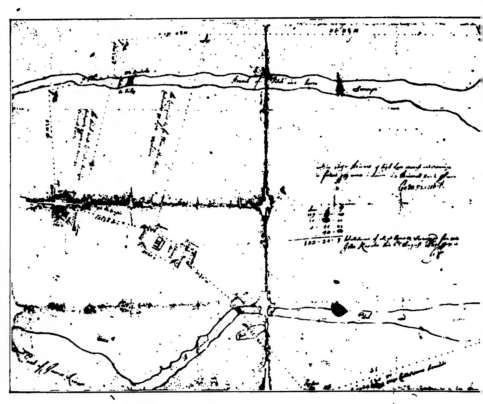

Plat by John Underhill for John Knowles of 133 acres, 35 chains and nine

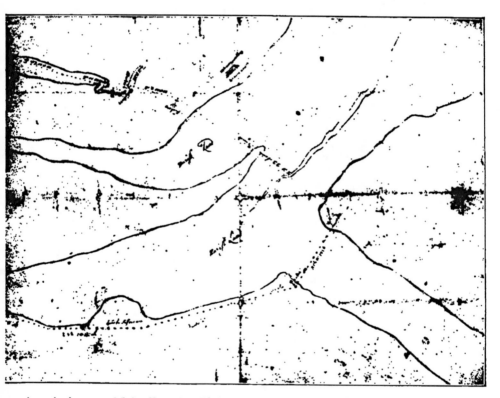

...owing the houses of John Knowles, William May and John Phipps in New Towne.

South West three fourths southerly ten chains to a marked persimmon at the end thereof and near a branch of Pitch and Tar swamp, thence over South East half easterly twenty one chains, 26 Decimal parts to a corner poplar in Lancelot Elys line, thence along the same east ¾ northerly 30 chains to Pitch and Tar swamp, thence along the same East one fourth northerly 13 chains, 74 Decimal parts, to a marked red oak near a small marsh, thence down the same South East Eight chains East South East 14 chains three primes including a small point formerly in difference, but found to belong to John Phipps, thence upon the edge of the high land to a marked saplin red oak by the side of a marsh gut, thence over the same North East half northerly 13 chains, 6 primes, to a marked persimmon upon a point against Mr. Nicholas Meriwether's cleared ground, thence over a marsh and sharp point of high Land North West 33 chains, 7 primes to a marked hickory upon the high land, thence West North West 8 chains to another marked hickory on the west side of a cart path, thence along the same South West half westerly two chains to a corner sapling red oak on the same side of the said path, thence West North West ten chains West North West half northerly ten chains North North East half easterly two chains to a marked sapling white oak on the North side of a branch of Pitch and Tar swamp & near Mr. Meriwether's fence, thence along the same side of the same branch West North West half northerly 14 chains to a corner white oak near a small branch, thence over the same West 2/3 northerly, 45 chains to a corner stake on the southerly side of a cart path to the Island House, thence West ⅜ northerly, 16 chains, 5 primes to a corner stake on the same side of the same path, thence South by West half westerly 6 chains to a corner stake on the North side of a branch of pitch and Tar swamp about 3 chains above a bridge, thence over the said branch West by South Eleven chains to a corner stake at the lower end of Mr. Walter Chiles' Ditch, thence up the same South half westerly 16 chains to a corner stake near and on the East side of said Ditch then South 2/3 westerly 4 chains to a corner stake 42 Decimal links from the South West end of Mr. Knowles' now dwelling house, thence South by West half westerly 2 chains and 21 Decimal parts to a corner stake near the South West corner of his old garden, thence East South East 3 chains to a corner stake at the other corner next to Mr. William May's house,

thence North North East 2 chains, 27 Decimal parts to a corner stake at the corner of the garden next the house formerly of John Phipps, thence East by South one chain, 16 Decimal parts to the place where it began." Dated May 6, 1665.

PATENT OF JOHN BAULDWIN FOR LAND AT THE WEST END.

To all &c whereas &c Now know ye that I yᵉ sᵈ Edwᵈ Digges Esqʳ do give and grant unto John Bauldwin fifteen acres & 69 Pches be it more or less lying in James Island between the main river & the back river bounded (vizᵗ.) ten acres of part thereof easterly upon Mʳ James his land north upon the back river and the land hereafter menconed west upon the main river and South upon the Slash which lyeth between the State house & ye s^d Mr James & five acres & 69 Pches the residue at the old blocke house begining at the head of a Marsh Swamp Issueing into the back river but running to the blocke house North ¾ west down behind Marsh belonging to the backe river Southerly to a red oak on a point near the first menconed land thence South ¾ west 4 Pches soewest ½ part North 36 Pches to the place it began. To have and to hold & c yielding and paying &c which paym^t is to be made &c dated the 4th october 1656.

Copia

Test Ralph Gough P^r C C Thacker
Cl Sec Off.

Patent of William Sherwood for Land at the West End.[1]

To all &c whereas &c now know Yee that I ye s^d Sr Henry Chichely Kn^t. His Maj^ts deputy Gòvern^r. &c give & grant unto Mr William Sherwood twenty eight acres & a half of Land lying at the mouth of James Citty Island and is bounded as followeth (vizt) begining at James River at the head of a great Slash & Issuing into the back River and down the s^d Slash East ½ a point Southerly Eighteene Chaines thence North ¾ point Easterly fower Chaines to the back River Marsh and up the Same to a Markt persimon tree under block house hill point thence under the said Hill West six Chaines to James River and downe it againe to the first Mencon'd Slash including eight acres & thence againe down the said Slash forty three Chaines to Mr Richard James Land and along it South twenty three Chaines to a branch of Pitch & Tarr Swamp thence up the said branch to James River and Up the River to the place it Begun Conteyning twenty & half acres the said Land Being formerly granted to John Baldwin by pattent dated the fowerth of October one thousand six hundred and fifty six for fifteene acres fifty nine perches more or less and now by a late survey found to Conteyne twenty eight acres and a halfe. And the said John Baldwin by his last will & Testamt. in writing under his hand & seal did give the said Land to John ffulcher and his Heirs forever which said John ffulcher by Deed under his hand & seale dated the two and twentieth of October one thousand six hundred seventy & seven acknowledged & recorded in James Citty County Court Sould & Conveyed the Same to the Said Mr William Sherwood and His Heires forever To have & to hold &c to bee held &c Yielding &c provided &c dated the three & twentieth day of Aprill Anno Domi, 1681.

Copia Test E Thacker P^r C C Thacker. C Sec Of

Endorsed 20: April 1681 Mr Sherwoods Patent for 28; Acres & ½ of Land.

[1] This tract was patented by John Bauldwin, see page 260, and was supposed then to contain only 15 acres and 69 perches. See plat on page 263.

DEED BETWEEN WILLIAM SHERWOOD AND FRANCIS BULLIVANT, SHOW-
ING THE LOCATION OF THE STATE HOUSE IN 1694.

This Indenture of Lease made the Sixth Day of January An° Dom.
1694 Between William Sherwood of James Citty Gent of the pt, &
ffran: Bulliuant of the Same place of the Other pt. Witnesseth that
the Said William Sherwood as well in Consideracon of the Sume of
Fiue pounds sterlin to him in hand paid by the sd ffran: Bulliuant, as
alsoe of ye rent & Couents hereafter menconed wch on the Tenants
pt is to be paid & pformed hath deuised granted & to ffarme letten
& by these prsents Doth Deuise grant, & to farme lett to ye sd ffrancis
Bulliuant A certaine p cell of Land conteining by Estimacon two Acres
be ye Same more or less. Scittuate lying & being in James Citty
bounded Westerly by James Riuer Southerly by the Slash or Branch
yt pts this Land & the State house, Easterly by the great Road, &
Northerly by ye Sd Slash that pts this Land & the block howse Land,
with all priviledges, proffitts, comodityes & Apptences thereto belonging (Except one halfe Acre of Land for a Landing & a Shore if the
sd Wm Sherwood or his Assignes shall haue Occasion for ye Same
next to the block howse Slash) To haue & to hold the Sd Land with
all Liberties priviledges & App tenances thereto belonging to the sd
ffran: Bulliuant his Exrs Admsrs & Assignes for & Dureing the Naturall
Liues of the sd ffran: Bulliuant & Joyce his wife, & William Hopkins
his Son in Law. Yielding & paying therefore Yearly & Euery Year
Dureing the sd term to ye sd Wm Sherwood his heirs or Assignes at
his Mansion howse in James Citty fower good fatt Capon at ye feast
of the Natiuity of our Lord Yearly, & tenn Dayes work Either in
harvest time or Otherwise Yearly And ye sd ffran Bulliuant Doth for
himself his Exrs & Admsrs Covent & Agree with the Said Wm Sherwood his heirs Exrs & Admsrs by these prsents That ye Said ffran.
Bulliuant his Exrs Admsrs or Assignes Shall & Will truly pay ye Sd
rent in manner before reserued & mncond, And he will not keep or
suffer to rainge in James Citty any hoggs or Swine unless they be rung
on penalty of paying tenn Shillings for Euery Such hogg, to ye Sd Wm
Sherwood his heirs or Assigns, And further that ye Sd ffran: Bulliuant
his Exrs or Assigs Shall & will within three Yeares next coming plant
an Orchard of at least fifty bearing Apple trees, & at ye end of ye Said
term leaue & Yeild up ye Same to ye Sd Wm Sherwood his heirs or
Assignes well ffenced with ye howses that shall be built on the sd Land
in good & tenantable rep e, And ye Sd Wm Sherwood for him his heirs
& Assignes doth Covenant & p mise with ye Sd ffran Bulliuant his
heirs Exrs Admsrs & Assignes. That he the Sd ffran Bulliuant his
heirs Exrs & Assignes paying ye rent & pforming ye Couents before
menconed shall peaceably Injoy ye Sd Land with ye Apptenances (Except before Excepted) Dureing ye Sd term, without the lett Suit
trouble or Interupcon of ye Said Wm Sherwood his heirs or Assignes
or any other pson by his means or pcuremt. In Witness whereof ye
Sd pties haue to these Prsent Indenture Interchangably Sett their
hands & Seals ye Day & year aboue written

                                        FFRA: BULLIVANT.

Signed Seald & Delur
in Prsence of
       Pr Perry & Edward Ross

APPENDIX.

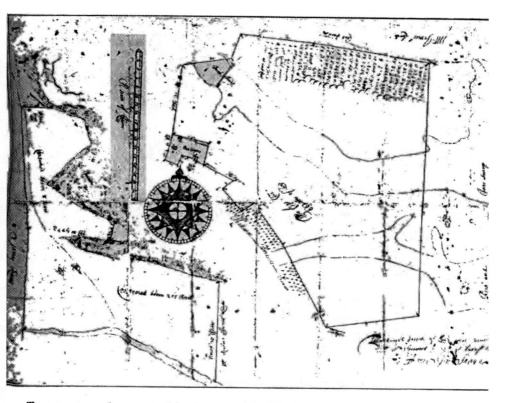

Two tracts on Jamestown Island surveyed for William Sherwood in 1680: 28 1-2 acres at west end, and 66 acres partly within and partly without New Towne. The plat shows Block House hill and the "Old Great Roade," and the houses of Walter Chiles (formerly Kempe William Sherwood's, (formerly the Country house), and William White's (formerly May's).

See Bauldwin's grant, page 260, and Sherwood's, page 261; also page 27. The tract to the right was intended to esent one-half of the land granted to John Knowles in 1065. See page 257.

DEED SHOWING THE LOCATION OF THE TURF FORT.

To all to whom these presents shall come Micajah Perry of London Merchant and John Clayton of Williamsburg in Virginia Esqr Send Greeting Whereas the said Micajah Perry by a certain Writeing or Letter of Attorney under his hand & Seal duely Executed Dated the Sixth day of November in the Year of our Lord One Thousand Seven Hundred and Ten Among other things therein Contained did Authorize the said John Clayton in the Name of him the said Micajah Perry to Bargaine Sell Assigne Transferr & Confirme all such Lands Messuages and Tenements of the said Micajah Perry as the said John Clayton should think fitt and to make Signe and pass all Such Deeds as shall be Necessary thereunto Now know yee That for and in Consideration of five pounds of Lawfull Money of Great Brittain by Edward Jaquelin of James City in the County of James City Gent To the Said Micajah Perry at & before the Executeing of these presents in hand paid the receipt whereof is hereby Acknowledged He the Said Micajah Perry by the Said John Clayton his Attorney hath Remised Released & Quitt Claimed And by these presents for himself and his heirs Doth Remise, Release and forever Quitt Claime to the Said Edward Jaquelin his heires and Assignes All the Right Title Interest property Claim & Demand of him the said Micajah Perry and his heires of in or out of all that Messuage or Tenement and half an Acre of Land be the same more or less Scituate & being at James City in the County aforesaid formerly in the possession of John Jarret Decd and bounded on the South by the River James East on the Old ffort North on the Land where the Mansion house of the said Edward Jaquelin now Stands and West on the Land late in the Possession of William Marable All which said Messuage and half Acre of Land now are in the Actual possession of him the Said Edward Jacquelin to have and to hold the Said Messuage and half Acre of Land to the Said Edward Jaquelin his heires and assignes for ever And the said Micajah Perry by his Said Attorney for himself his heires Executors & Admin^{rs} doth Covenant promise and Agree to and with the said Edward Jaquelin his heires & Assignes by these presents That he the said Micajah Perry and his heires Shall and Will from time to time and at all times hereafter within the Space of Seven Years Next Ensueing the Date hereof at the proper Cost & Charge of the said Edward Jaquelin his heires and Assignes make do and Suffer or Cause to be made done and Suffered all and every Such other Lawfull & reasonable Acts and things in the Law for the further & better Barring Extinguishing & Releaseing the right Title & Interest of the said Micajah Perry and his heires of and to the said Messuage and half Acre of Land or either of them as by the said Edward Jaquelin his heires or Assignes his or their Council Learned in the Law Shall be reasonably Advised Devised or required so as such other Acts or things do require or Containe no other Warrants than Against the said Micajah Perry and his heires and all Claiming under him or them. In Wittness whereof the said Micajah Perry by his said Attorney hath hereunto putt his hand and Seal this Ninth day of September in the Year of our Lord Christ One Thousand Seven Hundred & Twenty One.

MICAJAH PERRY   [Seal]

At a Court held for James City County September the 11th 1721 John Clayton Esq Attorney of Micajah Perry of London Merchant acknowledged this the said Perrys Deed for Lands &c: unto Edward Jaquelin Gent which at his Motion is Admitted to record

        Test
              Mich¹: Archer Cl Con

Endorsed:
Perry's Deed
     to
    Jaquelin
Brick house on yᵉ River.

PAPER SHOWING WILLIAM BRODNAX'S TITLES.

Patent to Willm Sherwood for 308 Acres in James City Island 1694. Dᵒ to Henry Hartwell for 2½ Acres in James Town 1689 sold to Willm Edwards by deed bearing date April 1695 & by Edwards to Willm Broadnax by Deed 1709

Patent to Jno Howard for 172 Perches land in James City 1694 begin at N E Corner Church Yard & running N. 87 Deg westerly 3 Chain & 90/100 to N. Bacons Land & along it N. six Chain & 8/10 to the Corner thereof thence South 85 & ½ Deg. Easterly one Chain & half to yᵉ great old Road & along yᵉ same to yᵉ first mentioned Corner

Bauldwins Patent for 15 & 69 perches in James City Island 1656 by him given to John Hulcher & by him conveyed to W. Sherwood who had it surveyed & took out a new patent Viz Patent to W. Sherwood for 28½ Acres at yᵉ north of J. C. Island which he gave by deed to his Nephew John Jarrett 1693 reservᵍ 2 acres & he sold to John Howard 1699. & by him sold to John Baird 1710 together with yᵉ ½ Acre granted to yᵉ said John Howard by patent described above; Both these Parcels viz yᵉ half Acre near yᵉ Church & yᵉ 28½ Acres at Block House Hill sold by Baird to Travis 1717, & by Travis to Brodnax 1719

Patent to Robert Beverly for 3 Acres 1 Rood & 6 Pole of Land in James City 1694 & by him sold to Willm. Brodnax 1718 for 110 £ Ster

Patent to Edwd. Ross for 5 Rood & Seven pole at yᵉ head of Pitch & Tar Swamp in James City

Patent to W. May for 100 A. Marish in J. C. 1667 called Goose hill

Patent to Briscoe for 12 Acres in J. C. 1683.

Chidleighs Deed to Edwards of 127 Pole in J. I. 1696/7 & by him assigned to Brodnax 1709

Baird Deed to Travis for the half Acre near yᵉ Church & 28½ Acres at Block House Hill 1717 & sold by Travis to Brodnax in 1719

37 A. granted by pat to Coll Swan & by Coll Swan Assignd to Richd Holder 1674 & given by Will of said J. Holder to his Sister Ann Holder together with 8 Acres more which were patented by sd Holder in J. C. Anne Holder married Briscoe; his Father by Will gave all his Lands in J. C. & heirs forever; one parcel contᵍ a quarter of an Acre in yᵉ Town Briscoe bought of Thomas Holiday yᵉ Extor of James Alsopp, who bought yᵉ same of John Barber

Bulliuant to Broadnax of 187 A. 1736.

PRIORITIES.

ILLUSTRATIONS.

INDEX

Printed in the United States
107845LV00002B/209/A

9 780548 261668